TT *HEROES*

- a personal selection

by

Mike Savage

© Amulree Publications & Mrs. R. Savage
First published 1997
Jacket design: Ruth Sutherland

ISBN 0 9521126 9 8
TT Heroes - a personal selection (softback)

.

Contents

To Marj, with thanks for all your encouragement
and to Harry, Bernie, Jeff, Stan, Tommy, Colvin, Geoff
Peter, Ellie, Eric, Colin, and the rest of the
Scoreboard Team.

Foreword

I had the privilege of knowing Mike Savage as a friend, and a working colleague, and his enthusiasm for Isle of Man Motorcycle Racing, and in particular the TT races is captured in this book.

We all have our first memories of this wonderful event, and Mike's are clearly defined on the following pages. Also we all have our favourite riders from 90 years - and Mike's selection may not agree with yours, or indeed mine, but the research he has obviously carried out to present his case is quite remarkable. There are certainly facts that are completely new to me and they make fascinating reading and show a rare insight to the riders he has selected.

For many years, from the commentary point in the Grandstand, I have looked down each June and September to see Mike carry out his work as Assistant Scoreboard Controller. In brilliant sunshine or in pouring rain, he carried out his duties in his own inimitable quiet style, checking carefully to ensure that the information on the Scoreboards was correct for the fans and competitors.

Sadly, his familiar figure is not there now, and is greatly missed. This book, however, ensures that his contribution to the TT will not be forgotten.

I hope you enjoy reading it as much as I did.

Peter Kneale, April 1997

The author (centre) presenting TT 80th year ties to Roger Marshall (left) and Mick Grant at the Great Northern Bike Show, April 1987.

1951: A lineup of TT winners at the only motorcycle road race meeting to be held at Goodwood. To win a copy of The History of the Manx Grand Prix 1923-1998, to be published by Amulree Publications in September 1998, identify all the above winners. Send your entries to: TT Heroes, Amulree Publications, Amulree, Glen Road, Laxey, Isle of Man, British Isles, IM4 7AJ by 31st December 1997. The first ten correct entries drawn will win a copy of the book.

Warm up

The sport that I love kills people. This book is a love story; it is not a romance.

Some 162 competitors have died taking part in races over the TT course. Yes, I know all the counter arguments. The figure includes the September Manx Grand Prix races as well as the TT. The deaths have occurred over an eighty-eight year period. Given the millions of racing and practice miles covered over that period the incident rate is lower than many short circuits, lower than other sports. All this cannot alter a basic truth: motorcycle racing is a dangerous sport.

It is important to be honest about this because Isle of Man TT = Most dangerous race circuit in the world = 162 deaths is now indelibly inscribed in the data bases of the sports' desks of every major newspaper. *The Observer*, for example, doesn't often cover motorcycle racing in any depth. But, when Wayne Rainey crashed at Misano in 1993, the paper clearly thought that an accident that might leave him paralysed for life was worthy of coverage. Rainey has never ridden in the Isle of Man. The Island ceased to be part of the World Championships in 1977. The incident had nothing whatsoever to do with the Isle of Man. But it took only the second paragraph for the Observer to say that Misano was not as dangerous as the Isle of Man where 160 riders have died over the years etc.. The data base has struck again.

Faced with this computerised hostility, and given the sensitivity of all islanders to criticism from outside, it is not surprising that Island residents tend either to apologise for the races or vigorously attack those responsible for the criticism. By doing so, however, we betray our own lack of self confidence. Defenders of the TT sometimes make the comparison between the races and mountain climbing. There are some parallels but the comparison is essentially a false one. Road racing is a unique sport and its risks are correspondingly singular. It is no use those of us who would never ride down Bray Hill at 150 mph trying to make a judgement about the acceptability or otherwise of those risks. Ultimately, the only ones who can make that judgement are the riders who compete in the races. So long as they feel the risks are acceptable, the races will continue.

What about us? Don't we have some higher moral duty to protect competitors from themselves? Shouldn't we at least stop encouraging or abetting riders? The answers to such questions depend upon whether you place personal freedoms above human life. We fought two World Wars to defend that principle. Nowadays we seem to be less sure it's true.

Such questions also raise queries about our attitude to motor sport, heightened by the tragedies of 1994. If we are honest enough to admit that motor sport is dangerous, we should be truthful enough to accept that this is part of the attraction. There is nothing shameful in that. It doesn't mean we have some blood lust or that we want to see someone killed or injured. But part of the attraction is the knowledge that competitors are pushing themselves and their machinery to the limit. It is their ability to ride/drive on the limit and survive that attracts our admiration and respect. The intensity of that experience also excites our passions and emotions. Motor Sport has the ability to move us in a way few other sports can.

This is not to say that we shouldn't make motor sport as safe as we can. But the element of risk will always be there and it will always be for the competitors to decide its acceptability. Unless we accept that danger is an essential element of the sport we risk undervaluing the sport itself - and seriously undervaluing the courage and commitment of those who take part in it.

It was my father who introduced me to the T.T., but it was the races themselves which grabbed my attention. There were a number of reasons for that. Excitement, emotion and passion were certainly some of them. It is impossible to talk to someone involved in motorcycle racing without feeling that passion. It is the passion that has riders and entrants returning year after year; that has some of them camping out in cold, wet, draughty tents to save money to spend on the bike; that has them working on their machines all night from the end of evening practice and then wheeling the bike out at 5 a.m. for three laps of morning practice before breakfast. The intensity of that passion, and the emotions which drive it, communicates itself to spectators and fans.

The race organisation also relies on emotion; a sense of camaraderie, groups of marshals and officials who may get together only a couple of times a year for the races, but who greet each other like the old and familiar companions they are.

This camaraderie is also expressed in loyalty; loyalty to the races, to the event, to your part of the organisation. You can see it in the beer tent after a race, a group complaining about some incident or firmly berating some other part of the organisation. Yet let anyone from outside criticise and the group will quickly close ranks and vigorously defend what they were previously condemning.

The TT's unique past gives us a sense of history, a sense of place, particularly for those of us who are Island residents. That, in turn, brings tradition and ritual, doing things because that's the way they have always been done, as a link with the past. When I became responsible for the Isle of Man Tourist Board's part of the organisation of the TT, I was temporarily panic stricken. There had to be a hundred and one things to arrange that I knew nothing about. I needn't have worried. Most of them happened automatically, without my having to do a thing. People who had been doing them for years, who had their tasks passed down to them like family heirlooms, simply turned up and got on with the job. The only problems would have occurred if I'd tried to interfere.

All this gives the TT the feeling of a club or a family. The enthusiasm you feel when you first join stays with you for the rest of your life. That is the real secret of the appeal of the TT. The passion, the excitement, the thrill we used to feel for so many new experiences, for life generally, is still rekindled by a revving engine, the smell of burning oil, the colour, the spectacle and, yes, the danger.

Long may it continue.

Mike Savage

Publishers Note

Late in 1996 I was contacted by Mrs Rene Savage enquiring whether I would be prepared to publish this book for her, in memory of her son, Mike, who passed away in September 1995. I was honoured to be offered this opportunity, which gave me immense pleasure.
The library staff of the Manx Museum are especially pleased to see the book in print, as Mike spent many happy hours there researching this book.
The words are all Mike's; some of the pictures are from his collection, but I am grateful to the following who allowed me to use photographs from their extensive archives:

Steve Colvin
Dennis Corkill
Island Photographics
S. R. Keig
Peter Kneale
Nick Nicholls
John Watterson

Bill Snelling, Laxey, May 1997

Foreword

In the middle of the Irish Sea, roughly halfway between England and Ireland, lies the Isle of Man. It has an area of just 225 square miles and a population of some 70,000. Most of them, and a good many of the millions of tourists who have visited it over the years, think it's one of the most beautiful places in the world.

Despite this, it is still little known in mainland Britain, particularly in the South. Say that you come from the Isle of Man and most people will think you mean the Isle of Wight, or one of the Channel Islands. If they associate anything at all with the Island it is likely to be kippers or tailless cats. That may be changing. The Island is now a thriving international off-shore finance centre.

For all but a couple of weeks each year, the Island is also a haven of peace and tranquillity. It has a singular quality of life, an unmatched sense of timelessness. It is often said, with justification, that the Island is twenty years behind the mainland. It is none the worse for that.

Every June, however, the Island, as it has since 1907, plays host to the Tourist Trophy [TT] races. These International races are unique. The race course is over 37¾ miles of normal public roads, on an Island only thirty miles by ten. The course has all the hazards associated with public roads, including hedges, stone walls and telegraph poles. The course rises from near sea level to close to the summit of the Island's only mountain, a difference in level of 1400ft. Practice takes place in the early mornings and evenings. Each race is run as a time trial, with riders setting off separately at ten second intervals to race against the clock as much as each other.

The transformation of the Island during TT has to be seen to be believed. The TT has a premier place in the history of motorcycle racing and the development of the motor cycle. It is still regarded with affection, even love, by motorcycle fans around the world. Each year some 45,000 people with 11,000 motor bikes invade the Island to be part of a festival of motor cycling. The largest influx happens almost overnight between the end of practice and the beginning of race week. For that period the Island becomes a sort of motorcyclist's haven/heaven where bikers are actually welcome and where the races are supported by a host of other motorcycle events; trials, moto cross, short circuit and drag racing, rallies, classic bike and sand racing. It's a true festival, in which the highlight remains the TT races.

This is a book about the TT and some of the men who have made it something special. It is a love story - a tale of my affair to date with the greatest motorcycle road races the world has ever seen.

None Braver

Handley's Corner came fairly early on. I must have been 5 or 6 when my father first pointed it out to me. We didn't have a car then but on holidays such as Easter my father would sometimes hire one as a special treat and take us off to some other, in my case unexplored, part of the Island. It was during one of these trips that he showed me the corner named after Wal Handley, the place where Handley had come off his machine during the 1932 Senior TT. The corner has long since been smoothed out but it remains a tricky S-bend.

I can still remember the note of respect in my father's voice as he told me about the great Wal Handley. My father can't have been much older than me when he saw Handley ride, but it was an impression that had clearly stayed with him over the years. Handley was the stuff of which legends are made. It was said at the time that a TT without Handley was like an egg without salt.

Television may have killed the art of conversation; it has certainly dulled the art of observation. These days I seldom notice things unless some television report or reporter is pointing them out to me. So it took me another 25 years to find the other TT course memorial to Wal Handley - and then it was by accident. I was reading about a memorial seat dedicated to Stanley Woods when it mentioned an earlier memorial to Walter Handley. A little research revealed that this memorial seat is on Quarterbridge Road, about a mile from the start of the TT course and about two minutes walk from the part of Douglas where I have lived all my adult life. I must have passed it thousands of times without ever noticing to whom it was dedicated.

-----oOo-----

Walter Leslie Handley was born in Birmingham in 1902. His father died when Walter was nine and the boy started work at the age of twelve. Towards the end of the Great War he tried to enlist in the Army as a dispatch rider. The Army rejected him; not because he was under age [which he was]. They were convinced he'd never make a good enough rider. It was a mistake the Army was to repeat over the years with a number of well-known TT riders.

Fortunately Handley's talent was recognised by another man who was to become a TT hero, H. R. [Howard] Davies later the founder of the H.R.D. company. In 1920 Davies advised O.K. boss Ernie Humphries that Handley had the potential to be a TT winner. It was a prediction Davies may have rued five years later when Handley beat him for the Junior TT victory.

Ernie Humphries made Handley his protege and employed him as a junior road tester. Handley got the chance to ride for O.K. in various trials and made friends with an engineer named Dougal Marchant, who was to build the Blackburne engines in Handley's O.K. and Rex Acme machines during 1925-1927.

Handley was a complex character. A loner, quiet, calculating and shrewd, he had a reputation for a quick temper as well as a good sense of humour. He was superstitious and always rode with a small stuffed monkey tied to his rear mudguard. He lost it in 1930 and was immediately inundated with replacements from adoring fans, but the original was eventually returned to him. During his prime he made money quickly but often gave it away with equal gusto. Whilst celebrating at a local hostelry after a race at Brooklands he is said to have thrown a whole handful of gold sovereigns into the air just to see the inevitable scrum that resulted.

In his racing career he broke a whole host of bones, including his back. A fracture to the base of his skull also left him without a sense of smell.

Wal Handley became one of the all-time TT greats. But his

Wal Handley with his 1922 TT debut O.K.

TT beginning was not an auspicious one. For 1922 the TT organisers, the ACU [Auto Cycle Union], had introduced a new separate Lightweight race for motor-cycles of 250cc capacity [the 250 cc machines had previously been a class of the 350 cc Junior Race]. The race was to be over five laps of the Mountain course, part of which was still little more than rough roads. The O.K. factory, which manufactured 250cc machines, decided at the last minute to enter a team in the race, in the hope of gaining valuable publicity. The factory

entered F. C. North [a TT veteran who had first ridden in 1911], and Neville Hall, a promising newcomer. Ernie Humphries also entered his protege, Wal Handley.

So it was, that on Wednesday 17th May at just after 5 a.m. on a cold, wet and misty morning, the young Wal Handley pushed out his O.K. machine, fired it up, leapt on board and shot off down the race course - in the wrong direction. Fortunately the marshals and officials managed to stop him at Governor's Bridge [about half a mile down the road], before he did any harm to himself or any competitor coming the right way round.

It was not a promising beginning. However, Handley soon showed what he was capable of. By the following Tuesday the *Motor Cycling* magazine was reporting that 'of the Lightweights, W. Handley, the youthful O.K. rider, distinguished himself by covering a lap at a speed only very little slower than the fastest lap in last year's race'. The next day Handley went one better and unofficially broke the lap record by over three minutes. By the Friday practice the motorcycle press were describing Wal's style as 'really brilliant'.

The race itself was held on the morning of Tuesday 30th May, and Handley immediately broke the lap record from a standing start. Over the rough and demanding course he averaged 51 mph, 5 mph faster than the previous year's best. He led nearest rival Geoff Davison [Levis] by eleven seconds. But the fairy-tale ending was not to be. A broken inlet valve at Sulby on the next lap put Handley out of the race.

There were 163 entries for the 1923 TT, a record for the races at that time. Amongst them was Wal Handley, entered by O.K., with his team-mate George Strange, for the Lightweight and the Junior events. Both races had been extended to six laps of the course, a severe test of man and machine with the road conditions of the time.

In practice Wal again showed good form, leading the Lightweights on the Saturday session and the Juniors on Monday, ahead of his former mentor Howard Davies. His luck was no better, though, in the Junior race itself. Starting No. 69 of 72 he rode out of sight of the Grandstand with two loud explosions. He retired on Bray Hill, just half a mile down the road, with 'engine trouble'.

It was often said that Wal Handley revelled in adversity, that he performed at his best when everything seemed against him. I'm not sure that that's entirely true or fair, but certainly he was a dogged and determined character. The first proof of that came in the 1923 Lightweight TT.

Handley set off at a cracking pace and broke the lap record at nearly 54 mph. At the end of lap two he was 3½ minutes ahead of second man Jock Porter [New Gerrard]. But by the next lap this had fallen to less than 30 seconds. On the fourth lap, perhaps trying too hard to retain his lead, Handley crashed, badly damaging his machine. He had lost half a handlebar, one of his footrests and the petrol filler cap on the top of the tank. Any other rider would have called it a day - but not Wal Handley. Steering with just one hand, one foot trailing and with petrol splashing into his face, he completed two more laps [over 75 miles], to eventually finish eighth.

In those days a Mr. J. R. Nisbet, a former Chairman and Clerk of the Course of the TT races, donated a shield, a sort of rider's gallantry award, to be given by the organisers to a rider who had shown 'such pluck, endurance or capacity to triumph over difficulties as to warrant some special prize'. That year it was awarded deservedly to Wal Handley.

After the TT Handley left the O.K. factory and signed up with the Rex Acme firm. Rex had begun as a car-making firm in Birmingham, but in 1900 they had moved to Coventry and begun making motorcycles. They had competed in the very first TT, in 1907, with Billy Heaton finishing third in the twin-cylinder class. In 1921 they merged with their next door neighbours, the Coventry Acme Motor Company, to produce a new range of Rex Acme machines.

The change in factory seemed to have brought a change in luck, as Handley won the Belgian 250cc TT a few weeks later. But it oh so nearly went horribly wrong. Handley was leading Geoff Davison [Levis], by six and a half minutes when Wal pulled into his pit at the end of the last lap. Handley was busy receiving the congratulations of a delighted Rex team when someone remembered that the finishing line was a hundred yards or so further down the track. Handley had to hastily re-start his machine and finally take the chequered flag, just ahead of Davison.

1924 saw another new class added to the TT races. An Ultra-Lightweight race for machines of 175cc was to be run over three laps of the Mountain circuit. What's more the event was to be a true race, with riders setting off in a mass start and first to the chequered flag winning. Wal Handley was the sole entry of the Rex Acme factory in the new class and the Junior and Lightweight races.

The Junior was held first on the Monday of race week. Handley started No. 22 in a field of 59 and made his usual good start. At the end of lap one he was in second position, but over one and a half minutes behind the flying leader Jimmy Simpson [A.J.S.], who was lapping faster than the Senior lap record. By the end of the second lap Simpson, who had now recorded the first ever 60 mph+ TT lap, had increased his lead over Wal to three and a half minutes. Handley was fifty seconds ahead of the third placed man. At the speed he was lapping there was a good chance Simpson's machine wouldn't last the distance and when it gave out Handley would be ideally placed.

Sure enough, on lap three Simpson's engine failed at Crosby. But Handley's lead was short lived. On the descent from the Mountain, Wal's engine also gave out and he was forced to retire. The race was eventually won by Kenneth Twemlow [New Imperial].

The new Ultra Lightweight race was held on the Wednesday. Despite fears of what might happen with a massed start, all seventeen riders got off safely on their first lap. Handley, who had been described at the start as being modestly confident, led at end of the first circuit with a lap at just over 51mph. Jock Porter [New Gerrard] was nine seconds behind. Wal had lost his lead when he skidded at the Bungalow but he soon re-gained it, passing Porter at Creg ny Baa in sensational style.

At the end of the first lap Handley drew into his pit to refuel. Porter went straight through and took the lead. By Sulby, however, Handley was making inroads and by Ramsey he was only fifty yards behind. At the end of lap two Porter made his pit stop, but, to everyone's surprise, Handley also pitted. It seems that his oil tank was leaking and he had to stop to take on more oil. Despite this handicap he set off in determined

pursuit of Porter. His efforts were in vain, however. He got no further than Bray Hill before the oil tank burst beyond repair. He returned to the grandstand on foot where he tore off his leathers and flung them away in disgust. Porter went on to win the race, but admitted that had Handley kept going it would have been a tremendous tussle on the last lap.

So Handley's last chance of TT success that year was the Lightweight race held on the Friday of race week. The race was run in conjunction with the Senior with the larger machines setting off five minutes ahead. For the twenty-one Lightweight bikes it was again a massed start.

Once more, Handley broke the lap record on the opening circuit, averaging 56.75mph. His lead over Jock Porter was some seven seconds but Porter reversed the positions on the next lap and led Wal by thirty eight seconds. At the end of the lap Porter came in to re-fuel, but, to general surprise, Handley went straight through. He had strapped an extra fuel tank on top of the normal one in the hope of stopping once to Porter's two fuel stops.

All Wal's strategy came to nothing, however, when the rocker broke at Ramsey on the next lap and, again, he was a TT retirement. Jock Porter faired little better, crashing at Glen Helen on the last lap when leading, and Eddie Twemlow [brother of Kenneth], went on to take the victory. So at the end of that TT week Wal Handley had now ridden in six TTs, led for some part of the race in five of them, but had finished in only one - in eighth place. His luck surely had to change sometime.

1925 was the year it all came right for Wal Handley - well, nearly all. Once again the Rex Acme concern had entered him for the Ultra-Lightweight, Lightweight and Junior TTs on Blackburne engined machines prepared by Dougal Marchant.

The Junior on the Monday got the week underway. Handley got his customary good start but early in the race he appeared to be in trouble when the indicator on the grandstand scoreboard clocking his progress appeared to show him stuck on the way to Ballacraine. Suddenly the indicator jerked forward. The observer had missed him at Ballacraine and he was actually tearing through the field. At the end of the lap he was second, only one second behind Freddie Dixon [Douglas], who had shattered the lap record by nearly one and a half minutes.

On the second lap Handley snatched the lead and, at the Grandstand was twenty three seconds ahead of Dixon and over a minute and a half ahead of Jimmy Simpson [A.J.S.]. Despite a pit stop for fuel, Wal's lead was up to one minute twenty-seven seconds at the end of lap three, with Simpson now in second and Dixon in third.

It was usually at this point that Handley's machine would cry enough, but not this time. On his next circuit Wal went even faster, setting a new record at 65.85mph. and extending his lead to two minutes twenty-seven seconds over his old friend Howard Davies [HRD], now in second. Re-fuelling at the end of the fourth lap, Handley still increased his advantage to over three minutes.

Given his TT history to date, Handley might have taken things easy on his last circuit and nursed his machine to the finish line. It wasn't his way. His final lap was only two seconds outside his new lap record and he took the flag three minutes forty-six seconds ahead of Davies - an emphatic victory. Davies' prediction of five years earlier had come true.

Wednesday saw the Ultra-Lightweight race, but the new class was already in trouble. For 1925 the ACU had imposed a weight limit of 150lb for these machines. But the previous year's machines had weighed half as much again. Most manufacturers felt it was impossible, and dangerous, to try to get down to the new weight limit. So there were just seven starters for the 1925 event over four laps.

The ACU had also abandoned the idea of the massed start, so the riders were set off one by one. In his now customary fashion, Handley lopped one minute ten seconds off the record on the opening lap to lead his old rival Porter by sixty-five seconds. On lap two, however, it was also back to old habits when Handley, trying to take Creg ny Baa too fast,

grounded the exhaust of his machine which promptly tossed him off. Wal picked himself and machine up and set off for the grandstand. He still led by seven seconds but the bike was misfiring badly as he started his third circuit.

Whatever the trouble was it soon cleared. Handley's third lap was only five seconds slower than his record whilst Porter was slowing dramatically. After a steady last lap, Wal finished four minutes twenty-seven seconds ahead of C.W. 'Paddy' Johnston [Cotton], who had grabbed second place from the slowing Porter. So Wal Handley became the first ever rider to win two TTs in the same week.

Handley was not entered in the Senior race which was run on Wednesday afternoon after the Ultra-Lightweight. Ten laps in one day on rough roads and no suspension were too much for any rider - even Handley. There was still the Lightweight race on Friday, however, and the chance of an unprecedented treble.

There were nineteen starters for the Lightweight and the pundits predicted another Handley/Porter battle. Wal made his usual electric start. Recording the first ever 60mph. lap by a Lightweight he led Porter by thirty-four seconds. Handley's second lap was only two seconds slower and when Porter retired at Ballacraine with a broken rocker, Wal led Paddy Johnston by over two minutes. Surely the treble was on.

But it wasn't to be. Handley's new found good fortune had finally run out. At the end of the third lap he was overdue. When he appeared at last he was touring, the bike's engine only just turning over and his riding helmet lying on the tank. As he crossed over the start line he shouted 'retired' and turned into the Paddock. It seems that as he approached the first warning board before Governor's Bridge his front tyre burst and he crashed, damaging the clutch too badly to continue.

If he had failed to do the treble, Wal Handley still left that year's TT with a host of records. He was the first rider to win two TTs in a week and the city of Coventry, home of the Rex factory, gave him a civic reception to celebrate. He was the first to win TTs on successive race days, a feat not equalled until Stanley Woods in 1935; and he was the first to make record laps in three TT races in a week, an achievement not equalled until Mike Hailwood 42 years later. In the Junior he had raised the winning race average by the largest ever margin from one year to another - 8 mph; and in the Lightweight he had recorded the first ever 60 mph lap. It had truly been Wal Handley's year.

Not surprisingly after the previous year's poor entry, the Ultra-Lightweight TT was dropped for 1926. However, Rex had now developed a V-twin 500cc machine for the Senior TT, so Handley was again entered in three races during that year's TT. Wal received the 500 machine on the Monday of practice week and spent all night up to 5.30 a.m. getting it ready to his satisfaction. Then he went out and did two practice laps on it. The hard work seemed to have paid off the following day when Handley was timed by the team in the high 60 mphs, two minutes less than the official time. He then left the 500 to one side to qualify his other two machines.

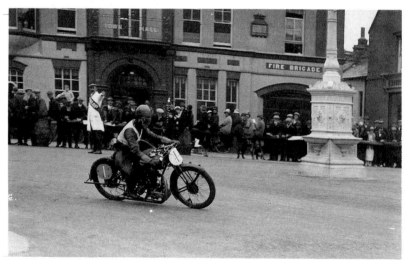

1926: Handley takes Parliament Square on his to his first TT win of the week.

With only two days of practice left Wal had still not completed the necessary number of laps to qualify his Lightweight mount. He set off determined to do so. He did a terrific leap at the well-known bump at the foot of Bray Hill and landed almost broadside across the road. Women screamed, and even the experienced marshals missed several heartbeats. To recover from the wobble was a superhuman effort that few riders could have managed, but asked later what had happened all the Rex Acme rider had to say was that he nearly parted from the bike. Handley qualified his machine.

In the Junior race Wal was first away by virtue of being the previous year's winner. He followed his now standard practice of breaking the record on the first lap and led Jimmy Simpson [A.J.S.], by twenty-two seconds. Simpson overhauled him on the next circuit and led Handley by twenty-six seconds with Alec Bennett [Velocette], third. Handley regained an advantage over Simpson but, with a record of 68.75 mph, Bennett overtook both of them on time and then passed Wal on the road as well.

By the end of the fourth lap Handley had real trouble with his machine. Damaged gears meant he only had top gear left after the third lap. He had been forced to stop twice to change jets on the carburettor and had to continually stop to adjust the front brake, which had caused him to skid at Governor's Bridge. He was still going well on the lower part of the course but the damaged gears were a real handicap going up the Mountain. Wal dropped to fourth place behind Bennett, Simpson and Freddie Dixon [Douglas], over nine minutes behind the leader. At the end of the sixth lap he had dropped to fifth behind Gus Kuhn [Velocette]. But with a superhuman effort on the last circuit, Wal hauled himself in front of Kuhn and Dixon again to finish in third place. Despite his troubles he had still managed to lap at nearly 66 mph.

By the mid 1920s the TT had become a truly international event and entries for the 1926 Lightweight included one from the Italian Guzzi factory with rider Pietro Ghersi. Handley started the race is his now accustomed fashion, breaking the record on the opening lap. But Ghersi had gone even faster, leading Wal by forty-eight seconds. At the end of the second circuit Wal came in to re-fuel, now three minutes behind the flying Italian. Handley's petrol pipe was broken and had to be repaired and he reported his front brake was 'wonky'. The delays first pushed him down to third below eventual winner Paddy Johnston [Cotton]. Then, on the fourth lap, Wal retired at Ramsey with a broken valve. Poor Ghersi was also out of luck. After he finished second behind Johnston's Cotton, the organisers disqualified the Guzzi rider for using a different type of spark plug from the one specified on his entry form. The Italian's protests were to no avail and it was to be three years before he returned to the TT races.

The Senior on the Friday was Handley's last chance for a win that year. Having had three machines to prepare [and probably fancying his chances more in the other two races], Wal had done very little practice on the Rex 500, nicknamed the 'Flying Bedstead'. He was unsure, therefore, what type of sparking plug would give him the best performance. In the end, he made the wrong choice.

For once there was no record opening lap, but Wal was in third place behind Jimmy Simpson [A.J.S.] and Stanley Woods [Norton]. On the next circuit, the plug choice rebounded. One plug ceased to work and the machine went on to one cylinder. Handley had to call at the pits at the end of the lap and it took seven minutes to effect a repair [presumably the plug was not very accessible]. The delay left Handley in twenty-second place. So began one of Wal's greatest rides.

It is said there has never been anything like Walter going down Bray Hill on that occasion. He was absolutely full bore, flat on the tank, using all the road. His speed was tremendous. Amazingly, by the end of the fifth lap Handley was back on the leader board in fourth place, to the cheers of the crowd on the stands. At the end of the sixth lap he was still fourth but only one second behind Frank Longman [A.J.S.]. On the final circuit he was up to second but the four minute lead of Stanley Woods was too much even for Handley. Second was where he finished.

He hadn't won, but it had been his greatest ride to date; the stuff of TT folklore. If Handley had been a star after his 1925 successes he was now a legend. The man himself was reported as disappointed that he hadn't won the Senior, but he confessed that his machine had required 'holding'.

Just to prove it had been no fluke Wal repeated the feat at that year's Brooklands 200 mile race . He lost seventeen minutes when a tyre went flat on the starting line, but came through the field to finish second, breaking a number of Brooklands records in the process.

The 1927 TT got off to a tragic start. The public roads which made up the Mountain course had always been officially closed for racing. Amazingly, however, there had been no such official closure for practice sessions. The organisers had relied on an informal arrangement whereby local residents knew the practices were on and took steps to keep out of the way. It was an accident waiting to happen, and when it did occur it was fatal. In an early morning practice session Archie Birkin [brother of Bentley driver Tim], collided with a fish lorry which was still on the course at Rhencullen and died from his injuries. Belatedly, from the next year onwards, the roads were officially closed for practice.

Wal Handley was now heading the Competitions Department of the Rex Acme factory and entered himself in the Junior, Lightweight, and Senior races. All didn't go well in practice. The Senior bike was fast; it had been timed in testing at a top speed of 102 mph. But the machine handled so badly that even Wal could do nothing with it. He sent the frame back to the factory in the hope that they could make some improvements, but there was too little time to make major changes and Handley had to scratch from the Senior Race.

Wal was hoping for better luck in the Junior Race. There was no opening record lap, but Handley still took the lead by fifty-eight seconds from Freddie Dixon [HRD]. Normal service was resumed on the second lap when Wal recorded a new record at 69.18mph. The lead over Dixon was up to eighty-two seconds with Alec Bennett [Velocette] in third position. The next circuit, however, almost brought disaster when Handley crashed at Quarterbridge. Despite being very shaken, and the bike having a bent footrest, Wal, as ever, had no thoughts of giving up. He picked himself up, righted the machine and set off down the course again. When he passed the Grandstand he was greeted with a resounding cheer, and he still led Dixon by some eighty-four seconds.

Handley called in for petrol at the end of the fourth lap, nearly three minutes ahead of Dixon. The Band, which kept spectators entertained when there were no machines in sight, struck up 'Bye, bye Blackbird' as Wal set off on his fifth circuit. His only remarks at the pit stop had been 'goggles' and 'Where's Alec?' He was right to be concerned about Bennett. On his fourth lap the O.K. rider had broken Handley's new lap record and was only 50 seconds behind. But on the next lap Bennett's engine gave up and Jimmy Simpson [A.J.S.] went into third. Handley kept his lead at the end of the fifth and, halfway round the last lap, was still comfortably ahead.

1927 Junior: Wal Handley (Rex Acme) leads Alec Bennett (Velocette) on the road at Ramsey Hairpin, but Bennett was to ran out the victor, whilst Handley, with various machine problems, struggled through to finish third.

But bad luck struck once more. The piston melted at Ballaugh and Wal was a retirement yet again.

Only the Lightweight was left. The race looked odds on to be a close run thing. Wal's main opposition seemed likely to come from Alec Bennett, riding for Handley's old team of O.K. Amazingly, after the harsh decision of the year before, the Guzzi factory had returned with a team of three riders and the best of these, Arcangeli, was also expected to be well in the hunt. One of the others, Varzi, was to become more famous as a driver for Alfa Romeo and Bugatti.

At the start of the race Handley got the biggest cheer after his disappointment in the Junior. And he was soon back to normal ways, breaking the record from a standing start. It was a good omen. At the end of the lap he led Bennett by over forty-five seconds. Wal's second circuit was slightly slower but he still increased his lead to two minutes with Arcangeli now in second. Handley's third lap was even slower but his lead increased to two minutes twelve seconds from Bennett who was in second again.

The combination of Wal's pit-stop and a new record lap by Alec Bennett reduced Wal's advantage to just fifty-three seconds at the end of the fourth circuit. Handley's response was quick and effective. He equalled his first lap time and extended his lead again to over a minute and a half. Clearly he was still worried by the threat from Bennett, however, for the next circuit saw him nearly fall at Ramsey but still be only one second slower than his previous lap. Wal was really trying. Would the cracking pace bring another breakdown and retirement?

It did, but not for Handley. Alec Bennett pulled in to retire at the end of the lap and Wal was left well ahead of the second man Arcangeli. Handley slowed, comfortable in the knowledge that his main rival had gone, and finished over eight and a half minutes ahead of the Italian rider. This time Guzzi retained their second place, no doubt having made doubly sure that the sparking plugs were the right ones. Handley's winning margin was his biggest ever.

Handley had left the Rex Acme factory and, for 1928, was a freelance professional rider, following the earlier example of his great rival Alec Bennett. His friend Dougal Marchant had joined the Geneva Motosacoche concern, and recruited Wal to ride for the factory in various continental events. For the TT, however, Handley was riding Rex machines and entered for all three solo classes. His Senior bike, however, had a Motosacoche, or MAG engine.

Wal was unhappy in practice with his Lightweight mount and, at the last minute, decided to take over his team mate Colgan's bike. The reaction of Colgan, who had finished third on a Cotton in the 1926 Lightweight TT, is not recorded. Handley was still unhappy with the new machine, swearing [literally], that its top speed was only 70 mph. Before the start of the race he called out to a practice leader Frank Longman, 'don't go too fast Frank, I want to get a replica'. Replicas were awarded in a percentage of the winner's time.

Handley started second on the road and, despite his previous dismissal of his chances, obviously felt that he could

The picture is uncaptioned, but could this be the 1927 Junior where he started number one, here he picks up the plot at Ramsey Hairpin.

1927: Wal Handley takes Parliament Square, Ramsey en route to his 1927 Lightweight victory.

make up with hard riding what his machine lacked in terms of speed. He took Quarter Bridge at such a speed that he ran right through the corner and on to the grass. He was soon in the lead on the road.

If the top speed of his bike was really 70 mph. then Handley must have been riding flat out almost all round the course, for his first lap average speed was nearly 62mph. He finished the lap in second place, thirty-nine seconds behind favourite Longman on the O.K. Supreme. Wal's rush of adrenalin had clearly slowed down by the second circuit. His lap time was a minute longer. However, he was still in second place three minutes behind Longman but a minute ahead of his team - mate Meageen.

Handley hit trouble on lap three. His oil pump stopped and he had to keep going with the aid of his foot operated oiler. As a result, he indulged in some exceptionally lurid riding. The *Motor Cycle* reported him as 'cornering like an inebriat-

ed panther'. Wal pitted at the end of the lap, still in second place.

Handley kept his position on the next two circuits, finishing lap five over five minutes behind Longman but nearly four minutes ahead of C. S. Barrow [Royal Enfield], now in third position. Nearly half the entry had still to pass the grandstand when Handley was reported as being at the Mountain on his sixth lap. But he was soon reported as passing Keppel Gate with a dead engine. After coasting on to Hillberry he retired. The connecting rod had broken. Wal walked back to the Grandstand to be greeted by sympathetic cheers.

He was out of luck too in the other two races. He was a non-starter in the Junior after failing to correct practice problems with the bike. The Senior was held in wet and foggy weather and as he set off, a spanner fell out from Handley's tool box [all machines had to carry a limited number of tools]. It was a bad omen. Wal got no further than a few miles before water in the magneto ended his race and he toured round for another retirement. It had been a miserable TT.

For 1929 Handley had a mix of rides. Part of the A.J.S. works team for the Senior and Junior [replacing Jimmy Simpson, who had moved to Norton], he was O.K. Blackburne mounted for the Lightweight race. He soon showed he'd got the hang of the A.J.S., shocking everyone during practice with a record lap on his Senior bike.

Unlike Longman's bike the year before, Wal's Lightweight O.K. was well down on speed and he was always struggling. At the end of the first lap he could manage no better than fifth, well behind leader Pietro Ghersi. Handley indulged in a characteristic plunge down Bray Hill at the start of the second lap, but by the end of the circuit he was still in fifth position. He improved to fourth after the third lap but, after a slow fourth circuit, he retired at the pits with a broken valve spring.

His Ajay's were much more competitive machines and this brought him better fortune in the Junior. He finished second at an average speed of 69.29mph. Wal could do nothing,

1932: Wal Handley (left) overtakes Leo Davenport (New Imperial) up the Ballahutchin, just past Union Mills. But it was Davenport who took the victory, with Wal finishing third after persistent plug troubles.

however about the winner Freddie Hicks. Setting new lap and race records Hicks took his new Velocette to the front on the third lap and from then on was never headed, beating Wal and that other TT star Alec Bennett by nearly a minute and a half.

It was the Senior, though, that had all the promise of being a really great race. There was the powerful Norton team of Stanley Woods, Jimmy Guthrie, Jimmy Simpson and Tim Hunt. A.J.S. had Wal Handley, Frank Longman, Tommy Spann and George Rowley [second in 1928 but originally included only as a reserve is the A.J.S. squad]. Sunbeam, winners the year before with Charlie Dodson, teamed the diminutive Senior trophy holder with the talent of Alec Bennett, then top TT winner with a total of five trophies.

If the TT has the power to delight and surprise it also, occasionally, has the power to disappoint. The anticipated battle

of the titans never materialised. The race was indeed a dramatic one - but for wholly unexpected reasons.

Guthrie was a non-starter. Perhaps in the circumstances it was just as well. Heavy rain before the start made the course very slippery. Handley, starting number 15, went off at a full lick but soon gave spectators a hint of what was to come. At Braddan Bridge Wal gave the assembled crowd a real fright and even had the marshals running in anticipation of the A.J.S. flying off the road. He got only as far as Greeba before he finally parted company with the bike, sliding across the road on his back.

Whilst Wal was coming to and picking his bike up ready to re-start, Douglas Lamb [Norton], crashed at the same spot, to be followed, in quick succession, by Jack Amott [Rudge], and Jimmy Simpson [Norton]. Although the damage to his own machine was negligible and he could have continued, Handley worked hard to clear the track and to attend to the injured riders. Then he raced on to Ballacraine to summon assistance. Sadly, Douglas Lamb died of his injuries and Jimmy Simpson sustained a serious leg injury which kept him out of racing for the rest of the season. It could have been far worse however, but for the intervention of Wal Handley. After the races were over the ACU wrote Handley a handsome encomium.

Once assured that a medical officer was on his way to Greeba, Handley toured back to his pit, his chances in the event having long gone. The race itself, however, continued to take its toll. The early leader was H. G. Tyrell-Smith [Rudge], but he crashed at Glen Helen on the third lap. After running repairs at the nearby Hotel, Tyrell-Smith rejoined the race, despite having cracked three ribs in his tumble. Matthews [Norton], crashed at Creg Willys and sustained a dislocated shoulder, a broken rib and slight concussion. The marshals at the site were ordered to transport the unfortunate rider by stretcher 'or door' to Crosby [about five miles away], where the ambulance would pick him up. Tommy Spann added to a day of woe for A.J.S. by coming off at Ballig with 'slight injuries'. Stanley Woods [Norton] crashed at Kirk Braddan, losing a couple of teeth in the process.

All through the mayhem and chaos, the two Sunbeams continued to circulate. Dodson repeated his Senior victory of the year before, beating his team-mate Bennett by nearly five minutes. The brave [or foolhardy], Tyrell-Smith took third place and Tim Hunt on the last remaining Norton was fourth, despite two crashes which broke both of the footrests on the machine. Not for the first or last time, the ability to stay out of trouble had proved as important as top speed.

By 1930, Handley had started his own motorcycle agency business in his home city of Birmingham. His friend Dougal Marchant had also left Motosacoche and joined the Belgian FN concern. The factory's full name was 'La Fabrique Nationale d'Armes de Guerre' and, as its name suggests, it had started as an arms company. By 1901, however, the factory was turning out motorised bicycles and from there went on to produce motor cycles. In the second TT in 1908, R. O. Clark had taken third place in the multi-cylinder class on his 5 hp FN. Handley was due to ride FN machines in the 1930 Junior and Senior races.

TT week that year got off to a bad start for Wal. It was common in those days [and sometimes today], for competitors to ride their race machines to and from their garage or workshop and the practice sessions. The local Police usually turn a blind eye on the absence of silencers or other requirements for a road machine. Often in trouble with the authorities, however, for some reason Handley had attracted the attentions of the boys in blue - perhaps for an unofficial practice session. So the beginning of the TT period saw Handley fined twenty shillings for failing to have an efficient silencer on his machine, and a further five shillings for failing to have a horn fixed.

Handley was quick to remark on the irony of being fined for making too much noise and too little. He added that he had never heard a quiet motor-cycle in the Isle of Man. Mr. W. Lay, the magistrate, agreed with Wal and said he intended to try and put a stop to such prosecutions. 'I am sorry to have to fine you. You are such a nice lot of fellows, and we are all so pleased to see you here, but you must comply with the law of the Island'.

More problems came during practice itself. The factory had been unable to get his FNs ready in time and he was forced to scratch from the Junior race.

Wal's mother travelled to the Island for the first time to watch him compete in the Lightweight event. Once again he was riding a Blackburne engined Rex Acme. At the end of the first lap Handley was in second place, half a minute behind South African Joe Sarkis [O.K. Supreme]. On the next circuit Handley broke the lap record and reduced the gap to just six seconds. Then his oil tank became 'inoperative' at Braddan and, yet again he was forced to retire. Riding number thirteen may have had something to do with it.

Having scratched from the Junior, Handley nearly had to do the same in the Senior. However, with the co-operation of the ACU, a way was found for him to take over a private Rudge entry [Jim Whalley's]. The Rudge concern then made him a member of their works team which consisted of Tyrell-Smith, Ernie Nott and Graham Walker. He couldn't have picked a better team to join that year. The Rudge team were to score a one, two, three clean sweep in the Junior and their 500 bike was no slouch either. Handley soon proved this in practice when, despite being unfamiliar with the machine, he averaged over 75 mph and cut fifty seconds off the Senior lap record.

The 1930 Senior TT was hailed at the time as the greatest ever. Handley enthusiastically returned to old habits and on his opening circuit broke the lap record by fifty seconds at an average of over 76mph.

On his third lap Wal went even quicker, averaging 76.28mph. Conditions then deteriorated to a downpour but Handley kept pushing on. As Graham Walker recalled later 'The fifth lap gave Wal Handley's bookmaker another excuse to visit the bar. Despite the heavy rain and mountain mist he waltzed round in twenty-nine minutes forty-four seconds to lead me by no less than three minutes and forty-nine seconds, poor Tyrell-Smith dropping back with a mysterious loss of performance'. Efficient pit and signalling work let Handley know where he stood and he knew he could slow down on the last lap when the fog really came down over the Mountain. He led for all seven laps and won by three minutes nineteen seconds from team-mate Graham Walker. Jimmy Simpson, the only works

1932: Wal Handley gets ready to fire his Lightweight Rudge to a third place finish, behind Leo Davenport (New Imperial) and Graham Walker (Rudge).

Norton to finish, came in a distant third nearly a minute and a half behind Walker.

Handley hadn't just won. He had set a whole host of records in the process; record lap and race records; first man to break the thirty minute lap barrier; first to complete two laps in under an hour; first to do four laps in under two hours. His average speed for the race was faster than the previous year's fastest lap. Most of all, he became the first rider in the history of the TT to win all four solo classes, a record not equalled until Mike Hailwood in the 1960s. He would never ride a better race.

If Handley had been on the wrong side of the Manx Authorities the year before, they made up for it in 1931. Wal

PRINCE GEORGE AT THE START OF THE SENIOR
T.T. RACE 1932.

1932: Wal Handley is introduced to Prince George before the start of the Senior TT. This is the race that put Handley on the TT map, literally - when he crashed at the bend that will forever be called 'Handley's Corner'.

had lost his U.K. driving licence after a conviction for a road traffic offence. It looked like Handley might be a non-starter for the TT. But the Island's Highway Board came to the rescue and issued Wal with a special short-term licence just to cover the TT period. It was a measure of his status as a TT legend, which had been enhanced still further by his crushing Senior win of the year before. The motorcycle press described Handley as the 'Valentino' of the Island - the greatest road-racing rider the world had yet seen.

Wal was again contracted to ride an FN in the Senior race. This time the Belgian machine did arrive but not until the middle of practice week. In the meantime Handley had not intended to ride, but the temptation proved too much. He borrowed his firm's Rudge, quickly converted it to racing trim and got in several respectable laps.

The FN arrived in time for Wednesday's morning session. It had a number of novel features, one of which was a windscreen. The A.J.S. riders, Freddie Hicks and George Rowley both carried little celluloid windscreens mounted above their number plates. But Handley's machine had a proper Triplex screen mounted in an aluminium frame and with a wire operated screen-wiper.

The bike was reputed to be the fastest on the Island but not to handle too well due to its high centre of gravity. Whether because of this, or unfamiliarity with the machine, Wal crashed the bike on the Mountain the first time out, breaking a handlebar and injuring his shoulder in the process. By the time his shoulder had healed he was short of time to qualify the machine

Handley determinedly set about trying to get in the necessary number of laps. The *TT Special* described him going down Bray Hill as 'Simply amazing! The huge machine is leaping, bucking, bouncing, but every incipient waggle is nipped in the bud, and the monster obeys the finest rider in the World'. However, in the last practice session, on Wal's fifth and final qualifying lap, the FN cried enough just two miles from the finish.

Handley was left in a peculiar position. He had qualified for the Senior on the Rudge. But FN were insistent. Wal was contracted to them and he would ride their machine or nobody's. Once again that year officialdom, so often his enemy, came to his aid. The ACU took pity on him and allowed him to ride the FN in the Senior.

It would be nice to record that the story had a happy ending. Alas, it was not to be. Handley set off at his usual meteoric pace, stormed down Bray Hill and approached the Quarterbridge bend at a high rate of knots, only to have the gearbox jam. Wal lost control of the machine and found himself sliding up the road. Fortunately he was unhurt. It was FN's last TT entry.

For 1932 Handley was back on Rudge machines in all three classes, part of a strong works team with Graham Walker,

Ernie Nott, and Tyrell-Smith. There were none of the practice incidents of the previous year and Wal was given a good chance in all three races.

The first lap of the Junior found him in third place behind the works Nortons of Stanley Woods and Tim Hunt. Determined to catch the Bracebridge Street pair, Handley broke the lap record on the next circuit at 77.36 mph, only to find that Woods and Jimmy Simpson [also on a works Norton], had gone even faster. A pit stop at the end of the next lap put Wal only six seconds outside his fastest time and, after the slickest pit-stop in Island history, he moved up to second when Simpson dropped out. He couldn't catch the flying Irishman, however, and had to settle for runner-up, over two minutes behind Stanley.

The Rudges were expected to dominate the Lightweight race, and this was widely regarded as Wal's best chance of the week for a win. Sure enough, Handley got off to his usual start with a record lap and first place. Plug trouble then intervened and pushed him down to second, seventeen seconds behind his team-mate Ernie Nott. The trouble having cleared, Wal's response was characteristic and effective. He set a new lap record, at 73.73 mph., and took eighty-nine seconds off Nott on a single lap. Then plug trouble struck again, and a stop to correct it dropped him down to fifth. As ever, there was no giving up. On his next circuit he raised the lap record yet again, to 74.08 mph, and took over fourth place. A further sterling effort brought him third but time was running out. He couldn't catch his team-mate Graham Walker or eventual winner Leo Davenport [New Imperial]. Handley's comments on his recurring plug troubles were said to be unprintable.

So, as so often, the Senior remained Handley's last chance of a TT week win. But this time he was up against it, for the Nortons definitely had the edge on speed. The opening lap saw Wal in third, five seconds down on Woods and eight on Simpson. He maintained his third place until the end of the third circuit. Then the public address system announced that he had crashed at 'Ballygallow'. He was a little knocked

about but not seriously hurt. A doctor was going out. Actually he had crashed at the first S-bend above Barregarrow when his bike's front brake seized. He had a few abrasions and was generally shaken up and was kept in Nobles Hospital overnight for observation. Later, through general acclamation and usage, the spot where he crashed became known as 'Handley's Corner', a permanent memorial to Wal on the TT course.

Wal Handley rode in the Island for three more years but he never again won a TT race. He came closest in 1933 when, with Rudge having withdrawn from racing, he rode an Excelsior 'Mechanical Marvel' in that year's Lightweight TT. The bike was an experimental 4 valve, two carburettor machine inspired by the successful Rudge. It came to the Island virtually direct from the Excelsior test bench.

Handley led on the first lap, ahead of his Excelsior team-mate Syd Gleave. But he dropped to second on the next lap and third on the following circuit. He climbed to second on lap five but then slipped to third by the end of the sixth. He retired on the last lap when the engine blew at Sulby. Syd Gleave went on to win.

In the Junior of that year Wal rode a 350 Velocette for his old friend and Velo boss Harold Willis. However he could do no better than seventh. He scratched from the Senior, practically at the flag, complaining of a bad leg. 1934 was Wal's only year with Norton, then all-conquering, when he replaced the injured Tim Hunt. In the Junior he was lying third behind his team-mates Guthrie and Simpson when he came off at Governor's Bridge and so damaged his nose that he was unable to continue or to race in the Senior. His final appearance in the TT was in 1935 when, once again he was in the Velocette team. In the first morning practice session, however, Handley crashed at Sulby and, in trying to re-adjust the chain and rear brake, lost part of his thumb and was unable to race. For Wal Handley the spark had definitely gone from the TT and, wisely, he decided to call it a day.

He had ridden in 28 TTs, won four times, finished second

three times and third twice. He had set the fastest lap of a race nine times and broken the lap record on many more occasions. He'd been the first to win all four solo classes, the first to do the double, and the first to set record laps in all three classes in a week. He had eleven TT replicas, a manufacturer's team prize and that Nisbet shield from 1923. It was a TT record anyone could be proud of.

After the end of his motor cycle career Handley turned to car racing. In 1934 he drove for MG in the car Tourist Trophy races at Ards in Northern Ireland. Fellow TT winner, Charlie Dodson, was one of his team-mates. But Wal had to retire with gear box problems. He returned to run his motor-cycle business in Suffolk Street, Birmingham.

Things were fairly quiet for three years. Then, on the 30th. June 1937 a strange entry appeared in the normal mid-week British Motor Cycle Racing Club [BMCRC], meeting at the famous Brooklands track. The entry was for Wal Handley and the entrants were BSA. It was a double surprise. Handley had retired from racing three years earlier; BSA had not taken part in racing since their disastrous TT entry in 1921, when they had entered six riders in the Senior race only to see them all retire.

1935: Wal Handley's last competitive race on the Island was the Mannin Mooar in this MG Magnette.

BSA had developed a new sports version of their 497cc Empire Star model, and competitions chief Bert Perrigo had persuaded Wal out of his retirement to try it. The race was a three lap allcomers' outer circuit handicap. The handicappers put Handley on the nine second mark, with the real Brooklands specialists on scratch. They should have known better. By the end of the second lap Wal had passed the rest of the field. At the finish he had won by a clear hundred yards at an average of 102 mph., and a fastest lap of over 107 mph.

It was the custom of the BMCRC to award a small gold badge, in the shape of a star, to anyone who could average over 100 mph. round the Brooklands Circuit. By his performance that day, Wal Handley won the award. So, when BSA decided to make a production version of the new bike, they called it, in celebration of Handley's achievement, the BSA Gold Star. It became, fittingly, the most famous sports machine the British motor-cycle industry ever produced.

Wal Handley was a keen and very competent pilot. So, when the Second World War broke out it was only natural that he should put his talent to good use. The autumn of 1941 found him a Captain in the Air Transport Auxiliary. As the C.O. he didn't have to fly but he did. He died on the 15th November 1941 when the Aircobra aircraft he was ferrying to an RAF station crashed on take off at Kirkbride Aerodrome. He was killed instantly.

Walter Handley is commemorated in the TT by the corner that bears his name, the memorial bench at Quarterbridge Road and the Walter Handley Trophy, formerly awarded for the fastest lap in the sidecar class.

Whenever TT fans get together the conversation will eventually turn to 'Who was the greatest TT rider of all? 'Was it Handley or Simpson, Guthrie or Woods, Surtees or Duke, Hailwood or Agostini, or, the man with the most TT wins, Joey Dunlop?' There will never be a definitive answer.

When it comes to Wal Handley, though, one thing is certain. As it says on that memorial bench at the side of the course, 'None ever passed this way more bravely'.

The Two Johns

My father swore it was true. I'd like to say I remember it, but I don't. Although my father wasn't averse to embellishing a good story, he wasn't a man to make one up, so there must be some truth in it.

We were standing at the top of the Butt in Onchan watching a practice session on the Clypse course. In the way that only small children devoid of inhibitions and discovering the power of embarrassment can, I was making my views known about the speed of the various riders who passed. Close by was a group of young men also watching the bikes and much amused at my comments.

One of them asked me who my favourite rider was. 'Geoff Duke', I replied emphatically. My father smiled with all the pride of one who has sired an offspring who is clearly wise beyond his years. Actually I was simply repeating his choice. I had never even seen Duke race. 'Who's the next best?', one of the others asked. 'Bob McIntyre' I replied quickly. My father looked further encouraged at his son's natural intelligence. 'What about John Surtees?' another asked, with a touch more humour than the others. 'Not as good as Duke' I said, with all the certainty of youth.

For some reason this caused a fair amount of amusement amongst the group, except for one young man, who just smiled at me. My father looked a little embarrassed. The young man smiling was John Surtees.

My first memory of John Hartle was less pleasurable and more dramatic, for me and certainly for Hartle. My father had taken me to watch the 1958 Senior TT. In those days the

1955: The Two Johns in team formation. John Hartle leads John Surtees in the Ulster Grand Prix.

warm-up for the race machines just prior to the race took place on the course itself, on a part of Glencrutchery Road just before the start and finish line. A series of dustbins were placed at intervals in the middle of the road and the bikes did slow circuits round the oval track created. We went to Glencrutchery Road to watch the warm-up and then, once the race itself had started, moved further down the road close to Governor's Bridge to see the riders exit from the dip.

After three laps my father suggested that we move back towards the Grandstand area to be sure of seeing the winners finish. It was a fortunate move. At the end of the next lap John Hartle, coming out of the dip at Governor's, lost control of his M.V. machine and crashed not far from where we had previously been sitting. The bike caught fire and was practically burnt out before the marshals arrived with fire extinguishers.

For three years the two Johns, Surtees and Hartle, dominated the TT and World Championship motorcycle racing generally. Surtees won five TTs and three 350/500 World Championship doubles. Hartle was a loyal and skillful number two.

In some ways they were very similar. Both had served apprenticeships in the motorcycle trade, Surtees at Vincents, Hartle at his local dealership. They started their works riding careers together in the Norton team and each had a healthy respect for the talent of the other. They also became good friends. Surtees was to recommend Hartle to MV and Hartle invited Surtees to become godfather to one of his children.

When it came to racing, the two Johns shared a common determination, an unwillingness to give up or give in and a firm will to win. With this in mind they were both consummate professionals in their approach to riding. They combined aggression in attacking corners and courses with the smooth rhythm so necessary to be successful in the Island. But there were differences too.

For all his rhythm, it was always obvious that Hartle was a trier. You could see that he was giving of his best and it was

this as much as anything that endeared him to race fans. Unfortunately he also seemed to be unlucky in his riding, almost jinxed. So often it would seem that everything was finally going to come right when mechanical breakdown or, particularly, injury would step in to spoil things.

John Hartle was a brave and tough rider who, on his day, could beat the very best for speed. He matched a rare, and sometimes raw courage to dogged determination and a tenacious, almost stubborn refusal to give in. Time after time he returned from injuries that would have finished the career of another rider; returned to racing at the highest level and the absolute limit.

His courage, which endeared him to race fans, made him a fine rider in the wet and a competitor to be respected in any conditions. Sadly his talents never really seemed to bring the rewards they ought to have done. Sometimes injury occurred at a crucial time. More often his successes and achievements were overshadowed, ironically, by the man who had such a great regard for Hartle's ability, his team - mate John Surtees.

Not that Surtees always got the recognition he deserved. But in the years the two Johns rode together, first for Norton and then for MV, Hartle was always seen as the number two, the junior partner.

It is worth remembering, then, that John Hartle won two TTs and finished second on five occasions. More impressively, he was in contention for a leader board place in every single TT race he rode in - a record any TT competitor would be proud of and which deservedly puts him amongst the all-time TT greats.

Surtees was more of a stylist. He really developed the high-speed drift form of cornering that improving tyres would allow and often made winning look easy. Unlike most riders he was not interested in luck or superstition. His easy style reflected thorough preparation and testing.

In the history of motorsport, John Surtees holds and deserves a unique place. An outstanding engineer as well as an outstanding rider, he won seven motorcycle World

Championships including three 350/500 doubles. He was first in 6 TTs and 32 other GPs, became the only man ever to win World Championships on two and four wheels and received the MBE for services to motorcycle racing.

For all this success, Surtees never seemed to receive the same sort of popularity as other TT heroes like Geoff Duke. A quiet, modest man he was certainly admired and well respected, but the public empathy was not the same. Perhaps he was unlucky in following Duke and being seen in some ways as taking over from him. Perhaps it was his wholly professional approach which contrasted with what was still seen as an amateur sport, or the unfair charge of lack of opposition in his later motorcycle career. Whatever the reason, only now perhaps, is John Surtees receiving the recognition he deserves.

John Hartle was born in Chapel-en-le-Frith, Derbyshire, in 1934. His father worked for a brake lining factory and when the young John left school he was apprenticed to a local

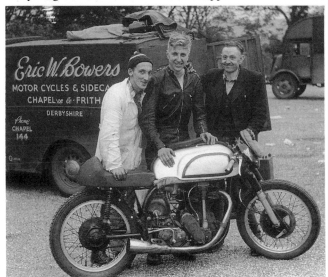

1954: John Hartle with the Eric Bowers equipe at Scarborough.

garage owner and motorcycle dealer. Eric Bowers soon spotted the talent of his apprentice and loaned Hartle the machines on which he started his racing career. At the end of his apprenticeship Hartle faced the prospect of National Service. But he was worried that joining the Army would mean an end to his racing. So Hartle opted to become a miner which, whilst it meant five years' service rather than two, would at least allow him some time to race. When he discovered, though, that the army would let him go on with his racing and give him a job as a mechanic and motorcycle instructor he left the mines after two years and joined the R.A.O.C. The Army stuck to its bargain and released him from time to time to ride for the Norton team.

Hartle made his Isle of Man debut in the 1953 Manx Grand Prix races in September, finishing 21st in the Junior on an AJS. In the Senior he took his Norton into 15th place and was part of the Louth and District trio who took the Club team award.

He returned to the MGP in 1954, this time finishing third in the Junior on his AJS, behind Derek Ennett [AJS] and Dave Chadwick [Norton]. In the Senior Hartle was leading the race when he ran out of fuel just 10 miles from the finish. In those days success in the Senior MGP was the 'fast-track' to the Norton works team and Hartle was invited to join Norton for the 1955 TT.

-----oOo-----

John Surtees was born on the 11th February 1934, the same year as Hartle, in Tatsfield, Kent. His father Jack was a well known sidecar rider, winning nine British Championships before his retirement in 1952. Jack Surtees had a motorcycle business in Croydon and it was not long before his son began riding. A Triumph Tiger was one of his first mounts. John Surtees learnt his chosen profession thoroughly, beginning at fifteen as an engineering apprentice with the Vincent Company.

The young Surtees was never too far from competition riding. Initially he partnered his father in sidecar grass track events, then entered his first solo class at fifteen, coming off whilst lying third. It was at road racing, though, that the young man's talent really shone. Aged seventeen, Surtees rebuilt a 500cc Vincent Grey Flash which he had rescued from the scrap heap and soon scored his first win on it at a meeting at Brands Hatch. But Surtees could see that the Vincent would soon be no good against the new featherbed Nortons. Using his winnings and the proceeds from the sale of the Vincent he bought a 500cc Manx Norton and spent four seasons riding to outstanding success on British short circuits. He was adopted by race fans as the 'King' of Brands.

Surtees wanted to make his Isle of Man debut in the 1952 Manx Grand Prix. At first, however, it seemed that he would be required by Vincent to help with a record-breaking attempt at Montlery. Then he finished sixth on his Norton in the 500cc Ulster GP. Though a fine result, this participation in a World Championship event debarred him from competing in the Manx Grand Prix. So, for his Island debut, Surtees had to wait for the next year's TT.

For 1953 Surtees was due to ride a 125cc EMC for Dr. Joe Ehrlich in the Lightweight [125] TT. Surtees success on short circuits, however, had also brought him to the attention of the Norton works team. When Syd Lawton was injured crashing his works Norton in practice, Surtees was offered the replacement rides. It was a remarkable [and unique], expression of confidence by Norton team manager, Joe Craig, in a young rider who had never ridden in the Isle of Man before. The Norton debut was not to be, however. Riding the EMC in practice, the forks broke at the left-hander just after Ballaugh Bridge and Surtees crashed breaking his wrist and putting

1955: John Surtees takes his NSU to a convincing win in the Lightweight Ulster Grand Prix.

himself out of that year's races. It was rumoured that, so afraid was he of Joe Craig's reaction, Surtees took the next boat home.

He was back at the TT in 1954, this time riding his own Nortons. He finished eleventh in the Junior and fifteenth in the Senior curtailed to four laps after appalling weather conditions. During the rest of the year he did well enough to keep Joe Craig interested. He led the Junior Ulster GP for four laps and diced with Geoff Duke's Gilera in the Hutchinson 100 at Silverstone. So in 1955, Surtees, as well as Hartle, found himself part of the Norton works team.

For 1955, Norton had already started to curtail their racing efforts. They competed only in the TT and Ulster GP. Their riders were free to race their own machines in other domestic races, which Surtees did to devastating effect. On a Sportsmax loaned to him by the NSU factory and his own 350 and 500 Nortons he was virtually unbeatable, winning sixty-five out of the seventy-two races he contested. This included a win at Silverstone over Duke and the Gilera.

The Norton team for the TT consisted of Surtees, Hartle and Jack Brett. Although they had experimented with various streamlining designs during the previous year, Norton rejected the use of the 'Dustbin' streamlining then being used by Guzzi and some private entrants, including Bob McIntyre's Joe Potts' prepared machines.

In the Junior Race McIntyre rode brilliantly on his 'dustbin' Norton, tussling with the two works Guzzis of Bill Lomas and Cecil Sandford. McIntyre and Surtees led after the first lap with Sandford in third place. On the next lap the Guzzi rider took second place from Surtees but the flying McIntyre was still in the lead. Bob kept ahead for the next two circuits until gradually Bill Lomas overhauled everybody to come home the winner. It was the first win in the Junior for a foreign machine and gave Lomas a unique double. He had also won the Lightweight 250 on the Clypse circuit - the first man to win two TTs in the same week on different circuits.

Surtees finished the Junior in fourth, just one second behind the Guzzi of Sandford. Hartle was a creditable sixth behind Australian Maurice Quincey. Surtees was part of the BMCRC trio with McIntyre and Sandford who won the Club team Prize for the Junior.

In the Senior race the Norton works team won the Manufacturers prize, even though the two Johns both had to push in to finish. Surtees had been lying eighth when he ran out of petrol on the last lap. He finished twenty-ninth. Hartle finished thirteenth after pushing in from Hillberry. Brett managed fourth.

The two Johns had a happier Ulster GP. Hartle finished second to Bill Lomas [Guzzi] in both the 350 and 500 races. Surtees finished third in the Junior but, more importantly, won his first GP, taking the 250 class on his NSU.

At the end of 1955 it seemed likely that Norton might pull out of racing altogether. Gilera had expressed some interest in Surtees but they too were having doubts about their future racing plans. Into the breach stepped MV Agusta.

Surtees had been brought to the attention of the MV factory by Bill Webster, a motorcycle dealer who had raced an early production MV 125 himself and been one of the first to recognise the potential of the MV bikes. Webster had also become something of a talent scout for the Italian factory.

After Surtees win in the 250 Ulster GP, the NSU factory had invited him to ride one of their machines in the Italian GP. Surtees retired in the race but his practice times had been enough to confirm his promise. He was invited to visit Gallarate, meet Count Agusta himself, see the set up and test the MV machines. After confirming with Norton that they were unlikely to run a team in 1956, Surtees signed for MV Agusta.

Those who dismiss Surtees' later MV successes as having been achieved against little opposition, forget that the ride for MV was hardly viewed at the time as an easy berth. There were plenty of people who warned Surtees not to join the Gallarate concern. Les Graham and Ray Amm, two of the finest riders of any generation, had both been killed riding for MV - Amm as recently as Easter that year. Carlo Bandirola had crashed several times that season due, it was said, to the poor handling of the big MV. Surtees, however, preferred to back his own judgement. Before signing, he tested the bikes at Monza and Modena. The factory agreed that there was too much movement in the frame but together they agreed how this could and would be rectified. New engines were also promised.

MV kept their promise, and for 1956 built new engines for their machines. The 500cc unit was rumoured to produce some 70 bhp at 11,000 rpm but was heavy at over 350 lbs. This unit was scaled down to produce a 350cc bike. This was said to produce around 50 bhp at 11,000 rpm. but was really heavy for its class, weighing about 340 lbs. Its main rival, the 350 Guzzi, was less powerful but weighed only 265 lbs and had the advantage of its wind tunnel tested streamlining.

Surtees used his engineering expertise to improve the handling of the MV's and increase their performance. The season started well with wins at a couple of U.K. meetings.

Sadly the exciting prospect of a Duke/Surtees Gilera/MV battle never really materialised, in this or any other season. Duke and Armstrong [Gileras] were suspended for the first six months of 1956 for supporting a riders' strike at the Dutch TT the year before. By the time they were back in racing misfortune had struck Surtees.

Although Joe Craig had now retired and Norton did not contest any of the continental GPs. Norton nevertheless decided that they would enter a team for the TT. There the ageing bikes might still perform well, their handling and reliability making up for their comparative lack of top speed. The TT team again included John Hartle and Jack Brett, backed up this time by Alan Trow, who had finished fourth in the 1955 Senior MGP.

TT practice did not provide an very good start for the new Surtees/MV partnership. Surtees hit a stray cow on the fast ascent after Sarah's Cottage and was lucky to escape with minor injuries. The cow wasn't seriously hurt. The MV was wrecked.

In the Junior race Surtees lay second to Lomas' Guzzi for the first five laps. Then Lomas retired at Guthries leaving Surtees in the lead by just one second from Australian Ken Kavanagh [Guzzi]. Unfortunately over-hasty pit work by MV, trying to give him an advantage over Kavanagh, had left Surtees without enough petrol to finish the race. He retired with a quarter of a lap to go, leaving Kavanagh to score another Guzzi win. Surtees borrowed some petrol from a spectator to get home, thus automatically disqualifying himself. Hartle's Norton was no match for the Italian machines but he had a good, fast but steady ride to finish third behind Manxman Derek Ennett on the works AJS.

The two John's did better in the Senior race. Conditions were far from ideal. The roads were dry but there was a strong wind blowing on the Mountain section. Nothing could stop Surtees, however. Despite starting No. 81, and being down on speed through having to ride a well-used practice machine [the race bike had been wrecked by the collision with the cow], he led from start to finish to win at a race average of 96.57 mph with a fastest lap of 97.79 mph. Hartle finished a fine second only ninety seconds behind the MV after two and three quarter hours of racing. Fourth on the first lap behind McIntyre [Norton] and Lomas [Guzzi], Hartle moved up as first McIntyre retired and then Lomas hit trouble. Hartle helped Norton win the Manufacturers team prize and was also a member of the winning club team of Winsford and District M.C.

Surtees went on to win the 500 class at the Dutch TT and the 500 Belgian round when Duke [Gilera] retired on the thirteenth lap with valve trouble. At the next GP round at Solitude, near Stuttgart, Surtees was trying hard to challenge Lomas in the 350 race when the front wheel of the MV slid away on a tricky surface and Surtees was thrown off. He hit some banking and badly broke his left arm, putting him out of racing for the rest of that season. It turned out, however, that his early season 500cc victories were enough to give him his first World Championship at the age of just twenty-two.

The season ended well for the other John. In a damp Ulster GP he won the 500 class, his first GP win, when Duke made a rare mistake and dropped the Gilera. This win and his second place in the TT were enough to give him third place in the World Championship, despite not having competed in any other rounds. When MV indicated that they might be looking for another rider for the big classes, Surtees recommended Hartle. MV, however, wanted McIntyre, only to see him sign for Gilera, their arch-rivals.

1957 was a disappointing year for the two Johns. The death of Joe Craig in March seemed to rule out any prospect of a works Norton for Hartle, whilst Surtees suffered early in the season from the slowness of his injured arm to heal fully

and a series of mechanical breakdowns. Both came to the TT looking for better things.

Norton had made 'works' bikes available to their former team riders through a number of agent/entrants. Hartle was entered in the Junior on one of these 'unofficial' works Nortons by Eric Bowers, the Norton dealer in John's home town . In the Senior Hartle was due to ride the experimental '90 bore' Norton.

Surtees rode the heavy MV-4 in the Junior but was never really in contention. The bike suffered from persistent plug trouble, necessitating two lengthy pit stops, and the best he could manage was fourth place. The race was led on the first lap by McIntyre on the new 350 Gilera. Then he too suffered from a bad misfire and was overtaken by Dickie Dale [Guzzi] and Hartle. Dale lost time repairing a broken fairing and on

1957: John Surtees at Union Mills on the 500 MV.

the fourth lap he and Hartle were dicing for the lead when both came off on a patch of oil at Quarry Bends. McIntyre went on to a comfortable win from Campbell [Guzzi] and Brown [Gilera] whilst Hartle's injuries were enough to put him out of the rest of the races. His ride in the Senior was taken over by Jack Wood, later the Clerk of the course.

For the TT's Golden Jubilee, the Senior race had been specially extended to eight laps - over 300 miles of racing. MV, Gilera and Guzzi had all brought new machines to the race. Surtees was hot favourite in the absence of Duke but others thought to have a chance were McIntyre on the Gilera and Dickie Dale on the exotic V8 Guzzi. For once Surtees made a tactical error. Tests of the MV on other circuits with a full 'dustbin' fairing had not been over promising. Perhaps because the MV fairing designers were really aeronautical engineers the bike had an alarming tendency to try to take off at high speed. The enclosed fairing also led to frequent over-heating problems. Weather forecasts for the Senior had predicted windy weather on the Mountain which with the full fairing would add considerably to the handling problems of the bike. These were already a cause of concern with the decision to carry nine and a half gallons of fuel for the longer race adding to the MV's already high centre of gravity. So it was decided to run the MV without its streamlined fairing.

In fact, fittingly for the Golden Jubilee celebrations, the weather for the Senior was absolutely perfect and McIntyre's Gilera, with its full 'bin' fairing was definitely significantly faster than the MV.

Surtees held second place throughout the race but could do nothing about the leading Gilera. McIntyre took the lead on time from the start and by lap five had made up the two minute starting difference to pass Surtees on the road. The Scotsman then eased off and Surtees re-passed the Gilera at Creg-ny-Baa, much to the excitement of BBC commentator Alan Dixon, providing the best 'sound bite' of the TT ever recorded. At the end of the race McIntyre and Surtees crossed the finish line virtually together. Surtees had almost equalled

Duke's record race average but had still finished two minutes behind McIntyre at his very finest.

From races in the rest of the season it was clear that the MV still had handling problems. Surtees suggested further modifications and developed his own duplex frame for the 1958 machines. Full frontal streamlining had been banned so that tactical problem had disappeared.

In the meantime, Hartle finished fifth in the 350cc World Championship on his borrowed Norton. More importantly, at Surtees' suggestion, Hartle was given a ride on the 250cc MV at the Belgian GP - and promptly won at record speed. When, at the end of the season, MV were again looking for a second rider in the bigger classes, Surtees' repeated suggestion of Hartle was happily accepted. The two Johns would be teammates again, in the world's most powerful race team.

The close season had brought a bombshell to motorcycle racing. Gilera, Moto Guzzi and Mondial all decided that racing had become too expensive to support. They would no longer run their works teams. For a time it seemed that MV might follow their example. But eventually Count Agusta decided to continue his involvement. The MV mechanics worked hard over the winter to try and eliminate the problems of 1957, and even found time to develop a six cylinder 500. However this was largely mothballed once the withdrawal of the other factories was known.

Surtees' new frame and fork layout improved the handling of the MV considerably, allowing Surtees to develop the power drift style of cornering he preferred. Hartle would support him in the 350 and 500 classes and, with factory opposition gone, they set themselves to beating records rather than just other riders. In this respect the TT was particularly important and the factory was anxious to do well after the disappointments of the previous year. The two Johns were to have mixed fortunes.

In the Junior Hartle got no further than the Bungalow on lap one before piston trouble put him out of the race. For a brief period Bob McIntyre [Norton] threatened to give the

MVs a challenge but he retired at Quarter Bridge on lap two. Surtees romped home over four minutes ahead of the privately entered Nortons of Dave Chadwick and Geoff Tanner. Terry Shepherd [Norton] finished a fine fourth despite having been twenty-sixth at the end of lap one.

In the Senior it was a similar story. Surtees led from start to finish recording his first 100 mph lap along the way. Once again McIntyre threatened to split the heavy MVs, taking second place from Hartle for the first three laps. Hartle did have the consolation of lapping at just over the 'ton', and being only the second rider to do so [he started ahead of Surtees on the road, making Surtees' ton lap the third]. When McIntyre retired on the third lap with engine trouble it looked like Hartle would be comparatively safe in second place. Then, when coming out of the dip at Governor's Bridge on lap four Hartle crashed the MV which burst into flames. Unfortunately the bike failed to live up to its nickname [it was called the 'Fire Engine' because of its red tank and fairing], and it was practically burnt out before marshals with extinguishers could reach it.

Hartle's accident put Alastair King up to second but he crashed at Kirk Michael on the last lap. Surtees eventually won by over five minutes from the private Nortons of Bob Anderson and Bob Brown.

It proved to be a remarkable season for Surtees. He won every single round of the 500 and 350 GPs except the Swedish GP where, with the World Championships already well won, MV decided not to compete. It was the first of three 350/500 World Championship doubles for Surtees. Amazingly he remained unbeaten altogether until, near the end of the season, Derek Minter beat him at Brands Hatch when the MV developed plug trouble. Despite his TT troubles Hartle performed his back-up role well, finishing second in both the 350 and 500 Championships. He also became the only man to ride the MV-6 when he tried it out in the Italian GP. Sadly he had to retire after a few laps with engine trouble.

For 1959 the two Johns were once again team-mates for the MV factory. At the TT, Surtees was looking to equal Stanley Woods' record of Senior/Junior doubles in successive years.

In the Junior it was the same old story. Surtees led from start to finish but McIntyre managed to split the MVs for a time. The MVs might have had the edge on top speed but the heavy 350s were really not at their best on the TT circuit and the much lighter, better handling AJS 7R, in the hands of a genius like McIntyre could give the works fire engines a real scrap.

McIntyre led Hartle for second for the first three laps, but then hit trouble on lap four and had to retire. If Hartle thought he was in for an easy second, however, he was soon disillusioned. The challenge was taken up by another Joe Potts entered Scot, McIntyre's close friend Alastair King. Hartle held off the challenge to finish second to Surtees, but only 10 seconds ahead of King. Surtees had broken the race record and finished four minutes ahead of the field.

Surtees' achievements were sometimes disparaged with the charge that he faced little opposition. But the sheer consistency of his results and the many records he continued to break along the way demonstrated clearly his skill, concentration and self-motivation. And if there were any doubts about his courage his next race answered those emphatically.

Bad weather had already led to the postponement of the Senior TT from the Friday of race week to the Saturday. The race started in the dry and Surtees had soon broken the lap record at 101.18 mph. Hartle had taken up station in second place and the thorn of the MV's, McIntyre, was in third. Then the weather changed quickly. The clouds rolled in, the winds picked up, low cloud enveloped the Mountain and the rain made the roads wet and greasy. Hartle crashed at Glen Vine early on lap three and was taken to Hospital with concussion. Conditions got worse but there was no sign of the organisers being willing to abandon the race. By the last couple of laps it was actually hailing so hard on the Mountain that the fairing of the remaining MV was pitted and discoloured. Surtees finished cold and exhausted with his hands almost frozen to the handlebars. He had to be lifted off the machine. When he had recovered enough to speak he said that he never wanted to ride in another race like that. His winning race speed at 87.94 mph was the lowest since 1949, but still astounding in the conditions. He finished five minutes ahead of Alastair King who, in turn, was five minutes ahead of Bob Brown.

If the 1958 season had been a remarkable one for Surtees then, in terms of results, the 1959 one was even more impressive. Surtees won all seven 500 GPs and all six 350 GPs - a unique record. It earned him the Sports Writers' Association's 'Sportsman of the Year' title and the BBC's 'Sports Personality of the Year' award. But his appearances in other races was restricted by the factory. Altogether he was only competing in about two dozen races a year. Unhappy with this level of activity, Surtees started to have his first serious look at car racing. Ken Tyrell gave him a drive in a Formula Junior Cooper and Surtees finished second to a promising youngster - Jim Clark.

Hartle was also unhappy, but for a different reason. It seemed he was out of favour with Count Agusta who had dropped Hartle from a couple of late season races in favour of the Italian rider Venturi.

Although attracted by the prospect of car racing, Surtees decided to have a further season with MV for 1960. Hartle and the Gallarate factory, however had come to a parting of the ways. MV offered Hartle a limited number of rides for the season [the Senior TT for example, but not the Junior], so Hartle decided to go his own way. Geoff Duke recommended Hartle to the new Honda team and Hartle was invited to ride a 250 for the season. But Hartle was contracted to Mobil oil and Honda to Castrol, so Hartle went back to racing his own Nortons, until the TT.

MV had made TT entries for the Junior and Senior for Surtees and Umberto Masetti. The latter had ridden in the 1955 Lightweight TTs, but on the Clypse circuit not the Mountain course. At the last moment, perhaps due to Surtees'

desire to have a more experienced TT partner, Hartle was invited by MV to ride their 350 and 500 machines. He gladly agreed. It was a fortunate decision. Determined to show the factory what he could do, Hartle had his best ever TT with MV machines.

One of John Surtees' ambitions was to become the first man to do the Junior/Senior double three years in succession.

1958: An exhausted John Surtees after the 1958 Senior TT.

MV had been experimenting with a lighter 350-4, but for the Junior race, Surtees decided to stick with the tried and reliable 'heavy'. It was a decision he may have come to regret.

For 1960 the length of the Junior and Senior TTs was reduced to six laps from the traditional seven. There were 80 starters for the Junior which was held in good weather conditions. A disappointment was the late withdrawal of Gary Hocking on the bored-out 250 MV twin. At the recent French GP the 282cc twin had handled much better than the heavier fours and had not been that much down on top speed. The bike had been expected to go well round the TT course, but there had not been enough time in practice to sort out some transmission problems and Hocking was a reluctant non-starter.

The now retired Geoff Duke dropped the flag to get the race underway. Bob McIntyre [AJS] was first on the roads. Surtees, the hot favourite, was number four and Hartle number twelve. Surtees soon passed the men in front of him and completed the first lap at 98.26 mph, nearly twelve seconds inside the lap record. Hartle took second place at 96.65 mph, thirty-seven seconds down on Surtees but thirty-two seconds ahead of McIntyre.

On the second lap Hartle passed McIntyre on the Mountain to take second place on the roads and on time. Surtees lapped at 99.2 mph, which included slowing down for his pit stop. It looked like the first 350cc 100 mph lap was on. But Surtees had problems. As he explained to his father in his pit-stop, a

1959: Surtees flies at Ballaugh Bridge on the 500 MV.

broken gear selector spring meant that first and third gears were jumping out. He still led the race, though, by forty-one secs. from Hartle, who also stopped for fuel. McIntyre was third, sixty-two seconds down on Hartle, and re-took second on the roads as the thirstier fire engine stopped for replenishment.

As Surtees, McIntyre and Hartle came through at the end of their third laps there was a buzz of excitement in the crowd.

Surtees' lead was down to twenty-two point eight seconds and he had been signalling frantically to his pit as he passed. Hartle's lead on McIntyre was down to forty-six seconds but now the Scotsman had to pit and Hartle regained second place on the roads. All through the next circuit Hartle continued to catch Surtees. By Creg-ny-Baa the lead was down to five seconds. By the Grandstand it was four point four and Surtees gave a 'thumbs down' to his pit. McIntyre was still third, now forty-six seconds behind Hartle but forty-four seconds ahead of Derek Minter [Norton].

Finally, at Sulby on the fifth lap, Hartle led the race on time, ten seconds ahead of Surtees. It seemed almost impossible, so great had been Surtees' recent domination of the TT and GP's. By the end of the lap Hartle's lead was up to twenty point two seconds with McIntyre in third one minute forty-five

1959: John Hartle at White Gates, Ramsey.

seconds behind the ailing Surtees. As the riders lapped the course for the last time the Grandstand's loudspeaker told the story. 'Hartle has Surtees in sight. Only twenty yards between them at Ballacraine'. Then, 'Hartle leads on the roads at Glen Helen by twelve yards'. The crowd at the Grandstand cheered loudly. Most wanted to see the other John win a TT at last. Hartle's indicator on the Scoreboard showed him at the Creg, then at Signpost. Soon he flashed across the line to the roars of the crowd -a TT winner at last. There to congratulate him were his wife June and children Nigel, Lesley and baby Julie, just ten months old.

Surtees was second but his last lap time was down to twenty-five minutes and he finished just twenty-six seconds ahead of McIntyre. How the Scot must have wished it was still a

seven lap race. Typically, Surtees was one of the first to congratulate his team-mate on his win. If he had to be beaten it should be by John Hartle.

Surtees confirmed afterwards that the gear problems had caused over-revving of the engine and subsequent loss of compression due to valve gear problems. They also led to the bike arriving at some third gear corners in neutral, without any engine braking to help him slow down! Hartle knew he was in the lead when he was given a plus rather than minus signal at Sulby on the fifth lap. His bike had been slightly undergeared and he had to sit up on some parts of the course to keep within the 11, 000 rpm limit. He nearly hit trouble on the last lap when a fly got inside his goggles and affected his eyes but he managed to keep going to the end of the lap.

Hartle's win was an extremely popular one, as shown in the marvellous reception he got at the Junior prizegiving. Hartle thanked his mechanics and team and 'Old Man Agusta, not a bad chap after all'.

If the 1960 Junior had been one of John Surtees' most disappointing TTs, the 1960 Senior was one of his best. It was as though he was determined to put the earlier disappointment behind him by producing a really breathtaking performance in the big race. He led from start to finish, looking almost as relaxed at the end as he had done at the beginning.

The opening lap set the tone for what followed. Starting number three, Surtees was soon ahead on the roads and lapped from a standing start at 103.03 mph, nearly 2 mph faster than his own lap record. Hartle was second, having lapped at 100.57 mph, but was thirty-two seconds down on Surtees and only fourteen and seventeen seconds ahead of Minter and McIntyre, both of whom had lapped at over 99 mph on single cylinder Nortons.

A tingle of excitement had run through the crowd as they heard the impressive speeds of the first lap. But the second lap was even more amazing. Bob McIntyre retired, but the young Mike Hailwood lapped at 100.37 mph on his single cylinder Norton. He was just beaten to the honour of doing the first 'ton' on a single by Derek Minter, who lapped at an astounding 101.05 mph on his Steve Lancefield tuned Norton. Hartle lapped at 102.05 mph, by far his fastest lap and well ahead of the previous lap record. But Surtees went even better. An incredible 104.08 mph, despite slowing for his pitstop, smashed the lap record and made nonsense of claims of easy MV wins. He led the race by fifty-eight seconds from Hartle with Minter a further twenty-eight seconds down in third spot.

At the end of the third lap Surtees lead had increased to one minute thirty seconds. Minter had retired after a series of lurid slides caused by a split oil tank spilling oil on the rear tyre, so Hailwood came up to third just twenty-four seconds down on the other MV. Surtees continued to lap at over 102

mph and Hartle at over the ton as the two Johns firmly demonstrated their class. At the end Surtees finished with a record race average of 102.44 mph, significantly faster than the previous lap record. It was the TT's first 100 mph+ race speed. Hartle, although two and a half minutes behind at the end, also broke the 'ton average' at 100.44 mph. Hailwood was nearly three minutes behind in third.

Surtees said afterwards that his ride had been comparatively uneventful. Hartle advised that the engine had shown some signs of tightening on the fastest stretches of Cronk-y-Voddy and Sulby, but this problem had disappeared when he eased the throttle. Surtees' win gave MV a clean sweep of all four solo classes. Surtees himself equalled Stanley Woods' record of four Senior wins and became the first man to complete a hat-trick of same class wins. Altogether he had won six TT's from 14 starts and completed the course in all fourteen events - albeit with a little help in one case.

Surtees went on to win the 500 GPs in Belgium, Germany and Italy and the 350 GPs in the Dutch and Ulster to give him a third World Championship double. Ironically, it was one of his last GPs that gave him a chance to show just how good a competitor he really was, and which provided another milestone for his friend John Hartle.

The 500 Ulster GP at Dundrod that year was described at the time as the most amazing race the Ulster had ever seen. Surtees took the lead from the start and it looked like being another comfortable win for the MV. Then, at the end of the second lap, Surtees dropped to 18th place with a broken gear lever. A three and a half minute pit-stop to replace it put Surtees down to thirty-third with just eighteen laps to go. It looked a hopeless cause and many a rider would have simply retired - but not Surtees. He set off in pursuit of the field and leaders McIntyre, Hailwood and Hartle.

Surtees broke the lap record on almost every lap and by half distance in the twenty lap race had worked his way up to eleventh place, still nearly three minutes behind the leaders. McIntyre and Hailwood then retired leaving Hartle, on a Bill

Lacey tuned Norton, the clear race leader. Everyone agreed that Surtees was riding a magnificent race but it was obviously a lost cause - or was it? On lap twelve Hartle was two minutes seven seconds ahead. On lap fourteen it was down to one minute fifty-seven seconds. Surtees was lapping consistently at around 99 mph, 3 mph faster than the previous lap record, and gradually whittled away at Hartle's lead. Then, with two laps to go, Hartle had to come in for a further fuel stop. It only took fifteen seconds but as he tried to get away, the Norton was slow to re-start. Finally the Norton fired, as though answering the crowds' prayers, and the final race was on. In the end it did prove too much even for Surtees and he finished second, just twenty seconds behind his former teammate. As the crowd went wild celebrating a great race, and the first GP win by a British machine for four years, Surtees strode up the track, a broad smile on his face, to congratulate an equally smiling Hartle. The two Johns had enjoyed themselves.

For 1961 Surtees decide to leave MV and motorcycle racing. The restrictions placed on him by MV had proved too much. He could understand MV wanting to keep their machines just for the big races but couldn't agree with a similar restriction on their riders. It might keep their riders free of injury but it also kept them short of race sharpness. So Surtees returned to the idea of car-racing. Initially he thought he might combine this with bike racing, but he soon found his new discipline would take up all his time if he was going to succeed at it.

In fact Surtees made the transition to world championship level car racing comparatively easily, something only done before by the likes of Varzi, Rosemayer and the great Nuvolari in the 1920s and 1930s. He also proved as skilled a car engineer as he had been a motorcycle one. Admittedly, the 1961 season driving for Coopers was a disappointment. But in 1962, Surtees finished fourth in the World Championship in a Lola of his own design. In 1963 he was invited to join the greatest team in racing, Ferrari, and later

that year won the German GP for Marinello. The Ferrari mechanics loved him. Few other drivers were prepared to spend long hours and get their hands dirty trying to find extra speed or cure a problem. They nicknamed Surtees 'Il Grande John', the great John, mistranslated by the U.K. Press as 'Big John'.

Surtees soon used the diplomatic skills he had learnt at MV to persuade Ferrari to improve his race car. Enzo Ferrari and Count Agusta were both proud autocrats, and Surtees knew that the key to getting changes was to convince the Commendatore that the idea had been the Commendatore's all along. In 1964 Surtees won the World Drivers' Championship - the first, and so far the only man, to win World Championships on two wheels and four.

Surtees left Ferrari after 1966 and a series of disappointing results. He joined the Honda team for a while and then in 1969 formed his own team. His World Championship results were patchy but the team did win the 1972 Formula 2 Championship with a certain Mike Hailwood as their driver. Surtees retired from racing in 1978 but remains very much involved in Classic Motorsport. He is a past President of the TT Riders' Association.

A heavy crash at Oliver's Mount in Scarborough put John Hartle out of racing for 1961 and 1962. For 1963, however, it seemed his luck had changed. Geoff Duke was convinced that the 1957 Gilera, with new brakes and tyres and other improvements, could still give Mike Hailwood and the works MV a challenge for the Championship. Duke had persuaded the Gilera factory to let him race the bikes under the 'Scuderia Duke' banner, with Duke acting as team manager. Always an admirer of Hartle as a road racer, Duke signed Hartle up with short circuit expert Derek Minter as the other team rider.

Early testing of the bikes confirmed that the 500 at least was still competitive. This was reinforced when, at an early season race at Imola, the Gileras came in first and second with Hailwood on the MV in third. Then Minter was badly injured in a crash at Brands Hatch whilst riding one of his own machines and a promising rider called Phil Read was drafted into the Gilera team.

The first GP of the season was at Hockenheim in West Germany. There was no 500 class but there was a 350 GP. It was soon clear, though, that the 350 Gileras were hopelessly outclassed, not just by the MV but even more by the 350 Hondas. Honda team leader Jim Redman nearly lapped Read in winning the race.

In practice for the Junior TT the problems with the 350s continued. One engine blew up and the practice times were well down on the Hondas and the MV. The start of the race itself was delayed and, when it did get underway, conditions were soon wet, cold and misty. Read retired as early as lap two. Redman initially led from Hailwood on the MV with Hartle in third place. Hailwood dropped out on the fourth lap with gear problems and Hartle took over second, a position he held to the end despite losing one cylinder on the last lap. He finished nearly seven minutes behind the Honda, but a minute and a half ahead of Franta Stastny on the Jawa twin.

It was clear that in the Senior, however, the Gileras were much more competitive. Hailwood attempted to undermine the Gileras by doing every practice lap on his big MV at over 100 mph. However, Hartle remained quietly confident that he could lap as fast as the MV-4. Hartle started the race fourth on the roads and it was soon clear that he was really trying. Using all his TT experience, and all of the road, Hartle went as fast as he could, narrowly missing banks and hedges. At the end of the first circuit he had lapped at 105.57 mph, an amazing speed on a seven year old bike. But Hailwood had gone even faster at 106.64 mph. He had the advantage of starting number five, just behind Hartle, and knew that he only had to catch the Gilera and stay with him to win the race. Once he caught Hartle on the first lap the race was effectively over, unless the MV hit mechanical troubles. It didn't, and Hailwood won at an average speed of 104.64 mph. Hartle was second at a very creditable 103.67 mph, and Read third at 100.10 mph. Hailwood always said it was one of his best races and he respected the challenge which Hartle had posed.

Overall, for all sorts of reasons, the season was a difficult one for Scuderia Duke. But Hartle won the 500 Dutch TT and finished second in the 500 Ulster GP. He finished third in the 500 Championship. Gilera, however, had seen enough and declined to continue their Championship efforts in 1964.

1963: John Hartle takes the Scuderia Duke Gilera round Quarter Bridge to second place behind Mike Hailwood (MV).

Hartle got off to a good start in 1964. Riding a Norton he finished third in the first U.S. 500 GP at Daytona, and there was talk of perhaps the loan again of a Gilera for the Senior TT. Then Hartle crashed heavily at a race at Imola, fracturing his skull and putting him out of racing for the next two years.

Hartle made a triumphant return in 1967, in more ways than one. For the Diamond Jubilee TT the ACU had included a race for production machines over three laps of the TT course. For the 750cc class, BSA, Norton and Triumph all entered machines. Triumph asked John Hartle, one of the few riders to have competed in the Golden Jubilee TT to ride one of their Bonneville twins. Hartle responded magnificently. With a display of high class, high speed, consistent racing he set the fastest lap at 97.87 mph on an almost standard machine and averaged 97.10 mph to win from Paul Smart on a Norton. He also won the Hutchinson 100 that year and finished third in the 500 World Championship on his G50 Matchless.

The prospects for 1968 looked even better. Worried by the threat of Renzo Pasolini's Benelli in the 350 class, MV looked around for someone to partner Agostini in the TT. Ten years after they had first done so, MV offered a works ride to John Hartle. He accepted gladly.

Hartle was to ride the MV-3 in the Junior and an MV-4 in the Senior. He was delighted with the opportunity so late in his career, and with the bikes themselves. But once more, just as things were looking good, Hartle's bad luck struck. Wednesday's Junior race was preceded by that year's Production Race in which Hartle was riding again for Triumph. Leading the race Hartle crashed at Windy Corner, robbing himself of another TT win and of the chance to ride the MV in the afternoon. He recovered in time to ride the big MV in the Senior but had gearbox trouble on the first lap and came off at Cronk-ny-Mona when he was unable to change down.

Hartle's appalling luck was to strike one more time, with tragic consequences. The 30th August 1968 saw Hartle competing in a race at the Oliver's Mount Circuit at Scarborough.

He had got off to a bad start but was coming through the field well and had just set the fastest lap. Accelerating out of the Hairpin the rider in front of him missed a gear and Hartle ran into the back of him bringing them both off. Hartle hit the scaffolding to a nearby footbridge and died from the resulting injuries.

I saw John Surtees again in September 1993. He had finally made it to the Manx Grand Prix - he was the organisers' Guest of Honour.

They say that in his racing days he could sometimes seem distant and hard to approach, so wrapped up was he in his racing. If so, he must have changed a lot. Now, he had a word for everyone he met, particularly the youngsters on the scoreboards. He was cheerful, friendly, clearly enjoying himself. He was everything you hope and expect an ex-Champion to be.

Standing again at the TT Grandstand must have brought back a lot of memories: six TT wins, seven World Championships, some great races, the fabulous sound of the MV-4. But I wondered whether, amongst those memories, there was also a thought for his former team-mate - for the other John - for the two Johns together.

I suspect there was.

The Record Breakers

You wouldn't do it now. If you were naming an eating place for bikers you wouldn't choose the Gay Heart Cafe. But that's what it was called then, and very popular it was too.

The building is at the Onchan end of Douglas Promenade, at the bottom of Summerhill. Built in the 1930s, the cafe, even then, was not named for motorcyclists but for the general tourists visiting Douglas each year in their hundreds of thousands. Nowadays it's L'Experience, an excellent local restaurant, particularly if you like French cuisine. In the 1950s the fare was a little more basic but no less appreciated for that.

Like most young Manx couples with a mortgage and a young family, my mother and father took extra jobs during the summer. The extra money they earned helped them get through the winter and paid for our birthday and Christmas presents. My father was a cinema manager. My mother waited on at the Gay Heart Cafe.

It was an extra burden to her but it was a godsend to me. The cafe was a main meeting and eating place for TT riders after an evening practice session. My mother was thus ideally placed to collect autographs for her race-mad son. She didn't disappoint. I still have the autograph book. The signatures are there, some in bold confident hands, some more hesitant, under newspaper pictures of the riders in question. Most of the top riders of the 1950s are there; Surtees, Hartle, Jack Brett, Alan Trow, Dickie Dale, Bill Lomas, Bob Anderson and Alistair King. There is a place of honour, though for the one I cherished most of all - Bob McIntyre.

-----oOo-----

The Golden Jubilee Senior TT was about to start. It was Friday seventh June, 1957. Fittingly, the weather was perfect for the specially extended eight lap race.

Bob McIntyre was outwardly as calm and cool as usual as he sat astride his 500cc four cylinder Gilera. The new, lighter machine had been delivered only part-way through practice week. It had pannier tanks to help reduce the need for refuelling during the longer race. McIntyre had chosen to ride the bike with its full 'dustbin' streamlining. In windy conditions this would have given handling problems. In that day's fine weather it added about 10 mph to the top speed of the machine.

Mac was No. 78, one of the last riders to start. It was a serious disadvantage since he'd have to spend most of the race passing slower riders. It did give him one advantage, though. John Surtees on the MV was starting two minutes ahead of him. All Bob had to do was reduce that gap and the race would surely be his.

In the absence of Duke through injury, Surtees was hot favourite for the race after his win the previous year. McIntyre might win, it was thought, if Surtees hit trouble.

Today, when the lap record for the TT course is 124 mph it is difficult to remember the excitement generated by the possibility of the first 100 mph lap. At the time, however, it had the same attraction as the conquering of Everest, the breaking of the sound barrier, the four-minute mile. There was something mystical about it. In 1955, Duke had come close, been announced as having done it indeed, only to have the timekeepers correct his lap speed to 99.97 mph.

McIntyre's Gilera-4 produced some 70bhp at 10,500 rpm. It was rumoured to have a top speed of 160 mph. It was surely capable of a 100 mph lap. But that was not on McIntyre's mind as he waited at the start. Beating Surtees, winning the race was all he was interested in. McIntyre had already won the Junior. He thought he could win again. But bitter experience had taught him the demands that the TT course could make on machines. To win he would have to go hard, as hard as he could. That would mean pushing the bike to its limit.

At the head of the field the flag dropped, the maroon sounded, the first bike fired. The race was underway. After what must have seemed like ages, McIntyre made his way to the start line. Push the bike back on compression, eyes fixed on the starter, heart thumping, flag raised - then dropped, push the machine, feel it start to fire, leap on board and accelerate, head down, towards that first dramatic plunge down Bray Hill.

Twenty two and a half minutes later he's back, flashing through the Grandstand, head down on the tank, flat out, machine sounding great, exhaust note reverberating between the Grandstand and the scoreboards. A buzz of excitement goes round the crowd. Has he done it? Was he quick enough? Then the announcement 'McIntyre has lapped at 99.99 mph'. A spontaneous groan from the whole crowd. So close, so very close.

On the machine Mac is unaware of his speed. He knows only that he is in the lead, but not by much. He should go faster on this, his first 'flying' lap, close further on Surtees, increase his lead.

At his signalling station at Sulby, Gilera stars Geoff Duke and Reg Armstrong confirm to Mac that he's leading. Press on to Ramsey, all those difficult lefts and rights, trying to remember the sequence, keeping the rhythm; smoothness is speed. On to the fast approach to the Town, the tricky surface in Parliament Square. Then the Mountain climb, the toughest part of the course for the machine, when the bike strains and pulls to get you up to the Gooseneck, Guthries, the Mountain Mile, the Mountain Box, the Verandah. Now it's the descent. You go up the Mountain on your bike, you come down on your nerves. It's a test of skill and courage. How fast do you go, dare you go? How late do you leave your braking?

All too soon you're at the Nook and then the slowest corner on the course, Governor's Bridge, tricky on the big fully-faired Gilera. Into the dip, accelerating out, watching the adverse camber, head down, flat out, screaming through the Grandstand to start all over again.

The tension in the crowd is collective, tangible. They're, willing the result. This time, it has to be. He must have done it. He must have. Then comes the announcement. The crowd at the Grandstand, the crowd all round the course, gasp, wonder, cheer with excitement, admiration, relief. McIntyre has lapped at 101.03 mph. It's been done. The 'ton' in the 50th anniversary of the TT.

If will-power alone could win races Bob McIntyre and Jimmy Simpson would be the greatest TT winners ever. No riders ever tried harder. They didn't just ride with determination, though, but with fire and spirit allied to great skill and natural ability; passion allied to intelligence and restraint.

They were both immensely popular. Fans knew that whatever happened, 'Bob Mac' or 'Jimmy S' would give their all. They might try to be cagey in practice to hide the true speed of their bikes, but when it came to the race itself they only knew one way to ride - flat out. They frequently led races and set the fastest laps only to see their machines cry 'enough' before the finish. They won only three TTs between them. They were labelled, unfairly, machine breakers. They became, instead, record breakers. In doing so they achieved not just the fame of winners, but the immortality of being first.

Simpson's achievement came from breaking not one barrier but three. In a seven year period he became the first man to lap the TT course at 60, 70 and 80 mph. Yes, there were road improvements and improvements in machines, but it was still an astounding feat. McIntyre will be remembered forever for that day in 1957. Their achievements are talked about long after you've forgotten who won a particular race. They brought more than excitement or admiration. They brought - bring - respect and reverence, a place in history.

-----oOo-----

Jimmy Simpson was one of the most popular riders of his time, perhaps the crowd's greatest favourite. He was also well liked and respected by his fellow riders and all those involved in motorcycle racing.

Known as 'Jimmy S' to distinguish him from his team-mate Jimmy Guthrie, Simpson was a highly spectacular but surprisingly safe rider. He rode in an era when teams often used a 'hare' who would be sent off at a speed which was bound to break his engine. The hope was that it would also break the engines of the team's main rivals as they attempted to stay with the 'hare's' pace. Simpson was often used for this purpose but he never lived down a reputation of being an engine breaker. He was an aggressive rider but never reckless.

Simpson was born in Birmingham in 1898. His father managed the Rudge Whitworth cycle depot, but his son was soon riding motorcycles, making his race debut at just 16.

In 1922 he made his first appearance at the TT riding his own Scott twin in the Senior Race. It was a vintage year for new recruits, for also making their TT debuts were Wal Handley and Stanley Woods. Simpson soon impressed in practice, and the press reported him as 'another pretty rider' - the only time that particular adjective can have been used about Simpson. In the final practice session he was third fastest in the Senior class. The Motor Cycle described him as a 'fairly promising newcomer'. In the race itself he had passed five riders who started before him when he was forced to retire at Barregarrow on the first lap with a split fuel tank.

Simpson was working then for his local AJS dealer Mr. W. Chapman. Mr. Chapman could see Jimmy's potential and persuaded AJS to give the young man a works machine for the 1923 Junior TT Simpson soon looked set to repay the factory when, in practice, he recorded the fastest lap.

In the race itself Simpson got off to a great start with a record lap at 59.59 mph, leading at the end of the first circuit

by twenty-three seconds from his team-mate Charlie Hough. On the next lap he increased his lead to eighty-six seconds over Bert le Vack [New Imperial]. Then, as he started down the fast Bray Hill at the beginning of his third lap, disaster struck. Simpson collided with Jacobs [Beardmore Precision], whilst trying to avoid a dog on the course. Luckily neither rider [nor the dog] was seriously hurt but Simpson was badly shaken. He returned to the Grandstand supported by friends, a wry smile acknowledging the congratulations on his narrow escape which had certainly shaken him more than a little. Later in the same race a second dog tried to race Vic Anstice [Douglas] down the same hill - but lost.

For 1924 Simpson was again in the AJS team, this time entered in both the Senior and Junior classes. In practice he again set fastest time in the Junior, his lap also being the second fastest by all machines. Indeed, his 350 bike seemed faster than the 500, on which he could manage no better than fifth fastest on practice times.

In the Junior race Simpson got off to another blistering start. Not only did he beat the Junior lap record, he beat the

Jimmy Simpson rode this very standard looking Scott on his TT debut in 1922.

Senior as well. In recording the first ever 60 mph lap, he went round at a staggering 63.19 mph. It was the fastest ever TT lap by a mile. He led Wal Handley [Rex Acme] by ninety-three seconds with Horton [New Imperial] third. All three men had lapped at over 60 mph.

By Creg-ny-Baa on the second lap Simpson was ahead on the roads. He roared through the Grandstand to record an even faster lap - 64.54 mph - and lead Handley by nearly three and a half minutes. Surely he couldn't keep this pace up? The answer wasn't long in coming. After five more miles Simpson's engine failed him at Crosby and he was forced to retire. Handley retired soon afterwards and the race was eventually won by Ken Twemlow [New Imperial]. Jimmy got a sympathetic cheer from the crowd as he appeared on foot at the Grandstand as the race was finishing.

For the Senior race, Simpson rode his 350 machine. It was rumoured that the AJS mechanics had deliberately detuned Simpson's engine to try and keep him from going too fast. Nevertheless AJS's plan was for Jimmy to act as the hare, allowing team-mates Frank Longman and Charlie Hough to ride for a finish.

The race didn't quite work out that way. Simpson lapped at 61.28 mph on his opening circuit but he was already down on Freddie Dixon [Douglas] and Alec Bennett [Norton]. On his second lap Simpson was even slower at 60.14 mph and was overtaken on time by Harry Langman on the works Scott. Jimmy was the first of the AJSs but he was hardly 'haring'. Perhaps the rumours had been right. Then on the third circuit Simpson fell at Laurel Bank. Despite the fall he retained fourth place but the carburettor had been damaged and a pit stop was needed to re-adjust it. The bike was loath to restart, never a healthy sign, and sure enough Jimmy retired at Kirk Michael on the next lap with a punctured carburettor float.

1925 did at least bring Jimmy's first finishes in the TT. He was third in the Junior, four minutes behind winner Wal Handley [Rex] but only forty seconds behind second man Howard Davies [HRD]. He also had his first and only race in

the Sidecar TT with fellow AJS solo star George Rowley as his passenger. They rode a 350 machine compared with the 500cc bikes of most of the other entries but they still finished fifth out of six finishers. The lightweight outfit took some keeping on the roads and Rowley's behind was often scraping the tarmac.

In the Senior he rode the new works 498cc AJS machine but after setting a new lap record of 68.97 mph and leading the race he was forced once again to retire. His team-mates suffered a similar fate.

Stung, perhaps by their poor showing in the previous year's races, AJS entered a team of six riders for 1926. As well as Simpson, the team included George Rowley, Charlie Hough and Frank Longman. Jimmy had recently been operated on for appendicitis and was only just fit in time to ride in the TT . As part of their policy of no expense spared for TT success, AJS decided that their riders would practice on one set of machines and race on a second set which would be new and only just run in. The Ajays went well in practice with lots of fast laps and only minor troubles. Simpson's speed was

1925: Jimmy Simpson and passenger George Rowley with their 350cc AJS outfit.

evident when he took over a Junior practice mount from team-mate Longman and lapped at over a minute faster.

After his performance the year before Simpson must have thought his best chance lay in the Junior. At the end of the first lap he was lying second, twenty-two seconds behind Wal Handley [Rex] but fourteen seconds ahead of Alec Bennett [Velocette]. Simpson went even faster on the next circuit, setting a new Junior lap record at 66.24 mph and took the lead from Handley. Then the almost unheard of happened. Jimmy Simpson found himself stuck for speed.

Jimmy's third lap was only six seconds slower than his record second one, but Alec Bennett on the Velocette had just been biding his time. Bennett set a new lap record at 68.04 mph to overtake both Simpson and Handley on time. On the next lap Handley was up to second and Simpson was relegated to third. Jimmy got up to second again when Handley hit brake and engine trouble but despite thrashing his AJS round the course he couldn't get anywhere near to Alec Bennett. At the end Bennett won by over nine minutes, though Simpson had averaged a respectable 63.90 mph and finished nearly two minutes ahead of Handley.

After the race Simpson confirmed that, whilst the machine had run well he could have done with it being a little faster. He had been forced to change three plugs. Otherwise the bike had given no trouble.

In the Senior it was back to the usual story. Jimmy broke the lap record from a standing start. His next lap time was greeted with a terrific cheer as it was announced that he had set the first ever 70 mph lap at 70.43 mph. He led the race by 90 seconds from Stanley Woods on the Norton. But Jimmy's fans at the Grandstand shook their heads in dismay . Surely there was no need for Jimmy to be that far ahead so soon. Their fears proved to be well-founded. Simpson continued his meteoric progress until Kirk Michael when his engine gave way and forced another retirement.

Not easily disillusioned, AJS sent an eight man team to the 1927 TT. Once again, Simpson was their main hope and

Rowley and Hough were amongst the back-up. Jimmy went well in practice on the Senior bike but it was rumoured the 350 was short of speed.

The rumours seemed to be borne out by the first lap of the Junior race. Simpson could manage no better than tenth. Gradually, helped by the retirements of others, he worked his way up through the field. Ninth on lap 2, seventh on lap three, fourth on lap four. By the fifth lap he was up to third but well behind the second man Dixon [HRD], and leader Wal Handley. He reduced the gap to six minutes at the start of the last lap but it still seemed a hopeless cause. The last lap seemed certain to be an uneventful procession. It wasn't.

First there was an unfortunate announcement. 'Jimmy Simpson has killed' - then an agonising couple of seconds whilst the nature of his victim was in doubt - 'a dog in Kirk Michael'. Then the announcement that leader Handley was in trouble. Simpson might yet take second. Then the announcement that Jimmy himself was in trouble at Ramsey with the chain off. In the end Simpson finished third, well down on winner Dixon but only forty seconds behind second man Harold Willis [Velocette].

The Senior started in poor conditions with mist on the Mountain. Simpson set off with a mascot of a small white toy dog on his bike. But, whilst it kept the canine hazards away, it failed to bring him luck. At the end of the first lap he was third behind Stanley Woods and Freddie Dixon. During the next circuit he and Dixon battled for second but were over two minutes behind the flying Stanley. Then Jimmy slowed to fourth and on the fourth lap retired at Windy Corner with engine trouble.

Still AJS were not disheartened. They claimed proudly that there 1928 engines were so well built that even Jimmy Simpson couldn't break them. It was to prove an unfortunate boast.

In the Junior the Ajays were no match for the faster Velocettes. Worse still, they proved to be unreliable. All six AJS machines retired. Problems had arisen in practice with sluggishness in valve closure. So, the factory had decided to fit the bikes with new springs for the race, even though these had not been tested for racing. The decision was a disaster. The inlet spring broke on every bike letting the valve into the cylinder.

For a while it looked as though things would be better in the Senior. Weather conditions were bad with wet roads and a good deal of mist and fog. Dixon, Woods and many others fell off and Bennett and Handley had mechanical trouble. The conditions didn't deter Simpson, though. Despite his tyres perpetually skating he lapped at 67.94 mph and led Joe Craig [later Norton team boss], by one minute thirty seconds. Jimmy increased his lead on the next lap with Craig still second, Simcock [Sunbeam] third and Charlie Dodson, also on a Sunbeam, holding fourth. By the end of lap three Jimmy was

two minutes eleven seconds ahead as he called in for his scheduled pit-stop. He even had time to apologise to his pit attendant for splashing him with petrol. Then on the next circuit it was announced that Jimmy's engine had packed up at Birkin's Bends. The crowd groaned its sympathy with the unlucky Simpson.

Disillusioned with his lack of success with AJS, Jimmy signed for Norton for 1929. His team-mates were Stanley Woods and Tim Hunt. In the Junior, Jimmy had mixed fortunes. He lapped at 69.94 mph from a standing start and led from team-mate Woods. Then Simpson slowed by seven minutes on his next lap due to problems with a partially seized front brake. Having sorted out that problem, Jimmy broke the lap record at 70.80 mph. Then he slowed again and retired on the fifth lap. Ironically, it was now Norton's turn to have valve spring problems. These affected the mixture and led to piston burn out in all three machines. Woods and Hunt also retired.

The Senior was held in difficult conditions. The roads were dry at the start but wet and greasy elsewhere, Greeba being one such spot. Greeba had developed a bad reputation with the riders. Several had been off there in practice. Six riders had come off there in the 1927 Amateur [forerunner of the Manx Grand Prix], albeit due to a riders' mix-up, and J. H. Veasey had been killed there in the wet Senior of 1923.

Greeba was to live up again to its reputation. Handley came off first followed shortly afterwards by Douglas Lamb. Whilst Handley was trying to clear the course, along came Simpson and Jack Amott [Rudge], battling neck and neck. Both skidded, hit the pavement and

1929: This Junior Norton gave Jimmy Simpson yet another retirement. He was featured on the 1982 set of TT stamps issued by the Manx Postal Authority.

crashed through a hedge in a heap. Amott broke his collar-bone, Simpson injured his leg and, as we have seen, the unfortunate Lamb died of his injuries. Simpson's injury was bad enough to put him out of racing for the rest of the season.

TT practice for 1930 saw Simpson going well on his 500 Norton, though the Rudges were the stars of the show. In the Junior class the 350 Nortons were down on speed. Jimmy could only manage seventh on the opening lap and dropped to eighth on the next circuit behind South African Don Hall [Velocette]. On the third lap his machine ran out of oil and the engine seized at the Gooseneck. Woods could only manage sixth and Hunt ninth as the Rudges romped home to a 1-2-3.

More surprisingly, it was a similar story in the Senior. Jimmy could only manage sixth at the end of the first lap, just behind his team-mate Tim Hunt. Pushing his motor as hard as he could, Simpson eventually got ahead of Hunt and up to fourth place, behind the Rudge trio of Handley, Tyrell-Smith and Walker. It was not that Jimmy was going slowly. His average speed was faster than the previous lap record. He just couldn't catch the flying Rudges.

On the fifth lap Tyrell-Smith's engine slowed and Jimmy moved up to third, just five seconds behind Graham Walker in second. Then the weather changed; light rain at first then heavy rain and thick mist. Jimmy sensibly settled for third and came home at an average speed of 72.70 mph, one minute twelve seconds behind Walker but two minutes ahead of Charlie Dodson [Sunbeam] in fourth.

Afterwards Jimmy confirmed that he'd flogged the bike as hard as he could but it was not enough to catch the Rudges. Desperate to get something out of the result, the Norton publicity men pointed out that it was Jimmy's first finish in a Senior, and that 'Norton have built a bike Jimmy Simpson couldn't break'.

In the Continental GPs that followed Jimmy was injured at the German GP. On his return to the team he set the fastest lap at the 500 Ulster GP and won the 500 class of the following Swedish GP. Then at the end of the season came a tragic accident at the French GP. A boy on a bicycle tried to cross the course during practice, despite being warned not to. Simpson couldn't avoid the lad. In the resulting accident the boy was killed and Jimmy suffered a broken leg.

By the time of the 1931 TT races Jimmy had only just recovered from his injuries. The Junior race was held on Simpson's birthday and it was hoped that this would be a lucky omen. Jimmy lapped at 73.88 mph from the off and led his team-mate Stanley Woods by sixteen seconds. He followed this up with a new Junior record lap at 74.42 mph and increased his lead over Stanley to forty-seven seconds. He made his pit-stop at the end of the lap and got away again quickly.

Despite the fuel stop, Jimmy's third lap speed was still 74.36 mph and his lead over Woods was thirty-three seconds - not too much and not too little. Surely this time Jimmy had got it right? The crowd certainly thought so as they willed him on to a first TT win. But on the next lap Jimmy slowed and his lead was down to twenty-three seconds. Worse was to come. On the fifth circuit Tim Hunt passed both his Norton team-mates and led Jimmy by fourteen seconds. Then the worst news of all. Simpson's indicator on the scoreboard stuck at the Mountain and it was announced he was touring.

Jimmy Simpson's bad luck had struck again - but not in the way that everyone thought. There followed one of the most bizarre moments in TT history. Jimmy stopped at the Bungalow with the machine reluctant to do more than crawl. He changed a plug but it made no difference. So, not knowing what was wrong with his bike, he decided to retire. Jimmy, never much of a mechanic, admitted afterwards that he just put it down to his usual bad luck and didn't look too hard for the source of the trouble.

Jimmy had a drink, lit a cigarette, signed some autograph books - then suddenly had an idea. He took out the carburettor jet and found it almost sealed with dirt. Jimmy cleared it and all the bike's power returned. A quicker diagnosis wouldn't have won him the race but it might have given him second.

Jimmy set off for the Grandstand at a real rate of knots and flashed through the start, as fast as ever, in twelfth place. He caught up four places on the last lap and finished eighth, helping Norton win the Manufacturers prize and the South Birmingham club to win the club team prize. Jimmy got a wild reception at the prize presentation when he came up to receive his replica.

The Senior was overshadowed by the death during the race of previous Junior winner Freddie Hicks. In the gloom that followed the news, Simpson's feat in recording the first ever 80 mph lap was almost forgotten. The opening lap of the race was sensational with five men all beating the lap record set just the year before. Simpson lapped at 77.56 mph and lay second behind Jimmy Guthrie, now also Norton mounted, and two seconds ahead of Stanley Woods. Simpson went even faster on the next lap. He lapped at 79.92 mph and led from Hunt by forty-one seconds with Guthrie back in third.

The third circuit saw Simpson pass the magic 80 mph figure, despite slowing down to make his scheduled pit-stop. His lap speed was 80.82 mph - clearly a little faster than Norton had counted on. For, as he came in for refuelling the engine stopped with three yards still to go. The tank was completely dry. Simpson was one minute thirty-four seconds ahead of Guthrie who also had a close shave when pitting. Guthrie left peeling off for his pit too late and had to pull over from the centre of the road. As he did so he was nearly collected by Syd Gleave who had assumed from Guthrie's line that he was going straight through. He missed Guthrie by inches.

Simpson started his fourth lap with a comfortable lead and his engine sounding fine. But then his indicator on the Grandstand scoreboard stopped at Kirk Michael whilst Guthrie's went on to Ramsey. Surely it wasn't engine trouble again? It wasn't, but that was little consolation. As Simpson approached the hump-backed bridge at Ballaugh the back wheel of his machine locked and Jimmy crashed into the bridge. The bike was hurled over the wall and into the river below, severely damaging the machine. Jimmy was badly shaken but was lucky to get away just a sprained wrist and bruises.

By 1932 Norton had an embarrassing, if welcome, problem. They were generally acknowledged as having the best bikes, certainly in the 500 class, and with a team of Woods, Guthrie, Hunt and Simpson, they certainly had the strongest team of riders - perhaps the strongest motorcycle works team ever. The only danger was that, in racing themselves, the Norton riders might let another team in. So, for the forthcoming TT races, Nortons decided on team orders. Their riders could race each other for the first three laps. Thereafter they were to hold their positions. This should have suited Simpson as he was always a fast starter but, as it happened, it didn't matter, except for it's effect on Stanley Woods' race tactics.

Jimmy went well in practice, unofficially breaking the Junior lap record. It was soon apparent that the Junior was to be his main target as he did very little practice on his Senior bike. Towards the end of practice week, Norton sent Simpson out on his Junior machine to do three continuous fast laps to test the fuel capacity of the 350 bikes.

The Junior race was held in good weather and on dry roads. At the end of the first lap Jimmy was only fourth, 34 seconds down on leader Stanley Woods. After the next circuit the gap to Woods had widened to forty-two seconds, but Jimmy was up to second place. For once he seemed to be biding his time and saving himself for a late challenge. At the end of the third lap the Rudges pulled in for fuel but the Nortons went straight through. Jimmy's experiment had shown that they could do four laps on a single tank; so they only had to stop once to the Rudges' twice. Jimmy was eleven seconds up on Wal Handley [Rudge] in third but fifty-three seconds behind leader Woods. It was a lot to catch up; and what about the team orders? In the event the question was academic. On the next lap it was announced that Simpson had left the course at

Governor's Bridge and was presumed to have retired. 'Engine trouble' had struck again.

The economic recession had reduced the field for the Senior to thirty-two starters. However, the occasion was made memorable by it being the first ever 'Royal' TT. His Royal Highness Prince George was the guest of honour. Royalty usually provokes the appearance of Mannanan's mist', cloaking the Island to protect its special guests from enemies. On this occasion, though, the Island's god was kind and the weather was dry and clear if rather windy up the Mountain.

It was Jimmy Simpson's 21st TT and the crowd was hoping that he would finally 'come of age' with a win. He got off to the best possible start, lapping at 80.11 mph and leading by three seconds from Stanley Woods. Handley [Rudge] was a further five seconds back in third. On the second circuit Simpson crowned the royal occasion by raising the lap record to 81.50 mph, but he was still only five seconds ahead of Woods. As he got his signal board at the end of the lap he acknowledged it with two fingers - presumably a victory sign. If so it was premature. Woods caught and passed his team-mate on time on the next lap to lead the race by fifteen seconds. When Jimmy called in at his pit to refuel, he complained that his clutch lever was sticking. He proved it by having trouble getting the machine away again.

At the end of the fourth lap Simpson passed the Grandstand lying flat on the tank. His engine sounded fine and he was travelling as fast as anybody. But he was still slowing. Woods was now sixty-nine seconds ahead as Jimmy risked gear changes only when he had to. Simpson, however, was still forty-six seconds ahead of his team-mate Guthrie in third. Simpson speeded up a little on the next circuit and reduced Woods' lead to sixty-three seconds, giving just a hint of a possible challenge. But the following lap he slowed again letting Woods increase his advantage to over a minute and a half and allowing Guthrie to close the gap to only fourteen seconds. On the final lap Guthrie overtook the stricken Simpson on

time and Jimmy had to settle for third at an average of 78.38 mph - far from bad in the circumstances.

That year's Senior presentation was held in the Palace Ballroom in front of nearly 8,000 people and was performed by His Royal Highness. The Prince congratulated Woods but also spoke of the prowess of Simpson and remarked that 'as usual' Simpson had set the fastest lap. The Prince brought the house down by adding that 'all will join in wishing Jimmy Simpson a winning TT ride in future'.

Would 1933 see a fairytale ending and the Prince's wish come true? For a little while it seemed possible. In the Junior, Woods led all the way, but was pushed hard by Hunt and Simpson. For once, however, Jimmy had saved his big effort for the final lap. He was well on his way to the first ever 80 mph 350 lap when the piston broke at Ballaugh and it was another retirement.

So to the Senior, widely rumoured to be Jimmy's last TT. The weather was kind again and the roads were dry. Jimmy started at his 'lucky' number 15, though it had hardly been fortunate up to now. His opening lap speed was 81.26 mph, just five seconds outside the lap record, and although he was in second it couldn't have been closer, with Woods only one second in the lead.

On the next lap Jimmy broke the lap record at 81.94 mph, but this was promptly beaten on the same lap by both Stanley Woods and Tim Hunt. Woods led by sixteen seconds from Simpson with Guthrie forty-nine seconds down on Simpson in third. Jimmy, now leading on the roads, was trying as hard as he could, but the gap to Woods gradually increased up to forty-six seconds. Still, Jimmy was well ahead of Guthrie in third and if anything happened to Stanley, well....

Unfortunately it was Jimmy, as usual, who hit trouble. He lost his front brake and had to settle for second, over a minute and a half behind Woods. Tim Hunt had overtaken Guthrie for third but was still thirty-six seconds behind Simpson.

At the Senior prize presentation Jimmy, receiving his replica, had to wait minutes for the cheering and clapping to subside before he could say anything. Putting aside any personal disappointment, he paid a handsome tribute to the winner Stanley Woods. 'I've been racing since 1922 trying to beat this Irishman', said Jimmy 'and I'm sorry to say he's too good for me'. He congratulated Woods and the Norton Team, and then added with feeling 'Believe me, ladies and gentlemen, I'd give my life to win it'.

Jimmy Simpson had contemplated making 1933 his last TT. How glad he must have been that he decided to give it one more try. In terms of race results it was his best year ever, and it produced some of his very best riding.

The 1934 Senior was held on Jimmy's 36th birthday. Simpson had already started working for the Shell-Mex Company and his boss, Captain Field, flew himself to the Island in a Tiger Moth in the hope of watching Jimmy win. Stanley Woods was now riding for Husqvarna. So Jimmy's team-mates were Jimmy Guthrie and Wal Handley.

At the end of the first lap Simpson was third behind Guthrie and Woods. On the next lap he reduced the gap to Stanley to fourteen seconds but then the gap widened again as Simpson complained of cramp in his right hand. By the fifth lap it was raining and Simpson's engine was misfiring badly but, for once, the problem cleared itself and, as they started their final circuit, Jimmy was still in third place, nearly three minutes down on Woods but four minutes ahead of fourth man Walter Rusk [Velocette]. On the final lap Woods' Husqvarna ran out of petrol and Jimmy finished in second place, well down on winner Guthrie but well ahead of Rusk in third.

So ended Jimmy Simpson's last TT. But the earlier races had been even better.

The week had begun with a titanic battle in the Junior between the two Jims. There were only ten seconds or less between them for almost all of the race, and they provided one of the finest TT battles of all time.

As they set off, Guthrie was reported as fastest at Bray Hill but Simpson as fastest round the Quarter Bridge. Simpson lapped at 78.26 mph but Guthrie was just two seconds faster. It was Guthrie who did the first ever Junior 80 mph lap on the next circuit, but Simpson was only ten seconds back in second, and Handley only a further four seconds away. At the end of the third lap the pace was such that Simpson came in for his pit-stop - forgetting he wasn't due to stop until the next lap. Because of the stop the gap to Guthrie widened to one minute, but after Guthrie's stop on the following lap, Simpson, who admitted he was riding flat out, reduced his team-mate's lead to only eight seconds. As they started their last lap the gap had edged up again to ten seconds but there was still a chance for Simpson to do it. The crowd watched the indicators anxiously, waiting to see if Simpson, as he had so often, would hit trouble whilst challenging for the lead. This time the bike kept going but, although he reduced the gap again to nine seconds, Simpson couldn't catch Guthrie. It had been a fantastic race, with both mens' race speed being only just short of the previous lap record. For Jimmy Simpson, though, the best was still to come.

For the first time in his racing career Jimmy had entered the Lightweight TT. The Rudge Company was in financial difficulties but Graham Walker had been able to secure the loan of race bikes for a private team. For the 1934 Lightweight TT, he persuaded 'Jimmy S' to join the team with Walker himself and Ernie Nott.

The Lightweight race was held in poor weather with mist on the Mountain. The Rudges were certainly fancied but so was Stanley Woods on a 250 Guzzi. Jimmy was riding his 'lucky' number 15, but it was a far from auspicious beginning. Simpson couldn't get the unfamiliar machine to fire at the start. He had to push it out of sight of the Grandstand before it responded. A cheer from the spectators and the noise of the engine confirmed that he was finally away.

At the end of the first lap of the seven lap race Jimmy was only fourth, ten seconds behind his team-mate Nott. Then he made an unscheduled pit-stop to change his goggles. A first TT victory looked a long way away.

The mist turned to rain on the second circuit, but Jimmy put up the fastest lap of the race so far. He was up to second now, seventeen seconds ahead of Nott and only seven seconds behind the leader Charlie Dodson [New Imperial]. Despite the misty conditions, Simpson completed his next lap over a minute faster than Dodson and, suddenly, Jimmy was leading the race. By the end of the fourth lap he led Nott by seventy-three seconds with Dodson well back in third. Graham Walker was up to fourth so all the Rudges were going well.

Jimmy made his second pit-stop, taking on oil and petrol, changing his goggles and setting off again in just thirty seconds. The crowd were desperate to see Jimmy win, and cheered him heartily on his way. On the next lap conditions started to improve but they were all the same to Simpson. Starting his last lap Jimmy had a comfortable lead of two and a half minutes over Ernie Nott. All he had to do - all? - was to keep going. Then an announcement - on unofficial timing the lead was down to one and a half minutes! Not again, surely? Surely this time Jimmy would-n't be robbed of victory.

The crowd at the Grandstand cheered every movement of Simpson's indicator on the scoreboard. The

loudspeaker commentary confirmed that the lead at Ramsey was still over two minutes. As Jimmy went up the Mountain for the last time the tension on the Grandstand was terrific. We can only imagine what was going on in Jimmy's mind after coming so close so often before. Listening hard for any change in the engine note, anything that would mean trouble striking.

On the Grandstand Jimmy's clock moved to Creg-ny-Baa. Then the light on the scoreboard showed he was at Governor's Bridge. The crowd prayed he wouldn't drop it. Surely he could push it in from there and still win? A

1934: A smiling Jimmy Simpson comes to the line with his Lightweight Rudge, was he aware that this was the machine that was to break his losing TT sequence?

machine was heard, then seen, then flashed across the line. He'd done it! The crowd, the Island went mad!

It was one of the most popular wins in TT history and must have brought particular pleasure to Graham Walker, a friend and great admirer of Jimmy Simpson. Nott finished second and, after Dodson had retired with engine trouble, Graham Walker came in third to make it a Rudge 1-2-3. Simpson fittingly took the fastest lap, his last, at 73.64 mph. No easing the machine home for Jimmy.

The Villa Marina has seldom been so full as for the Lightweight prize presentation that year. Jimmy Simpson, at his twenty-fourth attempt, had finally won a TT. He received a fantastic ovation and was carried shoulder-high around the grounds. At the Senior presentation later in the week he got a similar marvellous reception. In his response he announced his retirement from racing. On the start line for the Senior, he said, he'd felt that he was still the master of his machine and could still show the young lads how to ride. But after three laps he had begun to have doubts he was still the master and after seven laps he knew he wasn't.

Jimmy saw out the season with Norton with a series of Continental wins - the 350 Dutch TT, the 350 German, the 350 and 500 Swiss, the 350 Belgian and a win in his last GP, the 350 Ulster.

In 1935 Jimmy Simpson returned to the TT in his new capacity with Shell. During practice he was spectating at the 13th milestone with Wal Handley and Tim Hunt. 'You think the riders look dangerous this morning' said a marshal, 'You should have been here and seen last year's Senior. That man Simpson frightened the life out of us. He was terrifying'. Sensing some reaction from his listeners the marshal asked 'You weren't here by any chance?' 'I suppose I must have been' said Jimmy 'seeing that I'm that man Simpson'.

Having announced his retirement Simpson, unlike many others, never came back. He concentrated on his family and his work as Competitions Manager of Shell. He stayed with the company until his retirement except for a spell during the war as a Major in the RASC in charge of training dispatch riders. In 1948 he was commemorated by a trophy awarded, appropriately, to the rider of a solo machine making the fastest lap of a TT meeting. After a long career with Shell, he retired to the West Country. He died in December 1981.

In 1948 Arthur Birkett (left) presented the Jimmy Simpson Trophy to the ACU, to be presented to the rider making the fastest lap during the Junior, Lightweight and Senior TT races. Birkett and Jimmy are pictured here outside the Queen's Hotel, Douglas. The Simpson Trophy is currently presented to the rider setting the fastest lap of the meeting.

Robert McIntyre, 'Bob Mac' to thousands of motorcycle fans, was born in Glasgow some thirty years after Jimmy Simpson. Like Simpson he was a dedicated and widely admired rider who was sometimes seen as a machine breaker. In fact, unlike Simpson, he took considerable pains over his machine preparation and his outfits were always immaculate. But he did believe in pushing his machines to their limits. To him that was what racing was all about.

He started his competitive motorcycling in scrambles before switching to road racing. His road racing debut on a borrowed 350 BSA was in an amateur race in a public park in Kirkcaldy. Later he moved up to a 1931 Norton 500. Early in his career he started riding for Glasgow tuner Joe Potts. They got on well together and Mac and his close friend Alastair King were to ride Potts' tuned AJS and Norton bikes for many years. Although Joe Potts tuned the bikes, McIntyre was heavily involved in their preparation. Bob was never afraid to try new ideas, experimenting with 'home-made' all-enclosed fairings and with special pannier tanks to avoid pit stops.

Whilst most of Jimmy Simpson's races were on road circuits [there being few dedicated racing circuits around in the

1952: Bob McIntyre scorches down Bray Hill on his way to second place in the Junior Clubmans TT.

twenties and thirties], McIntyre was equally at home on road courses and short circuits, a superb rider on both. Very popular with the fans who knew he would always give of his very best, Bob Mac was also a great sportsman who would often give help and assistance to other riders. He had the true tenaciousness of a Scot and his refusal to give up often led to some memorable 'charges'. He was never reckless, though, and was cool and calm under pressure. He is widely regarded as the best rider never to win a World Championship.

McIntyre was a fan of the TT course but he also respected it. He made his Island debut in 1952 in the Junior Clubmans TT. These were races for club competitors held in TT week over the Mountain course, but over a reduced distance and on modified production bikes. They proved a useful training ground for some riders but they were never very popular with fans who didn't regard them as proper TTs. The Clubman races eventually moved to the Clypse course and, thereafter, to mainland short circuits.

McIntyre came second to Eric Houseley in the Junior Clubmans' event, setting a new lap record of 80.09 mph in the process. In September, Bob was back on the Island to compete in the Manx Grand Prix, the real training ground for the TT. Mac won the Junior class on his AJS 7R at a record race speed of 85.73 mph. Then, riding the same bike, he finished second to Derek Farrant in the Senior race. Farrant rode the prototype of the G45 Matchless amid much controversy about the trying out of a new 'works' machine in what was supposed to be an 'amateur' race.

McIntyre's performances in the Manx impressed AJS, who offered him a place in their works team for 1953. Mac gladly accepted, but he retired in the Junior with engine trouble and the season generally was a disappointing one. 1954 wasn't much better. Due to ride a G45 in the Senior TT, AMC [who owned AJS and Matchless] decided that Mac's bike should be given to another rider. McIntyre rode an AJS in the shortened race and finished fourteenth - the only member of the AJS team to finish. He scored a number of leader board

places in the other GPs, his best being a third in the 350 Ulster, but he was disillusioned and unhappy with the set-up at AJS and left the team at the end of the season.

For 1955, Mac returned to riding Joe Potts' prepared Nortons and, almost immediately, his fortunes improved. Norton, after a few experiments, had rejected the use of 'dustbin' fairings. But a number of private entrants, including Potts and McIntyre, had developed their own. The combination of Mac and fairing worked really well at that year's Junior. He led the race for the first four laps, from Surtees on the works Norton and Sandford and Lomas on the works Guzzis. Lomas had been recruited by Guzzi after a falling out with MV and it took him three or four laps to get used to the unfamiliar machine. Then he stormed through to take the lead and, eventually, to win the race. But McIntyre was a magnificent second ahead of Sandford on the other Guzzi.

In the Senior McIntyre finished fifth with another fine performance. He was beaten only by the works Gileras of Duke and Armstrong and the works Guzzi and Norton of Ken Kavanagh and Jack Brett respectively. It had been an excellent TT for Bob and he'd certainly attracted the attention of the foreign works teams.

For 1956, McIntyre rejected approaches from the MV, Gilera and Guzzi teams. Fiercely patriotic, he wanted to continue to ride British machinery so long as this was competitive. It was a decision he may have come to rue during the season. Riding his Potts' tuned Nortons he retired in both the Senior and Junior TTs. The Island was kinder to him when he returned in July for the first Southern 100 races on the four and a quarter mile road course at Billown near Castletown. Mac won the 350 class and set the fastest lap in the 500 class at 82.70 mph.

If 1956 had been a disappointing year, 1957 more than made up for it. At the beginning of the year Gilera were looking for a replacement rider for Reg Armstrong, who had retired. Geoff Duke was given permission to approach Bob McIntyre. Unbeknown to Gilera, McIntyre had also been approached by MV and had finally accepted that he would never be World Champion on the then British bikes. McIntyre decided to accept Gilera's offer and, when Duke was injured at an early season meeting at Imola, became Gilera team leader at that year's TT.

Gilera had developed new 350 machines for the 1957 season and they entered the Junior TT for the very first time. The bikes produced around 45bhp at 11,000 rpm and were rumoured to have a top speed of 145 mph. They were certainly competitive with the MV, Norton and AJS 350s. But like their MV competitors, the 350s were essentially scaled down 500s and very heavy. The Gilera weighed about 320lb compared with the works Guzzi's 240lb.

In the race McIntyre got off to a great start and led at the end of the first lap by forty-one seconds with a new lap record at 97.42 mph. Then a misfire slowed Mac, putting the bike on to three cylinders, and he was overtaken on time by Dickie Dale [Guzzi] and John Hartle [Norton]. After Dale hit a bird and had to repair a damaged fairing and screen, Hartle and Dale were dicing for the lead when disaster struck on the fourth lap. A patch of oil at Quarry Bends brought off first Hartle and then Dale. McIntyre, who after changing a plug and curing his misfire was catching both of them, re-took the lead and rode home to win from Keith Campbell [Guzzi] and Bob Brown, who had taken over Duke's Gileras. Mac won by three and a half minutes at a record average of 94.99 mph.

So to the Golden Jubilee Senior, held over eight laps. Mac's opening lap was 99.99 mph and put him into the lead. The second lap was the historic 101.03 mph, but still McIntyre didn't let up. His third lap was only 100.54 mph. But his fourth was his fastest - 101.12 mph, despite slowing for his pit-stop. He quickly re-filled, then shot off again on his pursuit of Surtees on the roads.

Disaster nearly struck on the next lap. A stone from the rear wheel of a back marker caught Bob on the forehead, between his goggles and his helmet. Dazed, McIntyre nearly vomited with the shock and pain. Somehow he managed to keep control of his machine and actually catch and pass Surtees on that lap. On his sixth lap Mac again lapped at over the ton but he was now getting frantic 'slow down' signals

1954: Bob Mac and Walter Zeller (BMW) in close company at the Bungalow in practice.

from Duke and Armstrong at Sulby. He eased off and Surtees re-caught and passed him. McIntyre knew that all he had to do was keep Surtees in sight and he would win, and that's just what he did. He and Surtees crossed the line virtually together, Bob winning by just over two minutes at a record race speed of 98.99 mph. McIntyre joined the select group of riders who had done Senior and Junior doubles in the same year.

Bob's 1957 good luck didn't last as long as the Dutch TT. He crashed, injuring his neck and forcing him to miss the Belgian GP.

He finished second to team-mate Liberati in the Ulster GP so the battle between him and Liberati for the World Championship came down to the Italian GP. McIntyre won the 350 race but was very sick afterwards and was rushed off to hospital. There it was discovered that his neck injury was not a strain but a dislocated vertebra which the 350 race had just knocked out of place again. Mac, unable to ride, had to settle for second place in both the 350 and 500 Championships.

McIntyre's season wasn't over, though. In September Bob and Gilera made an attempt on the World one-hour motorcycle speed record. McIntyre chose to ride the 350 Gilera because he thought it would be easier to ride at top speed all the way. The attempt was made at the bumpy Monza track

1957: Bob McIntyre through Union Mills on his way to the landmark 100 mph lap in the Senior TT.

and McIntyre was exhausted at the end of the hour. But he had taken the record at an average of 141 mph. The record was beaten by Mike Hailwood at Daytona in 1964 on the 500 MV. But Mac still holds the record for a 350 machine.

At the end of 1957, Gilera, Guzzi and Mondial announced their withdrawal from racing. So for McIntyre it was back to the Joe Potts' Nortons for 1958.

In the Junior TT Bob was initially third behind the MVs of Surtees and Hartle, then second when Hartle had to retire. But Mac's challenge ended when he was forced to retire at Quarter Bridge on lap two. It was a similar story in the Senior. Mac split the two MVs for the first two circuits, lapping at over 99 mph on his Norton. But he retired on the third lap with engine trouble. The Southern 100 was kinder to him. He won the 350 class from Terry Shepherd by a fifth of a second and finished second to Shepherd in the 500 class - by two fifths of a second.

For 1959, the ACU had introduced a three lap Formula One race for standard production racers only. It was really just a chance for a British bike to win a TT without the MV opposition. The race, which had separate 350 and 500 classes run concurrently, didn't prove particularly popular and, for the 500 class there were only sixteen starters. McIntyre, riding a Potts tuned Norton, started No. 6. He was in the lead on the roads by Ramsey, and never looked back.

Bob's first lap was at 98.35 mph and he led by 48 seconds from Bob Brown, also Norton mounted. Dickie Dale on the BMW, the only foreign machine in the race, was third not far behind Brown. Mac's second lap was only slightly slower than his first at 98.10 mph and he increased his lead over Brown to sixty-four seconds. Dale had retired and Terry Shepherd came up to third. McIntyre eased off on his last lap to win by seventy seconds at an average speed of 97.77 mph. His friend Alastair King, riding a Potts tuned AJS, won the corresponding 350 event.

In the Junior itself, McIntyre rode the same Potts 350 AJS as King had ridden in the Formula One. But the bike was now fitted with a more streamlined fairing. A system of seeding the top riders [so that the top riders started at the head of the field], had been introduced for safety reasons. Bob started No. 3, sandwiched between the MVs of Hartle No. 1 and Surtees No. 5. Once again he was to prove a thorn in John Hartle's side.

At the end of the first lap Hartle came through first on the roads with Surtees on his tail and Mac about three seconds behind. But on corrected time McIntyre was second, twenty-four seconds down on Surtees but fifteen seconds ahead of Hartle. The second lap was even more amazing. Bob actually passed Hartle, taking second place on the roads as well as on time. At the end of the next circuit Mac was forty-seven seconds down on Surtees but an unbelievable forty-three seconds ahead of the second MV. Surtees refuelled in thirty-four seconds, but McIntyre made his stop in twenty-four. By the fourth lap Surtees was only thirty seconds ahead of the amazing McIntyre on the roads. But it wasn't to last. At the end of the lap Mac came in to the pits to retire. The MV camp, and John Hartle in particular, must have given a huge sigh of relief. It had been one of Mac's greatest rides. But there was better to come.

In the 500 class Bob had practised on one of the experimental desmodromic Nortons. But for the race itself he stuck to one of his own Manx Nortons. Bad weather forced the postponement of the race to the Saturday. Weather conditions were reasonable on the first lap. Then it started to rain, lightly at first, then heavily. It also got colder until, finally, it was hailing on the Mountain.

McIntyre started first on the roads followed by Hartle No. 2 and Surtees No. 4. Mac managed to keep off the chasing MVs until Kirk Michael. At the end of the lap he was in third thirteen seconds behind Hartle. But Hartle called at the pits to change his goggles whilst Mac went straight through. The stage was set for another Hartle/McIntyre battle but, sadly, it was not to be. Bob had clutch problems and at the end of the second lap had to call at his pit to try and rectify the trouble.

McIntyre was nearly ten minutes in his pit and when he finally got away he was well down.

McIntyre refused to give up. Despite the appalling conditions, he stormed through the field to finish fifth, just thirteen seconds down on fourth man Derek Powell [Matchless]. Bob was only seven minutes behind his pal Alastair King in second, so but for his pit stop he would have finished second to Surtees. It was a fantastic ride and helped the Scottish ACU Team of Mac, King and Haldane [eighth] win the team prize.

Bob returned to the Island later in the year to win the 350 Southern 100. He also finished second in the 500 Ulster GP.

In 1960, Bob continued his role as the scourge of the MVs. The Junior [and the Senior] had been reduced in length to six laps. McIntyre experimented in practice with a big tank to avoid the need for a pit stop. The extra weight affected the handling of the bike too much and he decided not to use it in the race itself.

Riding his five speed AJS, Mac started No. 1. He was caught on the roads at Kirk Michael by Surtees, who had started No. 4. But at the end of the first lap Bob was still in touch, third, but only thirty seconds behind Hartle. On the next lap Mac was passed by Hartle on the roads but he repassed the MV when Hartle stopped for fuel at the end of the lap. During the next circuit Mac's AJS sounded as though it had a slight misfire and was a bit overgeared, but he still managed to keep ahead of Hartle on the roads. Bob was forty-six seconds behind the MV man and the positions remained the same during the next lap. But Surtees was in trouble and on lap five he dropped to second place, albeit nearly two minutes ahead of McIntyre. Bob sensed a chance and made a real effort to catch the stricken MV. But the gap was too large. Bob finished just twenty-six seconds behind John Surtees. How McIntyre must have wished it was a seven lap race.

Mac had finished at a race speed of 95.11 mph, the fastest ever by a single cylinder 350 bike. He got a terrific reception from the crowd at the Grandstand and at the Junior prize presentation. Typically modest, Bob didn't want to make a speech -

1959: Bob Mac and team mate Alistair King at the conclusion of their winning rides in the Formula One races.

he said he'd rather do another six laps - but he thanked Joe Potts and congratulated John Hartle on a wonderful ride.

In the Senior Bob rode his Norton and started together with Derek Minter. The two of them had a terrific dice around the course on the first lap, to the delight of spectators. Minter finally got ahead on the Mountain to take third place behind the two MVs with Mac just two point eight seconds behind in fourth. Then on the second trip over the Mountain Mac's machine gave occasional exhaust flashes and faltered in its normal engine note. Sure enough, Bob had to retire at Crosby on the next lap with ignition trouble.

As some consolation, McIntyre won the 500 race in the post-TT meeting at Mallory Park. But he was out of luck for once at the Southern 100 that year. In the main event of the meeting he soon took the lead and established a comfortable lead - so comfortable that he decided to stop at his pit for a precautionary top-up. Unfortunately Bob had forgotten that refuelling was not allowed in the Southern 100. So, although he finished well ahead of the field, he was subsequently disqualified. Bob took it like the sportsman he was.

For McIntyre, works rides were like London buses. For three years there had been no offers, now they all came at once. First Stan Hailwood tried to get Gilera to release bikes for Mac and Stan's son, Mike. Hailwood failed but Geoff Duke eventually succeeded in convincing the factory to loan machines to McIntyre. By then, however, Mac was already committed. He had signed to ride a works Bianchi twin in the 350 GPs and had also agreed through Honda's Irish concessionaire and former Gilera star Reg Armstrong, to ride a Honda 250-4. With his Potts Norton for the 500 class it was going to be a busy season.

The Lightweight [250] TT was now a five lap race over the Mountain course. Honda had decided to use a big six point five gallon tank to avoid the need for refuelling. It must have affected the handling of the Honda, particularly at the start of the race, but Mac showed no sign of it. He broke the lap record from a standing start at 98.83 mph and led the race by twenty-five seconds. Gary Hocking [MV], was second, about 100 yards ahead of Mike Hailwood [Honda] on the roads and 1.4 seconds ahead on time.

On the second lap McIntyre went even faster - close to becoming the first man to lap at 100 mph on a 250. His speed of 99.58 mph was 4 mph faster than the previous 250 record and five seconds faster than the 350 record. Bob now led the race by thirty-six seconds from Hailwood, who had turned the tables on Hocking and was now 100 yards or so and one point six seconds ahead of the MV.

On the third circuit the weather changed and the skies became more cloudy. Mac eased off, but only slightly, lapping at 99.26 mph. Hailwood was still thirty-five seconds behind in second place. Hocking had retired with mechanical problems and Tom Phillis was up to third. All the first six were on Hondas. Most of the other riders stopped for fuel at the end of lap three but the Hondas went straight through. Mac was still averaging 99.13 mph and was still thirty-three seconds ahead of Hailwood. But as he came through the Grandstand to start his fifth and final circuit he gave a 'thumbs down' to his pit.

The crowd on the Grandstand watched the scoreboard nervously as McIntyre's indicator showed he'd reached Ballacraine, Glen Helen, Kirk Michael, Ballaugh. Then the BBC Commentary position at Sulby reported he was overdue. A Honda came down the Sulby straight. Was it McIntyre? No, it was Hailwood in the lead. Then came news of Mac. He'd retired at Quarry Bends. A seized engine had caused a full lock broadside followed by a tremendous wobble but Mac had managed to stay in the saddle. Hailwood went on to win, one of his hat-trick of wins that week.

In the Junior Bob rode the works Bianchi. It was fast but tall, heavy and difficult to handle. Mac started No. 4 and was first on the roads by Ballacraine. By Ballaugh he led Hocking's MV by ten seconds, but gearbox trouble at Sulby put him out of the race.

For the Senior Bob was again riding No. 1, setting off with

the ill-fated Ralph Rensen - killed later in the race after a crash at the Eleventh Milestone. Mac made an opening lap at 99.14 mph but was only in fourth place. Hocking led Hailwood with Bob just point four of a second behind Phil Read. Only forty-four seconds covered the first six. On the second lap Mac was up to third, thirty-nine seconds behind Hailwood [Norton], but only one point four seconds ahead of Tom Phillis on the experimental Domiracer Norton twin.

Positions remained the same on the next lap but on the fourth Hocking's lead over Hailwood was down to fifteen seconds, whilst Phillis was in third but only one point two seconds ahead of Mac. Hocking's troubles got worse on the next lap and he dropped down the field to fifth. Hailwood led by one minute forty-eight seconds from McIntyre, who had just got ahead of Phillis again. The three held station on the last lap and Mac finished second, nearly two minutes behind Hailwood but with an average speed of 99.20 mph. Phillis, in a fine third place, was a further thirty-five seconds back.

McIntyre had mixed fortunes in the other GPs that year but he did win the 250 Ulster GP on his Honda and finished second in the 250 Dutch TT. In the 350 class he was also second in the Dutch and third in the East German round.

For 1962 Mac was signed by Honda to ride in the 125 and 250 GPs. But he was too big to be comfortable or competitive on the 125. Instead Honda decided to enter Bob in the Junior and Senior TTs on a bored out 250. The bike was to be fitted with an eight gallon tank to go the longer distance.

There were thirty-seven starters in that year's Lightweight [250] TT. McIntyre had headed the practice leader board with a lap at 97.68 mph. Bob started No. 8 in the race, with Derek Minter No. 1 and Jim Redman No. 10, both also on Hondas. On lap one Mac was eight seconds behind Minter at Ballacraine, but by Kirk Michael he was ten seconds ahead. By Ramsey, Bob was leading on the roads and on time and, at the end of the lap, he had lapped at 99.06 mph and was thirty-four seconds ahead of Redman and forty-four seconds ahead of Minter. Then just when it seemed another TT win

was possible Mac retired on lap two at the top of Barregarrow with ignition problems.

For the Junior Mac rode the 285cc bored-out Honda 4, as did team-mate Tom Phillis. Once again Mac had led the practice leader board and there was much speculation on whether the fast light Hondas could stay with the heavy MV-4s. On lap one Mac lapped at 98.65 mph to take fourth place behind the MVs of Hocking and Hailwood and the Honda of Phillis.

Tragically Phillis was killed on the next lap when he crashed at Laurel Bank. McIntyre moved up to third, averaging 99.44 mph but still a minute behind the flying MVs, both of whom had lapped at over 101 mph. Then on the next lap Bob was reported as coasting at Keppel Gate with a dead engine - a repeat of the ignition problems of the Lightweight. It was his last TT. He was a non-starter in the Senior.

In the rest of the season he won the Belgian 250 GP and was second in Spain, France, Holland and Germany. Then, at the wet Bank Holiday meeting at Oulton Park in August 1962 Bob crashed whilst riding an experimental 5-speed Matchless. He hit a tree and died later from his injuries. The whole of motorcycle racing mourned.

A Memorial race meeting for Bob McIntyre was held at Oulton several weeks later. It included demonstration laps by a number of celebrities including Geoff Duke on the Gilera. Ironically, the ride confirmed to Duke that the machines could still be competitive and led him to convince Gilera and introduce Scuderia Duke the following year.

Bob McIntyre is commemorated on the TT course by a flag marshal's hut not far from the Graham Memorial. Bob told his wife how he always pitied the flag marshal there having no shelter despite the sometimes appalling weather, and she thought it would be an appropriate memorial

In that famous Jubilee Year, when Bob McIntyre broke the 100 mph record, Jimmy Simpson took part in a pre-TT BMCRC meeting as part of a question and answer panel. There was a lot of criticism at the meeting of the decision to extend the Senior by an extra lap. The machines wouldn't stand it. It was too long. It would lead to too many retirements.

When his turn to speak came, Jimmy Simpson reminded the audience of the origins of the TT and of its object - to improve the touring motorcycle. 'Here you are admitting that the TT can still test and find weaknesses and that there is still scope for the TT in the development field, quite apart from the unequalled thrills and spectacle it provides.'

The audience was silenced. Who better could there be to defend the TT?

In its TT edition of the 13th June 1957, *The Motor Cycle* reported the first ever 100 mph lap. Bob McIntyre had achieved feat, it said, 'with such smooth skill that he must be bracketed with Geoff Duke - none less - as the finest rider

1961: Bob Mac at Quarter Bridge on the 250 Honda 4.

motor-cycle racing has ever known. McIntyre's performance was such as to make the vast crowds of spectators gasp in admiration and feel a trifle humble in their reverence of his mastery'.

1961: Bob McIntyre rides the 350 Bianchi twin in the Ulster Grand Prix.

The Voice of Motorcycling

You need help. The TT is the greatest motorcycle race in the world but the length of the course and its time trial format make it difficult to follow without some help. For many in the 1950s and 60s, the man who gave them that help, and also communicated to them his love of the sport and the event they were watching, was Graham Walker.

Those watching the races at the Grandstand had always had help. A large scoreboard was erected opposite the stands with the number on it of each rider. Underneath each number was a clock, the finger of which could be moved by boy scouts behind the boards. A telephone line around the course let officials ring in as a rider passed a particular point and the scouts moved the appropriate clock to show the rider's position on the course. Lap times were painted on slates and hung under the riders' numbers and other scouts tore off paper lap numbers to show what lap a rider was on. The system remains virtually the same today as it was when the present scoreboard was built in 1920.

In 1927, an additional service was provided. Loudspeakers were erected at the Grandstand and the first TT commentaries were broadcast. They were not a success. The nameless commentator clearly found out what most of us know. Commentating is very difficult, it's good commentators who make it sound easy. The experiment was abandoned part way through the race and the loudspeakers given over to playing 'In a Monastery Garden' and other equally inappropriate musical accompaniment.

The race organisers eventually found the right man for the job. The Reverend, later Canon, Stenning was a keen supporter of the TT and Manx Grand Prix races, in time becoming President of the Manx Motor Cycle Club. He had marshalled at Ballacraine, knew many of the competitors personally, and could communicate his love of the sport, and his admiration for the feats of the riders. Gradually the loudspeaker network was extended to other parts of the course so that more spectators could enjoy his commentaries.

BBC Radio began commentaries on the TT races in the 1930s. Initially these began as post-TT reports by 'Ixion' and other well known motorcycle writers. Then the BBC experimented with live broadcasts from around the course. Inevitably there were teething problems as they learnt by trial and error. But before long they were attracting the ultimate accolade from the fans - 'However did we manage without them?'

It was in the 1950s, however, that the BBC commentaries reached their zenith. With Commentators like Graham Walker, his son Murray and Alan Dixon, and with the greatly improved sound microphones able to pick up the thrilling exhaust notes of the bikes, they brought an extra dimension to the races - and some consolation to those stuck at home. Relayed by Mr Colebourn's loudspeakers at all the main vantage points and listened to on thousands of the new portable radios elsewhere, they added immeasurably to the fans' appreciation of the TT, and to the status of the races.

Sadly, like motorcycling's golden age of the 50s, they were not to last. By the early 60s the broadcasts were cut back to occasional bulletins and then axed altogether. Fortunately for race spectators, however, a new station was wiling to take over full coverage. Manx Radio began life in 1964, broadcasting from a caravan. But it was a condition of its franchise that it broadcast commentaries on the TT It did so - and has been doing so ever since. Its main commentator over all those years has been Peter Kneale, now deservedly known as the voice of the TT. But for many who listened in the 1950s that title will always belong to Graham Walker - and there were few men better qualified to commentate on the TT races.

-----oOo-----

Graham Walker was born in Scotland in 1897. A burly individual he was handicapped as a rider by his fifteen stone frame. But he never let it bother him and if anyone dared mention it he would point out that he had a brother who was six foot six inches and seventeen stone. Walker could often be forthright in his views but this was tempered by good humour and friendliness. He was well-liked and well-respected throughout the sport.

Walker was an intelligent and canny rider who, despite his size, was also something of a stylist. Careful rather than cautious he never took undue risks but was a particularly good rider in poor conditions. He usually started his races slowly to give the machine time to 'bed in' and to let the 'hares' blow up their machines. Then, whilst others were slowing or having problems, he would gradually move through the field. He was a great believer in the fable of the tortoise and the hare and, to emphasise the point, wore a little silver tortoise on his leathers.

He certainly went racing well-prepared. His bike usually carried a tool box containing an adjustable spanner, a small pair of pliers, a tappet spanner, a screwdriver, some copper wire, some insulating tape and some rubber piping. In the pockets of his leathers he carried some chain links, two spare plugs, some spare plug terminals, spring clips for the throttle, float needles and a magneto spanner. Tugged down one boot was a plug spanner and tugged down the other was a pipe and some tobacco - in case, as he said, he was unlucky but still conscious! He might have been a very professional rider, but Graham Walker always remained an enthusiast at heart.

He competed in twenty-three TTs and finished in sixteen of them. Apart from his debut ride and one other, he never finished outside the first six. He was very loyal and rode only three makes of machine in his TT career. He finished second three times and third twice and had one TT win.

Walker started his motorcycling career in trials and hill climbs and joined the Norton factory in 1919, to compete in these and the occasional road race. In 1920 he was part of the Norton team at the first post-war TT races, along with Noel Brown, Jimmy Shaw, Manxman Duggie Brown and Charlie North. His TT career nearly got off to a disastrous start when he hit a sheep in practice, but he wasn't seriously injured.

Walker's machine was a standard production model with a few modifications and a top speed of about 75 mph. During the Senior race he impressed with his style. But from the second lap the machine began to give trouble and he could manage no better than thirteenth in a time of five hours twenty-four minutes fifty seconds and an average of 41.83 mph.

In 1921 Walker was in charge of assisting the Norton private entrants in the TT and was not due to ride himself. However he took over the Norton ride of H. Minton who had crashed heavily in practice at Ramsey and been taken to hospital. Minton was posted 'missing' in the Island after he disappeared from hospital after walking in the grounds. The mystery was finally cleared up by a telegram from Minton's home town in England announcing his safe arrival.

Minton's machine didn't bring Walker much luck and he retired in the Senior. He was not alone. Of the fifteen Nortons entered only three finished. The rest suffered mainly from valve trouble.

For 1922, Walker was Competitions manager of Nortons in charge of the private entrants and under strict orders from 'Pa' Norton not to race himself. Walker, however, thought there was no harm in keeping his hand in, just in case. So he practised on a borrowed machine. It nearly all went wrong when he had a spill at Ballacraine early on in practice but, fortunately, he was unhurt. He showed up well in practice, being one of the fastest 500s, and when Vic Horsman crashed in practice on the Thursday and put himself out of the race, the temptation proved too much. Walker took over the ride. He finished fifth in the race itself, the best finish by a Norton. When he got back to the factory nothing was said about the disobeyed instructions.

Sadly he and Norton were to part company in 1923. The disagreement arose over the type of forks to be used on the Norton racers. Walker wanted to use a different make which, he was convinced, would considerably improve the handling of the Norton. But Nortons wouldn't allow it. So, despite being Norton's Competitions Manager, he entered his own private Norton. Walker proved to be right, of course. The factory eventually accepted the need to change the forks, but by then the damage was done.

1923 saw the introduction of a TT race for Sidecar outfits and Walker entered on a 588cc Norton. The race was over three laps and most of the riders had never raced a sidecar in anger before. Walker showed the difficulties of adapting when, in practice, he tried to take Creg-ny-Baa flat out on his solo as he did on the sidecar and nearly came to grief accordingly. Of the sixteen starters in the Sidecar TT only six finished. Amongst these was Walker and his Manx passenger Tommy Mahon who finished second, one minute forty seconds behind winner Freddie Dixon [Douglas], but one minute ahead of team-mate George Tucker. Walker averaged 52.50 mph for the race, faster than the winning race speed for the Lightweights.

Walker had ridden a Lightweight Excelsior in practice but didn't compete in the race itself, which was run concurrently with the sidecar event. In the Senior he finished fourth. Of the official Norton team, Graeme Black finished second, but Walker finished ahead of Simister [fifth] and Shaw [seventh]. At the end of the season Walker left to join the Sunbeam factory.

Graham Walker didn't compete in the 1924 TT but went on later in the season to win the 500 Swiss GP on his new Sunbeam. He was less lucky in his return to the TT in 1925, retiring in both the Sidecar and the Senior races.

1926 was better. Walker was part of the winning British ISDT Trials Team, and he was back as a finisher in a TT. During practice he again made himself useful to his fellow competitors - giving Frank Whitworth [of Rudge-Whitworth] a lift from Sulby to Ramsey after Whitworth's bike had seized and helping Syd Crabtree repair his Wallis and get it back to the start. Walker was pleased with his Senior Sunbeam but caused some amusement by putting blue and yellow rubber balls in his saddle springs to act as shock absorbers. The idea must have worked, however, because Wal Handley also adopted it.

In the race itself Walker made his usual cautious start, but by the fifth lap he was up to twelfth. By the next lap he was

1923: Graham Walker and locally recruited passenger Tommy Mahon swing their Norton outfit round Ramsey Hairpin. The northern part of the circuit was still dust-bound roads, tarmacadam was only used for the Douglas area only.

up to eleventh, thirty-two seconds behind Jackson [HRD] but over a minute ahead of Macaya [Norton]. At the finish he was tenth, thirty-three seconds behind Kenneth Twemlow [HRD] and eighteen minutes behind the winner Stanley Woods, but still fast enough to get a replica. He was also part of the BMCRC trio with Frank Longman [third] and Pat Driscoll [nineteenth on a 350 Chater-Lea], who won the Club team prize.

In 1927, Walker was Competitions manager for Sunbeam and also riding in the Junior and Senior TTs. In the Junior he was out of luck. Twelfth at the end of lap two, he retired on the next lap with engine trouble.

Before the Senior race Walker was calmness itself on the start line, enjoying a final cigarette before the off. After the usual slow start he was up to twelfth by the end of lap three, averaging 63.87 mph. At the end of the next lap he was up to eleventh averaging 64.01 mph. The fifth circuit saw another place gained, tenth at 64.5 mph. By lap six he was up to eighth and at the finish he was fifth. His average speed had increased to 64.73 mph and, though he was twenty-four seconds behind Jimmy Shaw [Norton] in fourth place, he was one minute thirty-four seconds ahead of Freddie Dixon in sixth.

To add to his delight the Sunbeam team of Walker, Charlie Dodson [eighth] and Birch [sixteenth] won the Manufacturers' team award. Walker also went on to win the 500 German GP that year.

Graham Walker joined the Rudge factory in 1928 and was entered on their pushrod ohv 500 machine in the Senior TT. The race was held in poor conditions with wet roads and mist on the Mountain. At the end of the opening lap Walker and Simcock [Sunbeam] were having a terrific dice on the roads and Walker was tenth on time, just one second behind his team-mate Tyrell-Smith, making his TT debut. On the next circuit Walker was up to sixth, thirty seconds behind Tommy Simister [Triumph]. Simister fell on the next lap and Walker was up to fourth, and only three seconds behind Tyrell-Smith

in third. Difficulties for Tyrell-Smith put Walker up to second on the next lap, albeit a minute or so down on the leader Charlie Dodson [Sunbeam].

As the riders started their sixth laps the weather was improving a little. Dodson had a comfortable lead but, perhaps deceived by the improved conditions, he fell, giving Walker a lead of over two minutes. As Walker started his last lap, an elusive TT victory was almost in his grasp. His indicator showed he'd reached Ramsey safely - but then it stopped, whilst Dodson's went on to the Mountain. The drama wasn't over. Dodson fell again at Keppel Gate, but remounted to win. Walker, it was announced, was at the Gooseneck 'not going too well'; he retired there. Despite what must have been his bitter disappointment Walker picked up the stranded Mainwaring who had also retired at the Gooseneck, and together they toured to the Grandstand on Walker's bike.

As some consolation Walker went on to win the 500 Ulster GP on his Rudge racer, known thereafter as the 'Rudge Ulster'. He also won the 500 Dutch TT on the same machine.

Walker was back at the TT the following year to see if, this time, he could make it a win. But his Rudge started No. 46 in the Senior, leaving him plenty of riders to pass along the way. He was conscious that his size meant he had to use more power than others in the climb up the Mountain and, the night before the race, admitted 'I'm too heavy'. Nevertheless he was determined to give every effort in his search for a TT trophy.

For once he got off to a fast start. At the end of lap one he was second., having lapped at 71.16 mph. He was 19 seconds down on leader Tyrell-Smith and 16 seconds ahead of Ernie Nott, giving Rudge a 1-2-3. After the next circuit he was still second, eighteen seconds behind his team-mate, but Nott had dropped back and Charlie Dodson was up to third. Then a lengthy pit-stop put Walker down the leader board to sixth.

Walker responded magnificently, setting his fastest lap of the race at 71.58 mph and recovering second place, thirty-one seconds down on Dodson who was now in the lead. It looked all set for a repeat of the previous year's battle - until Walker retired at Ramsey on the next lap with a broken push rod. Once again he had the consolation of winning the 500 Ulster GP later in the season.

1930 was to be Rudge's great year, and a good one for their racing chef d'equipe, Graham Walker. The TT began, as usual, with the Junior. Rudge had originally planned to build just one new machine for the race which Tyrell-Smith was due to ride. Then factory manager John Pugh decided to enter a full three man team with Walker and Nott. The only way three machines could be made ready in time was to use up all the available spare parts, leaving no spares for emergencies.

After the first practice session it was obvious that Rudge had a problem with the new 350s. The bikes were very quick but all three had developed piston trouble. Their designer, George Hack, calculated that the pistons would last just 8 laps without disintegrating. It was a seven lap race. So new pistons were fitted to the bikes on the final morning practice session and they did one slow lap to bed the pistons in. On Hack's calculations this left a seven lap margin for the seven lap race.

Rudge ordered Tyrell-Smith to go flat out at the beginning

Walker, per et fils. Graham Walker relaxes in the paddock after finishing second in the 1932 Lightweight. Standing alongside is son Murray, himself no mean off road rider with a gold medal in the International Six Days Trial, who now upholds the Walker families reputation as a peerless motorsport commentator.

in the hope that their main rival, Charlie Dodson on the Sunbeam, would chase him and break down. Walker's bike had seized in that last practice session and he was ordered not to exceed half throttle until he passed the usual seize point at Creg-Willy's Hill. Then he was not to exceed three quarter throttle for the rest of the lap.

Sticking to his orders, Walker was only fourteenth at the end of the first lap whilst his team-mate Tyrell-Smith followed his orders and led the race. By the next lap Walker was up to twelfth and on the third circuit he was lying ninth, just behind Stanley Woods [Norton]. On his fourth lap Walker broke the lap record at 70.46 mph and rose to sixth, only three seconds behind team-mate Ernie Nott. By the next Walker was fourth, behind Tyrell-Smith, Jimmy Guthrie [AJS] and Nott. Guthrie retired on the next lap and the Rudges started their last lap in the first three positions. But would their pistons hold?

At the Rudge pits it must have been a long and anxious wait. But eventually all three machines came home. Hack's calculations had been spot-on. The piston on Walker's machine was split almost all the way down and the bike would hardly have gone another mile. They had finished though, and in the first three positions, romping away with the Manufacturers' team prize. Afterwards Walker, who'd finished third, said that, like a good soldier, he had only ridden to orders. He was surprised he had gone as fast as he had. He confirmed that this was his last TT - a statement he was to repeat for the next four years.

For the Senior race, the Rudge team was strengthened by the addition of Walter Handley. The combination of Handley and Rudge proved just too much for the opposition. Walker, however, set off to his usual race plan. Tenth at the end of lap one, he moved through seventh on the next to third on the third lap, behind the flying Handley and Tyrell-Smith but only just ahead of Jimmy Simpson on the first of the Nortons.

For the fifth lap the spectators could have done with one of Walker's commentaries. News of the race was scarce after the Mountain telephone box broke down and the one at the Creg was demolished when Jamaican rider F. C. Isaacs crashed into it on his Norton. The two telephone operators had to be taken to hospital for treatment.

Walker was averaging 73.80 mph and was now up to second as Tyrell-Smith slowed. By the sixth circuit Walker was only four seconds ahead of third place man Simpson. Then the rain came down heavier and heavier and Walker pulled away from Jimmy to finish second, one minute ahead of the Norton star. Despite the conditions Walker had averaged 74.10 mph for the race. Afterwards Walker expressed himself somewhat forcibly about the rain on the last two laps. Being a married man with a family, he said, he took no risks. His only complaint was that the rear mudguard had come adrift and rubbed on the tyre for the last two laps.

1932: Big Man - Small Bike. Graham Walker pushes his 250 Rudge into life, the winner the previous year, Graham finished second this time.

Despite his statement of the year before, Graham Walker was back at the TT in 1931, and with a new machine. Walker had always maintained that his size needed a 350 or 500 to carry him over the steep Mountain climb. But now Rudge had produced a 250 version of their radial valve engine, so successful in the bigger classes. Walker agreed to give the 250 a go. It was a good decision.

The week began, though, with the Junior. Walker followed his standard race plan. By the third lap he was up to eighth, averaging 71.07 mph and twelve seconds behind F. A. Renier [Velocette]. By the fourth lap he was up to sixth behind Stanley Woods [Norton]. Jimmy Simpson's retirement put Walker up to fifth on the penultimate lap but he was well down on Stanley Woods and fifth was where he finished. It had been Norton's race, with Hunt and Guthrie first and second and Woods taking fourth. Ernie Nott was the best of the Rudges in third place. At the prize presentation Walker congratulated the Norton Team 'speaking as a one-time Norton man myself'.

The Senior was started in fine weather but the roads were wet and greasy from the rain earlier in the morning. Walker's race followed its usual pattern. Eleventh on the second lap he had a fine battle with Emery [Sunbeam] in moving up to ninth, then eighth, then sixth. By the sixth lap he was fifth but well behind his team-mate Ernie Nott in fourth. They held positions on the last lap with Walker finishing six and a half minutes behind Ernie Nott, despite an average speed of 73.98 mph [nearly as fast as Wal Handley's winning average the year before]. The race was another Norton benefit with Hunt, Guthrie and Woods taking 1-2-3. Walker and Ernie Nott had some consolation, however. They and fellow Sunbeam MCC Club man Simcock [eighth on an O.K. Supreme], won the Club team prize.

It had been a different story in Wednesday's Lightweight race. Walker had not been fancied before the race, reflecting his own doubts about his suitability for a 250. The *Motor Cycle* preview was typical, suggesting that 'The Age of Miracles would not be past if a 250 engine could carry Graham Walker's fourteen and half stone to victory'.

The race was held in perfect conditions. Walker started nine and a half minutes after his team-mate Ernie Nott and, for once, Walker got off to a fast start. He was third at the end of lap one, lapping at 68.58 mph. Nott led from Tyrell-Smith and all the first nine men had unofficially broken the old lap record.

On the next lap Nott made it official, breaking the lap record at 71.28 mph and leading from one minute forty seconds from team-mate Tyrell-Smith. Walker was third, a further thirteen seconds back. The third lap saw Ernie Nott go even faster - 71.73 mph - and Walker get ahead of Tyrell-Smith. The positions remained the same for the next two circuits with Nott building up a healthy lead of over four minutes over Walker. On the sixth lap Nott had caught Tyrell-Smith on the roads and only had to stay with him to win easily. But Ernie couldn't resist passing Tyrell as they came through the Grandstand. Walker came through some time later to get a two fingered signal from George Hack, presumably meaning 'You're second'. He had pulled back twenty-four seconds on Nott on the previous lap but Ernie was still over three and a half minutes in the lead, and with only one lap to go.

Nott seemed certain to win. But it was his turn to have the bad luck and Walker's to benefit. At the Grandstand the loudspeaker announced '17, Nott, is off his machine 1 mile on the Ramsey side of the Mountain Box'. Then, to the delight of his supporters, 'Nott is moving again'.

'Nott is touring in' - groans of disappointment.

'Nott has passed the Bungalow going fairly well' - puzzlement? What did 'fairly well' mean?

Tyrell-Smith finished at speed. Walker was still on the Mountain climb and, with a nine and a half minute starting difference and no commentary points around the circuit it was difficult for spectators to judge the position. Walker was certainly gaining on Nott, but would it be enough to win?

'Number 17 going well at the Creg'.

'Number 17 past Hillberry going very well'.

'Number 17 at Governor's Bridge'. Then, dramatically,

'Number 17 has just come off at Governor's Bridge'.

Nott remounted and finished at speed. For miles he had been holding a broken push-rod with one hand. A few minutes later Walker finished to win and to huge applause. Whilst everyone felt sorry for Nott, Walker's was a hugely popular win. Rudge had finished first, second and fourth with Ted Mellors [New Imperial] finishing ahead of the unlucky Nott. In the end, Walker's winning margin had been a comfortable two minutes twenty-six seconds at a record race speed of 68.98 mph.

At the presentation of the Lightweight Trophy, Walker said sportingly that whilst he was pleased at having won a TT after his many years of trying, the race by rights was not his but Ernie Nott's.

Whatever temptations there may have been for Graham Walker to hang up his leathers after his first TT win, Walker shook them off, and returned in 1932 with the Rudge team to see if he could repeat his TT victory.

In the Junior he reverted to his usual strategy. Ninth on the third lap and eighth on the fourth, he was up to sixth on the next circuit, thirty-two seconds behind Charlie Dodson on an Excelsior. Another retirement for Ernie Nott put Walker up to fifth but he couldn't close the gap on his old rival Dodson and had to settle for fifth place, over three minutes ahead of Les Archer on a Velocette.

In the Lightweight, the hot favourites were Walker's Rudge team-mates Nott and Handley. The Rudges were late for the weighing - in, carrying out last minute speed trials on a secluded road nearby.

At the end of lap one Handley led from Nott, Emery [Cotton], Crabtree [Excelsior] and Leo Davenport [New Imperial]. Walker was sixth, twenty-eight seconds behind Davenport. On the next lap the Cotton slowed whilst Nott took over the lead from Handley. Walker was fifth, now thir-ty-eight seconds down on the New Imperial. A pit-stop by Davenport put Walker up to third on the next lap but his own stop put him back down to fourth on the following lap.

Then on the fifth circuit Handley slowed with plug trouble. Davenport passed both Nott and Handley to take the lead with Nott second, Walker third, Jack Williams [Rudge] in fourth and Handley fifth. At the end of the lap Davenport pitted again and was away in seventeen seconds chased by the four Rudges. Nott pulled out all the stops and gained a twenty-two second lead over the New Imperial. Then it happened again. Nott had to retire on the last lap whilst leading the race and Davenport went on to win by eighty seconds from Walker, with Handley third.

After the race Walker's main complaint was that there had been too little air in the pneumatic cushion on the rear mudguard. He expected to have to eat his breakfast next morning standing up. At the presentation he paid a handsome tribute to Davenport and New Imperial and sympathised with Ernie Nott who, he said, was rapidly catching Jimmy Simpson in the bad luck stakes.

The 1932 TT saw the first 'Royal' Senior. The race was another Norton clean-sweep with Woods, Guthrie and Simpson taking 1-2-3. Walker held eighth place at the beginning behind team-mate Tyrell-Smith, then gradually moved up to sixth behind his old adversary Dodson. But once again he couldn't get past Charlie and had to settle for sixth place. Despite their 1-2-3 in the race, Norton didn't win the Manufacturers' Team Prize - Hunt not Guthrie had been in their nominated trio. Instead, the award went to Rudge with Nott [fourth], Walker [sixth] and Tyrell-Smith [eighth]. Nott, Walker and Simcock [ninth] again won the Club team prize for the Sunbeam MCC. Walker was also given the honour of proposing the vote of thanks, on behalf of the riders, to HRH Prince George who presented the prizes.

By 1933 the worldwide economic depression had hit the British motorcycle industry hard, and Rudge were one of a number of firms to have financial difficulties. The Company

announced that it would no longer partici-
pate in competitions but 500cc machines
would be loaned to the Graham Walker
syndicate, whose riders were walker, Nott
and Tyrell-Smith. The riders, all of whom
were Rudge employees, would be given
time off for racing.

The Walker team entered for the Senior
but with little hope of staying with the all-
conquering Nortons. Walker rode to his
usual pattern and was eleventh by the time
of his pit-stop at the end of lap three. He
was up to tenth on the next lap but also
back in his pit again - surely an ominous
sign? It was. Gearbox trouble slowed him
and he took thirty-eight minutes for his
next lap. Although the next was faster,
Walker retired on the last lap. Nott was
again the best of the Rudges, finishing
fifth behind the Norton quartet of Woods,
Simpson, Hunt and Guthrie. Tyrell-Smith
managed ninth.

By 1934 Rudge were in receivership. But 'Old Father
Graham' as Walker was now affectionately known, arranged
to borrow 250cc machines for the Lightweight TT. Rudge
had also constructed a limited number of 500cc production
racers for sale at a price of £90. It was claimed that the
machines produced 35bhp at 6,000 rpm and Walker agreed to
ride one of the bikes in the Senior as a demonstration.

The Lightweight gave Walker one of his best rides, and the
spectators one of their most memorable spectacles. Stanley
Woods on the Guzzi started just ahead of Graham Walker and
they were together on the roads for most of the race.
Spectators were treated to the sight of a real scrap on the roads
between two of the TTs most popular, and most skillful per-
formers. Both riders said afterwards they had never enjoyed
a battle so much.

*Graham Walker was often heard - but rarely seen. The voice of the TT in the
1950s, Graham hangs nonchalantly out of the press box at the TT to give another
of his masterful commentaries.*

At the end of the first lap Walker was in eleventh place and
as he went through the Grandstand, he flippantly raised both
hands from the handlebars. By the third lap he was up to
sixth, whilst Stanley Woods, who had hit trouble after a fast
start, was now only just ahead of Walker on the roads.
Walker got up to fourth place on time but couldn't shake off
the Irishman and they circulated together for the next three
laps. At Hillberry the crowd had a real thrill as Stanley tried
to cut inside the Rudge, got into the gutter and nearly lost it.
During the battle both riders held out their hands at corners to
show the other which line they were taking. Walker was even
reported as patting Stanley's back when they were taking a
bend at Lezayre at around 80 mph. By the sixth lap Walker
was fourth, five minutes down on Charlie Dodson in third but
only thirty-one seconds in front of Stanley Woods on corrected time.

On the last lap it was Charlie Dodson's turn to retire. Walker finished only a few yards behind Stanley Woods on the roads but twenty-eight seconds ahead on time. Graham's third place at 67.97 mph gave Rudge another 1-2-3, with Jimmy Simpson winning from Ernie Nott. Once again the 250 Rudge had given a TT veteran his only TT win.

At the presentation Walker apologised for collecting another replica. 'The fact is' he said 'they make these motor-cycles so reliable that even an elephant can't break them'.

In the Senior Walker made his usual slow start. After all, he was riding the machine as a demonstration and that meant riding for a finish. He was eighteenth at the end of the first lap but gradually worked his way up the leader board by steady riding at around the 70 mph average. By the end of lap four he was in ninth, sandwiched between the works AJSs of Harold Daniell and Tyrell-Smith. Positions remained the same until the last lap, when a combination of Walker's fastest lap of the race and the retirement of others put him up to a fine sixth place. He had averaged 70.59 mph and was beaten only by three works Nortons and two works Velocettes. He finished ahead of the two works Ajays. Not a bad result for a demonstration ride on a production racer.

At the prize presentation Walker was in more sombre mood than normal. He announced that it had been positively his last TT. To the cries of 'No!' he replied 'Definitely', for he had now achieved all his TT aspirations that mattered. He had:-

Won a TT

Seen Jimmy Simpson win a TT

Been on the leader board in his last Senior

Completed a collection of 15 replicas

Seen promising youngsters come through; and

Managed to get the same crash hat passed by the ACU for the tenth year in succession!

This time he kept his promise.

Graham Walker stayed at Rudge for a while, but when the business was sold in 1938 he took over the editorship of the weekly *Motor Cycling* magazine and served in that capacity for twenty-five years. During the Second World War he also organised a scheme for TT riders and others to become Dispatch riders. He and his son, Murray, became the BBC's motorcycle commentators from 1949 to 1962.

Graham Walker proved a magnificent commentator. He had that rare ability to paint a picture and convey excitement whilst never intruding or detracting from your enjoyment. When you heard Graham Walker you knew you were in safe and knowledgeable hands. His son, Murray Walker, followed his father's example, and has continued to this day to serve with distinction as the BBC's main motorsport correspondent.

The year after Graham Walker's 1931 TT win, the following verses by Bob Holliday appeared in a *TT Special* feature 'Alice in Manxland'.

'You are old Father Walker, 'his young son cried,
'And your hair has become almost white;
Yet year after year round the Island you ride-
Do you think at your age it is right?'

'In my youth, 'Father Walker replied to his son,
'My wife said I'd not stand the strain.
But now that at last the Lightweight I've won,
Why I'll do it again and again!'

Sadly Graham Walker wasn't to win another TT But in the 1950s he did help establish a motorcycle gallery in the National Motor Museum at Beaulieu. The gallery contains a wide variety of machines including the original Rudge Ulster - the machine on which Walker won the 1928 Ulster GP. The exhibition is named the Graham Walker Gallery - a fitting memorial to a great rider, a great enthusiast, and the 'Voice of Motorcycling'.

The Masters

I can still hear it now. The tone of respect, almost reverence, in my father's voice. We were watching the warm-up for the 1958 Senior. There was a BMW, a black bike with a white fairing matched by the rider's black leathers and white helmet; Number 20. 'That's Geoff Duke' said my father, and you knew he wasn't just imparting information. He was inviting you to marvel.

Duke was a legend then, 'a phenomenon' the motorcycle press had called him. Motorcycle racing owes him an enormous debt. There were many good riders in the immediate post-war resumption of racing - Les Graham, Artie Bell, Harold Daniell, Bob Foster - but when Duke exploded on the scene in 1950 it was something different. Just as the Coronation seemed about to usher in a new Elizabethan age, so Duke brought a whole new era to motorcycle racing. With his mastery on the track, his smooth, effortless riding style, his professionalism, his good looks and his intelligent and articulate comments he simply moved road racing up a gear or two. It became a major, nationally recognised sport. As a young British World Champion on British bikes, Duke captured the public's imagination. He generated a much wider public interest than those who had always followed the sport. Even today, people who know nothing else about motorcycle racing know the name of Geoff Duke.

Alec Bennett never achieved that sort of fame, but in his own way he too raised the status of the rider, if not the sport itself. A great talent, it was not for nothing that many opponents' first question at their pit stops was 'Where's Alec?'

Duke and Bennett were both supreme stylists who made racing, and winning, look easy. Their neat, effortless riding inspired their contemporaries. Newcomers tried to model themselves on The Masters. They seldom succeeded.

Duke and Bennett were intelligent sportsmen; they rode with their heads. They were determined to win, but never took unnecessary risks. They won by the margin they needed to, and didn't break any records unless they had to. It didn't matter whether they won by a few minutes or a few seconds. Winning was enough.

Both were supreme professionals but both obtained their success over a comparatively short period. Bennett competed in only twenty-nine major events in his whole career. He won thirteen of these, five of them TTs. Duke's five TT wins and seven World Championships were won over the six year period 1950-1955.

They were both quietly spoken but strong willed, modest but determined to succeed; both were shrewd businessmen inside and out of racing. They were superb tactical strategists, but with very different tactics, reflecting the varying mechanical fears of their separate eras. Duke would often try to demoralise the opposition with a really fast first couple of laps [a tactic later borrowed and employed equally successfully by Mike Hailwood]. Then, when the opposition had settled for second, he could ease off and save the machine for the finish.

Bennett did the opposite. He would often shrewdly estimate the pace at which the race would be won and gradually work up to that pace, letting his machine 'bed in' and other faster starters break down along the way. Duke and Bennett, though, had one thing in common. They always seemed to have something in reserve - the ability to go faster if they needed to. That, their speed and their superb riding style is what made them The Masters.

-----oOo-----

Alec Bennett was born in Craigantlet, Belfast in 1896. His family emigrated to Canada when Alec was a young boy, and he gained his early motorcycle racing experience in British Columbia. He was Province Champion at the age of sixteen.

He returned to Britain soon after the outbreak of the First World War as part of the Canadian Expeditionary Force. He started the war as a dispatch rider and ended it flying Bristol fighters in the Royal Flying Corps. After demobilisation he decided to stay in England and got a job as a motorcycle test rider with the Sunbeam factory at Wolverhampton. He was soon drafted into the Sunbeam race team alongside Tommy de la Hay and George Dance.

Alec made his TT debut in 1921, riding for Sunbeam. He had a novel way of learning the long Mountain course. Bennett simply followed team-mate George Dance round at speed with his front wheel close to Dance's rear one. By the end of practice Alec was confident enough to be riding on his own - but his TT career nearly didn't start at all.

The Friday morning practice session was held in high winds. As Bennett approached the Waterworks, the wind caught his Sunbeam and drove him into a stone wall. But for a recent ACU directive requiring all riders to wear crash hel-mets the consequences could have been serious. As it was Alec suffered from bad concussion and cuts and abrasions around the face. After a few days in bed he decided to start in the Senior despite the doctor's advice.

Although Bennett still had a tendency to return to his dirt track origins and broadside the odd corner, his method of learning the course had obviously worked. After four laps he was in the lead of his first TT. Then a missed gear change led to a stretched valve and the Sunbeam started to lose power. Bennett stopped to make adjustments but there was nothing he could do. A combination of the lost power and fatigue from his injuries meant he could finish no higher than fourth. Still it had been an amazing debut, and he confirmed his promise by going on to win that year's French GP at Le Mans.

For 1922 Bennett was to ride the new side-valve, long-stroke 500 Sunbeam. He went well in practice and after his performance the previous year he was very much fancied. Geoff Davison of *TT Special* fame complained that, when he visited the bookmakers, he could get no better odds on Bennett than 'evens'. The bookies' odds were justified. Bennett led the race from start to finish, though he said afterwards he had been forced to nurse his engine throughout for fear of it seizing. Nevertheless he won by over seven minutes from Walter Brandish [Triumph], with a record average of 58.31 mph, sixteen minutes better than the old race record. He had also set a record lap at 59.99 mph - just short of the first ever 60 mph lap. Later he repeated his win in the 500 French GP.

By 1923, after some disagreement in the Sunbeam camp over who should be the Number one rider, Alec had moved to the Douglas factory. The move gave Bennett the chance of rides in the Junior and Senior TTs. At the end of practice he had qualified his Junior bike but hadn't qualified on the 500, being a few seconds too slow on his best lap. Nevertheless, as the previous winner, he was allowed to start.

In the Junior, Bennett got off to a slow start but by the fourth lap he was up to fifth, fifty-five seconds behind Manxman Tim Sheard [AJS]. On the next lap De la Hay [Sunbeam] ran into the back of Bennett at Governors Bridge and fell, but Bennett was able to continue and by the Grandstand was up to fourth place, twenty-eight seconds behind Harris [AJS]. At Braddan Bridge Bennett was reported as being in hot pursuit and leaning his Douglas over at a terrific angle, but it wasn't to last and he retired on the last lap with engine trouble.

The Senior was run in drenching rain, the first wet TT since the 1912 Junior. Bennett was going well early on, lying second after the first lap. But he was slowed by a variety of problems. Despite having lost his front mudguard, a real disadvantage in the pouring rain, he carried on, eventually coming home in tenth place. Soaked through, he arrived at the Grandstand to find the place deserted. There was no-one on the stands, no flag marshal with the chequered flag and not even anyone in the refreshment tent. The conditions had been so bad that everyone but the timekeepers had gone home.

In 1924 Alec opened his own motorcycle dealership in Southampton, and this was largely the reason that he restricted his racing. Rather than ally himself with any one particular factory, he also became a freelance, allowing him to ride for different makes within the same TT meeting, something almost unknown at that time.

In the new Ultra-Lightweight race for 175cc machines Bennett had signed to ride a Villiers-engined Diamond. But he was dogged by magneto trouble throughout and, for once, got slower as the race went on. He eventually finished ninth at an average of 38 mph, forty-five minutes behind the winner Jock Porter [New Gerrard] and between the two remaining Wee McGregor machines in their only TT appearance. Bennett said afterwards that he learnt more about the course on this ride than on any other - presumably because he had more time to look around.

For the Senior he was engaged by Norton boss Bill Mansell to ride the new works Norton. Despite an unspectacular practice performance it was generally felt that Bennett had been hiding his speed and he was a firm favourite to win.

Bennett's opening lap was at 62.23 mph, well ahead of the old lap record but still only enough to put him in second place nearly a minute down on Freddie Dixon. On the second lap he nearly came off at Governor's Bridge when he approached the corner much too fast. Alec was still over a minute behind Dixon, but well ahead of third man Harry Langman on the Scott. During the next two laps Bennett was hampered by a loose petrol filler cap which eventually came away altogether. But he managed to rig a running repair with a handkerchief and finished the fourth lap still in second place, one and a half minutes behind Dixon but nearly two minutes ahead of Langman.

Then Dixon hit trouble. A stop to change a plug put Bennett in the lead. On the final lap Bennett drew away and came home to hearty cheers from the crowd, many of whom must have backed the favourite. Alec crossed the line at such a speed that he missed the usual return gate for riders and went straight through to Parkfield Corner several hundred yards down the track, where he was mobbed by avid autograph hunters.

Bennett won by one and a half minutes from Langman with the unlucky Dixon in third place. Alec's race speed was a record 61.64 mph, despite the Norton, at 327lbs, being one of the heaviest machines in the race. Bennett said he had taken no chances and had saved himself for the last two laps. Apart from the filler cap he had no real problems. Once he knew he was leading he eased off accordingly.

It was Norton's first TT win since Rem Fowler in 1907. At the Senior Prize Presentation 'Pa' Norton got a tremendous cheer when, supported by Bennett, he collected the TT trophy. 'Pa' Norton was dying of cancer and passed away the following April. Bennett went on to win the French and Belgian 500 GPs and only failed to win the Ulster GP when he ran out of petrol on the last lap.

In 1925 Bennett was again engaged to ride for the Norton works team in the Senior with team-mates Tom Simister and Joe Craig. In practice he again showed his potential, unofficially breaking the lap record by over forty seconds at almost 66 mph. In the race itself he started with a record lap of thirty-three minutes fifty seconds. But with a comfortable lead he hit a patch of oil at Governor's Bridge and fell, bending the footrest so it grounded on right-handers. The fall dropped

A. Bennett "Norton" 1925 T.T. Race 3rd in Senior Race

Alec back to sixth place, but he worked his way back through the field and eventually finished third, despite not being able to lay the bike over in the corners at the angle he would like. Bennett finished at an average speed of 64.65 mph, 3 mph faster than his winning average the year before, and he was only a minute down on second place man Frank Longman [AJS].

After the TT Alec again won the French 500 GP, but was unlucky once more in the Ulster, having a puncture when leading.

In 1925 Velocette had introduced a new 350cc ohc model for sale. One of the dealers handling the new Velocette was Bennett's motorcycle business. Alec was so impressed with the bike he persuaded Percy Goodman to engage him to ride one in the 1926 Junior TT. His arrangements with Norton didn't prevent this since Norton at that stage, didn't have a racing 350. The contract with Velocette was really only rewarding for Bennett if he won, but Alec was confident this would be the case.

Bennett went reasonably well in practice but, as usual, he was holding back. Before the race he told friends he thought he could lap at around thirty-three minutes - 68 mph - well ahead of the lap record. He was true to his word. At the end of the first lap Wal Handley led from Jimmy Simpson with Bennett in third place, fourteen seconds down on Jimmy. To the dismay of the crowd Bennett then pulled in to his pit. But it was a planned stop. Bennett had decided to pit early for tactical reasons.

The position remained the same on the next lap. Then Bennett decided it was time to open up a little. He set a record lap at 68.04 mph and passed both Handley and Simpson on time to take the lead. On the next circuit he passed Handley on the roads and took the lead there as well. Alec was now over two and a half minutes ahead of Handley with Simpson fur-

1926: Attracted by the potential of the new Velocette, Alec Bennett rode it on a no-win-no-pay basis in the 1926 Junior. His winning margin of over ten minutes demonstrated the machines potential to the world.

ther behind in third. By the fifth lap Handley had dropped back and Bennett led Simpson by over eight minutes. Pitting for the second and last time, Bennett had a glass of lemonade, changed his fly-covered goggles, refuelled and got off in just twenty-two seconds.

Bennett took things easy on the last two laps but was still faster than the winning speed of the previous year's Senior. He almost came to grief when he crashed at the Nook on the last lap; but he was able to remount and continue and crossed the line before many of the other riders had finished their sixth lap. His winning race speed was a record 66.70 mph and his fastest lap was a record 68.75 mph. He finished ten and a half minutes ahead of Simpson on the AJS.

Bennett confirmed that he had taken the first two laps very easily and had kept some speed in reserve in case he had to get a move on. His fall at the Nook [known for a short time afterwards as Bennett's Corner], was down to a very smooth rear tyre. He had badly bruised his left elbow in the fall but was able to carry on. The race Medical Officer, Dr.Woods, confirmed that Bennett was so fresh he might have been start-

ing a race instead of finishing one.

Gus Kuhn and George Povey had finished fifth and ninth respectively on their Velocettes so they took the Manufacturers' Team Prize. Bennett celebrated his win by dancing at the Villa Marina. He thought ballroom dancing was an excellent way of relaxing after a race in the saddle and enabled him to start the next day feeling perfectly fresh.

Bennett rode for Norton again in the Senior but this time he was out of luck. As usual, he started slowly, lying eighth on the second lap just behind Ashby on the P&M. He accelerated up to fourth on the next lap but then had to retire between Ballacraine and Kirk Michael with clutch trouble.

Bennett was back on the Velocette for the 1927 Junior, a firm favourite for a repeat win. Lying fourth after the opening lap, Bennett climbed to third place behind Handley [Rex] and Dixon [HRD]. But he could make no impression on the leaders. Four minutes behind Handley and sixty-six seconds in arrears of Dixon he retired at the Creg on lap five with engine trouble.

Alec had also contracted to ride an O.K. Supreme in the Lightweight. He had a bad start. The mechanical oil pump failed on the first lap and he had to use the hand pump to prevent the machine seizing. Nevertheless, by the second lap he was lying third, three seconds behind Arcangeli on the Italian Guzzi but two minutes down on leader Handley. Bennett, though, didn't give up. On the next circuit Bennett got ahead of the Italian by seven seconds and on the fourth lap he broke

Seven years after his initial win, Alec Bennett was still faithful to Sunbeam. He finished second in the 1929 Senior behind team-mate Charlie Dodson. Bennett is the only rider to have won TT races on side-valve, overhead-valve and overhead camshaft powered machines.

the lap record at 64.42 mph to reduce Handley's lead to just under a minute.

By the end of the Fifth lap the gap to Handley had widened again to one minute forty-seven seconds, but Bennett had completed all his pit-stops whilst Handley had one more to make. Alec could still do it. Then on his sixth lap Bennett's clock was slow to move to the Creg, and when it finally did so it was announced that Alec was touring in. When he arrived the stands greeted him with sympathetic applause. He had retired with engine trouble probably caused by the oil pump problem.

For the Senior Bennett was riding for Nortons again on the new Walter Moore designed ohc model. His team mates were Joe Craig and Stanley Woods. The bikes seemed to go well but Alec suspected the clutch wouldn't last both practice and the race and he had it changed at the end of practice. Alec didn't pass this information on to Woods, whom he saw as his main rival. Nor, for some reason, did Norton.

In the race itself Bennett got off to a slow start with clouds of blue smoke. At the end of the lap he was only fifth, ten seconds down on Ernie Nott [Rudge]. Bennett moved up to fourth on the next lap and third on the next. He was now only forty-six seconds behind Freddie Dixon on the HRD. But at the front, Woods was running away with the race. Dixon slowed on the fourth lap and Bennett came up to second. But Woods was over four minutes ahead of his team-mate and, effectively, the race looked all over.

Then came an announcement. Woods had retired - with clutch trouble! Bennett made his pit-stop at the end of lap five and was told he was in the lead. Tommy Spann [Sunbeam] was in second but over four minutes behind. Bennett eased off whilst Spann also hit trouble. Starting his last circuit Bennett led Tommy Simister [Triumph] by seven minutes. This time there were no last lap falls and Alec came home a comfortable winner - and the only Norton to finish. Woods' reaction is not recorded.

Bennett's winning speed of 68.41 mph was a race record and he won by over eight minutes from Jimmy Guthrie [New Hudson]. Simister was back in third. It was suspected that Bennett had gauged that a 68-69 mph average was enough to win and had ridden accordingly. Alec said he had no trouble apart from a little misfiring during the last three laps. On the last lap he had slowed and taken no risks. He was looking forward to returning home to Southampton. His son, Pat, expected him to win every race and was put out Alec hadn't won the Junior and Lightweight; Alec was anxious to explain that he had done his best.

The race had an unfortunate sequel. A Norton mechanic went to collect Bennett's machine from the finishing enclosure. The throttle stuck open, the mechanic fell off and the bike careered into the crowd, several of whom were slightly injured.

The Velocette that Bennett rode in the 1928 Junior was the first machine with a positive stop foot gear change. It gave Bennett an added advantage and he won the race easily, beating the lap record three times and finishing over five minutes ahead of team-mate Harold Willis. Despite a very strong wind on the Mountain, his fastest lap was 70.28 mph, close to the absolute lap record, and his winning average of 68.65 mph would have won that year's and the previous year's Senior. No wonder the gear change mechanism was soon adopted by the other teams.

In the Lightweight Alec again was O.K. mounted. But, in a wet and misty race, he was slowed from the beginning by magneto trouble. Whilst other riders were finishing their second lap, Bennett toured in to the Grandstand to retire at the end of his first.

He was out of luck in the Senior too. Riding for Norton, he was strongly fancied to repeat his win of the previous year. But a broken valve rocker on the first lap led to retirement at the Thirteenth Milestone.

1929 was Bennett's last full year as a professional racer, and for the first time he was out ridden in a long-distance race. In the Junior, riding once again for Velocette, he started slowly as usual and speeded up towards the end of the race. But, for once, he'd miscalculated the winning speed, and as he tried to come through Freddie Hicks and Wal Handley were already too far ahead to be caught. Bennett's race average of 68.97 mph was faster than his speed the previous year when he had won so easily. But he misjudged how much others had improved in twelve months. Alec finished in third place, two minutes nineteen seconds behind Hicks and just under a minute behind Handley.

There was still the chance of the Senior. This year he was riding for Sunbeam who, in poor conditions, had won the previous year's race through Charlie Dodson. As always, Bennett rode with perfect style but had a bad start and seemed, once again, to have misjudged the winning speed.

Plug trouble meant he got away badly and was over two minutes behind the leader at the end of lap one. By the end of lap two Alec was only eleventh, but by lap five, with a speed of over 72 mph, he had moved up to third, four minutes behind Dodson in the lead, but only sixteen seconds down on

Tim Hunt [Norton] in second place. On the next lap, riding quickly but smoothly, he got fourteen seconds ahead of Hunt on the next lap but was nearly five minutes down on Dodson. Alec settled for second place.

Alec finished four minutes forty-eight seconds down on his team-mate but said he was happy with the result. Apart from the plug trouble on the first lap he had no serious difficulties. His average speed of 70.51 mph was certainly respectable; but 'respectable' was never good enough for a Master like Alec Bennett. He retired at the end of the season.

Bennett was persuaded to ride a KTT Velocette 'for fun' in the 1932 Junior TT. It was a disappointment to his many fans when he could finish no better than eighth. Thereafter he concentrated on his business until his retirement. He died in 1973.

Alec Bennett waits to flag in the winner of the 1948 Lightweight TT.

Geoffrey Duke was born in March 1923 in St. Helens, Lancashire. His father ran a bakery and confectionery business and the family frequently visited the Island for holidays, though not at TT time. Geoff's first visit to the TT was in 1939 as a spectator for the Senior.

Geoff Duke celebrates his first win on the TT course. He outsped the rest of the entry to win the 1949 Senior Clubman race. Pictured with Geoff is Dr Steve Darbishire.

In 1940, Duke joined the Post Office as a trainee engineer. Then, aged nineteen, he joined the Army as a dispatch rider. Trained by Hugh Viney, an outstanding trials rider, he became a Sergeant Instructor and was later chosen for the Royal Signals motorcycle display team - the White Helmets.

On demobilisation Geoff went to work for BSA and also rode for their trials team. He was spotted by Irish racing star Artie Bell and offered a job by Nortons - as a trials rider. In 1948 he entered for the Clubmans but was rejected as being too inexperienced. So his Isle of Man road racing debut came in the 1948 Junior Manx Grand Prix. Riding a 350 'Garden Gate' Norton he was lying second to MGP star Dennis Parkinson [Norton] for the first two laps. On the third lap he took the lead but a split oil tank on the next lap caused the bike to seize and forced Duke to retire on the Mountain Mile.

After this performance there was no problem with his entry for the 1949 Senior Clubmans. Duke rode an International Norton and won the three lap race from Alan Jeffries [Triumph] with a record lap of 83.71 mph and a record average of 82.97 mph. Duke emphasised his liking for the TT course in the 1949 MGP meeting. This time, after a spill and clutch trouble, he finished second in the Junior to Cromie McCandless, but won the Senior from McCandless with a record average of 86.06 mph and a record lap of 87.48 mph.

Duke's performances were more than enough to convince Norton that they should add him to their racing team in 1950. Norton had new machines for the 1950 season with a new frame designed by Rex McCandless. For the TT Norton's 'A' team consisted of Bell, Duke and Johnny Lockett, with Harold Daniell and Australians Hinton and Morrison making up the 'B' team. In practice it seemed that of the new bikes, Bell had the fastest 350 and Duke the fastest 500.

There were 100 starters for the Junior race. Velocette had won the Junior for the past three years, and Bob Foster on a works machine was the firm pre-race favourite, but the new Nortons dominated the event. Despite Duke's best efforts, Artie Bell led from start to finish and won by seventy-seven seconds at a record average of 86.33mph. Duke was second and Daniell third, Lockett finished sixth to give Norton the team prize. At the prize giving, Daniell praised the handling and comfort of the new bike and said it was just like riding a featherbed. The name stuck, and the bikes were forever known as Featherbed Nortons.

The weather was perfect for the Senior and it seemed certain to be a fast race. This time it was Duke who led after the first lap, with Daniell twenty-nine seconds behind in second and Bell and Lockett battling for third. Duke, noticeably quicker and smoother than anyone else, was never challenged as he set a new lap record of 93.01 mph on his second lap and raised this to 93.33 mph on his fifth lap. By the last lap Duke had caught up the two minute forty second starting difference between Bell and himself and they crossed the finishing line together. It was almost a close thing, though. Duke's tank was virtually dry at the end.

Duke's race speed of 92.27 mph was faster than the old lap record. Bell finished second, and Lockett third so Norton romped away with the Manufacturers' team prize. The BMCRC trio of Duke, Dickie Dale [seventh] and Cromie McCandless [eighth] also won the Club team prize.

In the later GPs Duke and the rest of the Norton team were dogged by tyre troubles, but Geoff did manage to win the 500 Ulster and Italian GPs and the Italian 350 GP. Duke finished second by just one point to Masetti [Gilera] in the 500 World Championship, and second to Bob Foster [Velocette] in the

The all-conquering Norton team for the 1950 Junior TT, from the camera: Artie Bell, Johnny Lockett and Geoff Duke.

350 Championship.

1951 saw considerable improvements in the 350 Norton which was now producing around 36bhp at 8,000 rpm. In ideal conditions, Duke led throughout the Junior. Breaking the lap record on the first lap [at 89.75 mph], he increased this to 91.38 mph on the next lap. Thereafter, with the opposition demoralised, Geoff could afford to ease off, though his winning speed of 89.90 mph was still a record. Duke finished over three minutes ahead of Johnny Lockett with Jack Brett, on another works Norton, a further forty-seven seconds back in third.

In the Senior it was much the same story. Duke, starting number 1 by virtue of his win the year before, had a clear road ahead of him and used this to the best advantage. After a quick opening lap Geoff led by forty seconds from Lockett and Bill Doran [AJS]. After a record lap of 95.22 on his second circuit, Duke was well ahead, an advantage increased by the misfortunes of some of his rivals. Brett came off at the Gooseneck, Les Graham [MV] retired with valve gear problems and Lockett retired on the last lap with a broken chain. Duke won from Doran by four minutes twenty-two seconds with McCandless on a private Norton in third place. So Duke became only the fourth man to do a Junior/Senior double, and the first post-war rider to achieve the feat. For once Norton didn't win the Manufacturers' prize, but the Birmingham M.C.C. trio of Duke, Albert Moule [eighth] and E. R. Evans [twelfth] did win the Club team prize.

1952: Geoff prepares for a practice lap.

Junior he was an easy winner despite persistent cramp in his leg. He opened with a lap at 90.27 mph and followed this with a 91 mph lap. Having seen off the opposition he then eased down but still won at a new race record speed of 90.29 mph.Norton team-mate Reg Armstrong was second, one minute twenty-seven seconds behind, with AJS's Rod Coleman third a further minute and twenty seconds back. It was beginning to look as though no-one could beat Geoff Duke on the Isle of Man.

In the Senior race Duke's main opposition was expected to come from Les Graham on the MV. Duke's engine began to misfire intermittently on lap one, but he still led the race. Gradually, over the next three laps, Duke increased his lead over the MV star to more than a minute, setting a fastest lap of 94.88 mph. Then Duke had clutch trouble at Governor's Bridge on lap four and rode into the pits to retire - his first non finish in a TT. The race was won by Reg Armstrong despite his chain breaking as he crossed the line. Graham finished second, twenty-six point six seconds back on the Norton. He had lost the race when he overshot his pit at a pit stop, losing precious seconds in the process.

Duke went on to repeat his dominance in the Continental GPs. He won the 350 Belgian, French, Ulster and Italian GPs, whilst in the 500 class he was first in the Belgian, Dutch and Ulster rounds and fourth in the Italian GP. He won both the 350 and 500 World Championships, the first man ever to hold both titles in the same season. At the end of the year he was voted 'Sportsman of the Year' and awarded the RAC Seagrave Trophy for his achievements.

Duke had been approached to ride for Gilera for the 1952 season, but instead he elected to stay with Norton. In the

Duke easily took his second 350 World Championship, winning the first four races including the TT. But the 500 class was a tough struggle between Duke on the Norton and Masetti on the Gilera. Masetti won the Dutch and Belgian GPs where the Gilera was much faster. Then, on the thirteenth July, Duke crashed at a non-championship meeting at Schotten and dislocated his ankle. It took a while to heal and put Duke out of riding for the rest of the season, leaving Masetti free to take the title.

The season had been far from all bad, however, and Duke had also had his first experience of car racing. He drove a DB2 for Aston Martin but only had four races before the accident at Schotten. Duke was also awarded a well deserved O.B.E. in the New Year's Honours list for his services to motorcycle racing.

By the beginning of 1953 Duke was disenchanted with Norton. The single was being out paced in the World Championships and it was increasingly clear that the promised four cylinder machine was not being developed. Initially, he looked at car racing full-time with Aston Martin. Then an offer from Gilera lured Geoff back to his first love - motorcycle racing.

After testing, Duke made a number of suggestions for modifications to the forks brakes and frame of the Gilera. The revised version was nicknamed the 'Nortonised' Gilera. The other Gilera riders for the GPs were Dickie Dale, Reg Armstrong [also lured from Norton], and Alfredo Milani.

In the Senior, Duke started No. 67 whereas Les Graham on the MV was No. 18, a considerable advantage. Duke opened with a lap record of 96.38 mph and led Graham by fifteen seconds. Then, as Duke came down Bray Hill for the second time he saw a smouldering machine at the side of the road. Tragically, Les Graham had crashed and been killed.

In the race, Ray Amm on the works Norton took up the challenge. The Norton was out paced over most of the GP courses, but in the Island its superb handling still made it competitive with the Gilera, especially when ridden by the spectacular Amm. On his second circuit, Duke raised the lap record to 97.20 mph and was thirty-eight seconds ahead of Amm. But for once the opposition was not demoralised. Instead, Amm responded with an even faster lap - 97.41 mph.

At the end of the third lap Amm made his pit-stop. Duke went straight through. Striving to make the most of this advantage, Duke gave the Gilera a little too much power on a piece of molten tar coming out of Quarter Bridge. The bike flipped sideways and threw Geoff off. Duke was unhurt but the tank of the bike was too damaged to continue. The rest of the Gilera team fared little better. Armstrong had valve and chain trouble, Dale also came off and Milani was generally unhappy on the Isle of Man course. Amm went on to win from team-mate Brett with Armstrong in third. Duke was honest enough to admit that the fall had been his own fault.

The other GP rounds, however, proved the wisdom of Duke's change of team. He won the 500 Dutch, French, Swiss and Italian GPs and finished second in the Ulster to win another World Championship. Team-mate Armstrong finished second in the Championship.

The 1954 Gilera was narrower, lower and handled better and Duke was optimistic for the season. The Gilera team was a strong one with Duke and Armstrong joined by former World Champion Masetti. At the French GP, first of the season, Duke retired but he was confident things would be all right at the TT and was anxious to give Gilera their first TT win.

Nortons knew that, despite the brilliant riding of Amm, they would be struggling to stay with Duke and the Gilera. They experimented with the 'kneeler' fully-streamlined model but were unsure it would pass muster with the TT scrutineers. So they settled for Amm riding the so-called 'proboscis' Norton with extended streamlining at the front, and pannier tanks fitted to allow Amm to do all seven laps without a pit-stop. It was a crucial decision.

There will always be arguments amongst TT fans about which was the best ever TT race, but there is no doubt which was the most controversial. The start of the 1954 Senior was delayed by an hour and a half because of poor weather conditions. When it did get underway, the weather was still appalling, with driving rain and visibility on the Mountain down to fifty yards or less. At the end of the opening lap Duke was fourteen seconds ahead of Amm but confidently expecting the race would be stopped. It wasn't. In the terrible conditions Amm was using a 'foot down' style of cornering at some points and seemed willing to take more risks than the World Champion. At the end of the second lap Duke's lead was down to two seconds, and by the end of the third Amm led by twenty-eight seconds. It was then that the controversy occurred.

The organisers had met at the end of the second lap and had decided that the race should be stopped. But, with an unfortunate disregard for the riders' safety, it was decided not to stop the race until the end of the fourth lap. By then the race would have gone sufficient distance to allow World Championship points to be awarded!

To compound this surprising decision, the organisers chose not to tell the riders' team managers or mechanics what was going to happen. So, at the end of lap three Amm, as intended, went straight through. Gilera, though, called Duke in for his pit-stop, something they wouldn't have done if they had known the race had been cut to four laps. Duke reduced Amm's lead on the next lap but as the flag came out at the end lap four, Amm had won by sixty-six seconds.

In the aftermath of the race there were all sorts of recriminations. It was not generally known that Amm had intended to do the whole race non-stop. In the absence of this knowledge, there were ugly rumours that Norton had been forewarned of the organisers' decision and had been able to advise Amm not to stop at the end of his third lap. These rumours were untrue but Gilera felt strongly they'd still been cheated and should have been advised of the organisers' decision. Whether Duke could have caught Amm on that last lap is open to argument but he should have had the opportunity. Many more felt that the organisers' should have stopped the race straightaway as soon as they felt the course was too dangerous, and not waited until another couple of laps had passed - by which time, ironically, the weather was starting to improve.

It seemed that Duke had gone from the man who couldn't be beaten in a TT to the man who couldn't win one. But he put aside his disappointment and won the 500 Belgian, Dutch, German, Swiss and Italian GPs to take his fifth World Championship. The 1955 season held out the promise of a tremendous battle between Duke on the Gilera and Ray Amm who had signed to ride the MV-4. Tragically,

1955: Geoff takes St Ninian's Crossroads flat out on the 500 Gilera.

it was not to be. Amm, a close friend of Duke's, was killed on his debut for MV after a crash at an early season meeting at Imola.

Duke retired in the Spanish GP [the first GP of the season], but won the 500 French GP in his approach to the TT. He also raced his Gilera at the North West 200 meeting in Northern Ireland where he raised the lap record to 99.98 mph, so close to the magic 'ton'. It was a portent of things to come.

In the absence of Amm and the MV, Duke's main opposition in the TT was expected to come from Gilera team-mate Reg Armstrong, and Ken Kavanagh and Bill Lomas on the works Moto Guzzis. Duke and Armstrong practised on the full 'dustbin' fairing machines but, for the race, decided to ride the 'naked' Gileras. Duke took the lead from the start with Armstrong in second place, and the positions remained the same as the race progressed. The main interest switched to whether Duke could be the first to lap the course at 100 mph.

At the end of the third lap Duke came in for his pit-stop. He was quickly away again. The crowd waited anxiously for his lap time - and then it was announced. Duke had lapped in twenty-two minutes thirty-nine seconds - the first 100 mph lap. The crowd erupted with cheers and applause. It was surely fitting that Duke, the greatest rider of all time, should be the first to do the magic 'ton'.

Forty minutes later, came another announcement. The time of twenty-two minutes thirty-nine seconds equated to 99.97 mph. Duke hadn't done it after all. There were groans of disappointment and not a few boos.

Meanwhile, unaware of the controversy, Duke had a race to win. Despite an attack of cramp Geoff managed to keep a comfortable lead over Armstrong. A full-lock slide at 136 mph just after Bishopscourt on the sixth lap nearly put paid to Geoff's chances but he held on and came home at a record race speed of 97.93 mph to win by two minutes from Armstrong in second. Kavanagh was third, over two and a half minutes behind Armstrong. The BMCRC had entered a club team of Duke, McIntyre [fifth] and Surtees - who pushed in to finish twenty-ninth - and this trio took the Club team prize. There can never have been a better club team of riders.

Duke went on to win the German and Dutch 500 GPs and to win his sixth World Championship. But the Dutch race was not without incident. The privately entered riders found themselves in dispute with the organisers over start money and threatened to boycott the race. Duke and the rest of the Gilera riders felt obliged to support the privateers as the latter had supported the British works stars in a similar dispute at the 1953 Italian GP. But Duke's action was to have unfortunate repercussions the following season.

As a punishment for their support of the Dutch TT riders, motorcycle racing's governing body, the FIM, suspended the licences of Duke and others for the first six months of 1956. As a result Duke missed the 1956 TT. He was back in action at the Belgian GP in July but, when leading Surtees on the MV, retired when a piston broke. At the Ulster GP he made a rare mistake and dropped the Gilera when leading in damp conditions. Geoff was back to winning ways in the Italian GP, but by then Surtees had done enough to win the 500 World Championship.

1957 was no more successful. With Gilera's permission Duke approached Bob McIntyre and persuaded Mac to join the Gilera team for the season. The combination of Duke and McIntyre would have been a formidable one but, again, it was not to be. Duke crashed at an early season meeting at Imola and injured his shoulder. At first it was diagnosed as a fairly minor injury. Then it became clear it was a major dislocation and Geoff would be unable to compete in the TT.

Altogether, Duke missed four of the six GPs that season and, although he was back for the last two GPs, he was still not fully fit and could manage no better than third at Ulster and second in Italy. Then, at the end of the season, Gilera announced their withdrawal from racing. With it, Duke's era of domination came to an end.

Duke was back at the TT in 1958, however, to try his luck

again on what was now his home circuit [he was now an Island resident]. In the Junior he was entered on a Reg Dearden prepared Norton. It went well in practice and Duke lapped at a competitive 94 mph. But Norton persuaded Dearden to change the engine for an experimental 80 bore one - and then to change it back again to a standard unit - with no time left to test the machine. The bike got no further than Sulby on lap one before Duke had to retire.

For the Senior Duke had arranged to ride a works BMW on which Walter Zeller had gone so well in the 1956 and 1957 TTs. But Geoff found it difficult to adapt to the very different riding style needed for the BMW, which could not be leant into the corners to the same extent as the Norton or Gilera. Then the brakes faded at the end of the second lap and Duke was forced to retire at the pits. The season did end on a triumphant note, however, when, with MV not competing, Duke

1958: BMW mounted, Geoff takes Signpost Corner in fine style in the Senior TT. Brake trouble halted his ride.

won both the 350 and 500 classes of the Swedish GP on his Dearden tuned Nortons.

1959 was Duke's last TT. He was entered in the Lightweight on a 250 NSU but the engine seized in the first practice session and Duke was a non-starter. He had no bike for the Senior so his only ride that year was in the Junior.

Riding his Norton, Duke was lying sixth at the end of the opening lap, fifteen seconds behind Alastair King. By mid-race he was still in the same position but only two point six seconds behind Bob Anderson [Norton] with whom he was having a terrific dice. On the fifth lap he got ahead of Anderson and, with the retirement of McIntyre, found himself in fourth behind the two

1959: Geoff Duke takes his lightweight Junior Norton through Whitegates, Ramsey.

MVs and King. He remained in that position to the end, finishing at an average speed of 93.10 mph, fifty seconds behind King but forty-seven seconds ahead of Anderson. The crowd were pleased to see him back on the leader board and, once again, he was amongst the trophies. The Isle of Man's Southern MCC trio of Duke, Dave Chadwick [sixth] and George Costain [twenty-third] won the Club team prize.

Geoff Duke retired at the end of the 1959 season. He tried car racing for a while but retired after a crash in Sweden at the end of 1961. In 1963 he formed the Scuderia Duke team which raced the 350 and 500 Gileras in the world championships. He was involved later in the Manx Line, which brought competition and better standards to the sea links to the Island, and he has always kept his interest in the races and campaigned for the establishment of a short circuit on the Island for car and motorcycle racing.

I count myself very lucky. Like most of my generation, television has brought me the chance to see and appreciate sporting genius on an unprecedented scale. I have seen Muhammad Ali box, Jackie Stewart race cars, Gary Sobers and Ian Botham play cricket, and Pele and Best play football. I've seen Gareth Edwards and Mike Gibson play rugby, Jack Nicklaus play golf, Seb Coe run and Daley Thompson prove time and again he was the greatest all-round athlete in the world. However good television coverage is, though, it can't beat the experience of actually being there. I'm still prouder to be able to say, therefore, that I saw Geoff Duke ride in the TT races.

There are those that argue that both Bennett and Duke stayed on too long; that they should have retired whilst they were still at their peak. But that is to ignore just how high those peaks were. At their best both were simply unbeatable - and acknowledged as such by their contemporaries. They won in a style that put them in a different class from anyone else. Such brilliance, genius, is often short-lived and can go as quickly as it appears. When it's over we shouldn't be disappointed. We should just give thanks for the rare privilege of having witnessed a sporting Master.

1963: Geoff Duke and the Scuderia Duke Gilera at Jurby Airfield with riders John Hartle and Phil Read.

The Iron Man

-----oOo-----

Freddie Dixon holds a unique TT record. He's the only man ever to win TTs on two, three and four wheels. He was born on the 21st April 1892 in 31, Alliance Street, Stockton-on-Tees in Durham. One of eight children, he left school at 13 and went to work in a local garage. The firm had the agency for Indian motorcycles and Dixon started his riding on these machines. He developed a liking for the American style bikes and later insisted that his race machines should be fitted with footboards, a twistgrip throttle, a foot operated clutch and other features of the U.S motorcycles. He was seventeen when he bought his first motorcycle and started taking part in local hill-climbs.

Freddie Dixon was a character in an age of characters - full of fun sometimes, full of mischief at others and a tough customer who would stand no nonsense from anyone. He believed in living life to the full and his antics earned him the nickname of 'The wild man of the North'. He was a hard man who liked a drink, although never before a race, and a strong man both in physique and character. He was doggedly determined and had terrific stamina.

He disliked fussy officialdom but tempered his opposition with a keen sense of humour. Told he must wear goggles when racing - he usually rode without them - he came to the line wearing a pair from which the glass had been removed. No-one said a word.

He was a brilliant engineer although largely self-taught, and worked as a designer with Douglas and JAP. He was always willing to get his hands dirty and was meticulous in the preparation of his machines. Later he showed the same attitudes in the preparation of his racing cars.

In May 1912, Freddie, then twenty, told his parents he was going away for a couple of weeks. He failed to mention that he was going to the Isle of Man to take part in the TT races.

He made his TT debut in the Senior on a Middlesbrough-built single cylinder Cleveland Precision, and sponsored by a Middlesbrough businessman. It was an undistinguished start. His first lap took over fifty-five minutes, nine minutes slower than the leader Frank Applebee [Scott], and he was well down the field. His second lap, an even slower seventy-nine

Freddie Dixon's TT career started in 1912. The Cleveland was built, in Cleveland, by Egerton Price, who later became Mayor of Middlesborough in 1922.

minutes, showed he was obviously in trouble and his third lap took him over two and a half hours. He finally retired at Quarter Bridge on the fourth lap with broken timing gear.

Although he then joined the New Hudson factory, the 1912 Senior was Freddie's only pre-war TT race. During the Great War Freddie was in the Army and reached the rank of Staff-Sergeant. After his demobilisation he set up business in Middlesbrough as a motorcycle dealer, including the local Harley-Davidson franchise.

It was 1920 before the first post-war TT could be held.

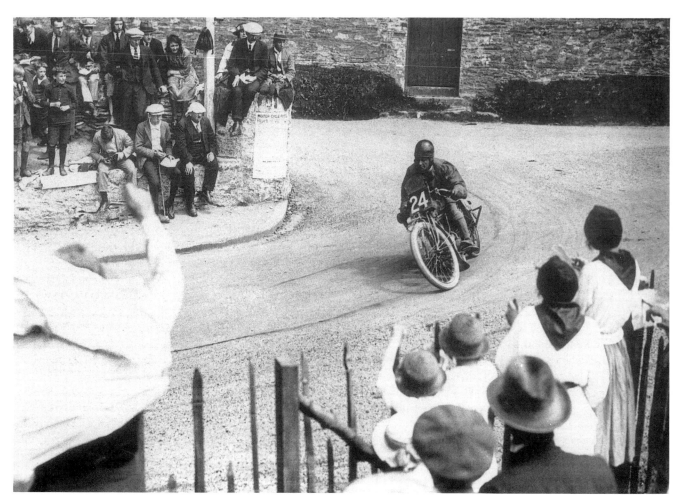

Freddie Dixon on an Indian at Governors Bridge.

Even then the effects of the war were still being felt. There was a shortage of machines and, more tragically, of riders, and only twenty-seven riders came to the start for the Senior race. One of them was Freddie Dixon on an Indian.

That year saw the introduction for the first time of the 'dip' at Governor's Bridge. The short, adverse camber, semi-circular section of road with its tricky descent and then ascent turned the preceding corner into a tight downhill hairpin bend which caught many riders out. Amongst them was Freddie Dixon. On his second lap he and two others riders approached the corner too fast. Freddie skidded violently under braking, almost hitting the wall, then skewed his machine dirt-track style onto the opposite lock to turn left and accelerate away down the dip. It wasn't the fastest or neatest way to get round Governor's Bridge but it was certainly spectacular.

More trouble lay in store just up the road when Freddie arrived at his pit just before his bike. Coming in to the Grandstand for his pit-stop, the rear brake on the Indian jammed and Freddie crashed heavily ten yards or so short of his pit - and in full view of the spectators. Dixon skidded up to his 'cage' on his shoulder to be followed shortly by the bike. Fortunately neither were too badly damaged. A few repairs in the cage [so called because the pits were surrounded by chicken wire] and he was on his way again.

Dixon had been lying eleventh at the end of the second lap but by the third he was up to sixth, thanks partly to the retirement of first, second and fourth placed riders George Dance, Alfie Alexander and Eric Williams. Freddie was thrilling the crowds all round the course with his lurid but exciting cornering style. But mechanical problems intervened. By the end of the fourth lap he was down to tenth and on his next circuit he passed the Grandstand slowly [for Freddie] in eleventh place. He hung on to finish twelfth at a race speed of 42.84 mph, nearly an hour behind winner Tommy de la Hay [Sunbeam].

For 1921 Freddie was back on the red Indian. During practice he continued where he had left off the previous year, thrilling and terrifying spectators at the same time. His cornering was spectacular but it was also fast - he lapped at over 53 mph in practice, not far short of the lap record. It was also safe, at least for Freddie. His pit lane crash the year before was to be his only TT crash until his final race. Nevertheless, he was frequently viewed by the race pundits as an accident waiting to happen.

In the Senior Freddie led the race for the first two laps until a misfire caused by a broken valve spring put him down the leader board. After stopping for repairs, Freddie came back through the field to take second place, but he couldn't catch Howard Davies on the 350 AJS. Freddie finished second, two minutes thirteen seconds behind H.R.D. at an average speed of 54.02 mph. Dixon's team-mate Bert le Vack was in third place, thirty-one seconds back.

In July of that year Freddie made his debut at Brooklands, the circuit that was to become his favourite and the scene of many Dixon triumphs over the years. He rode a 998cc Harley-Davidson in a 500 mile race. In practice he had found the saddle of the bike too slippery so he tried to improve its grip by covering it with sandpaper! In the race this proceeded to wear its way through Freddie's leathers and then drew blood from Freddie's backside. He had to stop to remove the sandpaper. Not long after he got going again, Freddie had a flat tyre and came off at high speed. But, typically, he just picked himself up, rode to the pits, repaired the machine and carried on - to finish second. There were seldom any uneventful races where Freddie was involved.

By now Dixon was also riding in some continental races, including the 1921 Belgian GP. He finished third. The race had been sponsored by the local FN armaments and motorcycle manufacturers and the Company presented sets of pistols to the first three in the race. After a night of celebration Freddie used his for target practice on his local hotel, to the terror of his fellow guests.

Freddie was back on an Indian for the 1922 TT, but, as

usual he'd made his own modifications to the bike. He had improved both the rear and front brakes and included a device, operated from a handlebar control, for lengthening or shortening the brake cable to the front brake, allowing him to change the strength of response of the brake for a given movement of the brake pedal.

Freddie went well in practice and unofficially broke the lap record at over 57 mph. As always he rode with a style of his own. On the bumpy parts of the course he rode moto cross style; he stood up on the footboards he always insisted on and let the bike buck beneath him. Spectators who saw his cornering style suggested that he actually lifted the front wheel round the corner at some points. Certainly he used his physical strength to help haul his bike around. He was no stylist, but it was certainly effective. The pundits doubted, however, that he could manage six laps without coming to grief.

The race itself was dominated by Alec Bennett on the Sunbeam. Dixon was lying third at the half way point and, on the next lap, moved up to second place, only fifty-three seconds behind Bennett having just lapped over two minutes faster than the Sunbeam star. But Freddie slowed again on the fifth lap and retired at Ramsey on the last lap with a flat tyre. It was said the air was blue with Freddie's comments on his bad luck.

For 1923 the ACU introduced a race for sidecar machines. There were only fourteen entries but they included eight makes of machine and a mixture of single and twin cylinder bikes. They also included Freddie Dixon who, true to form, had come up with an ingenious modification of his own.

Freddie had fitted his Douglas bike with a banking sidecar of his own design. The mechanism was operated by the sidecar passenger who pulled a long lever on the outside of the 'chair' which lowered or raised the sidecar wheel for right or left hand bends . The outfit was banned at first by the scruti-

1923 Sidecar TT. Harry Langman (Scott) approaches Braddan Bridge on the third lap of the race, miles too fast. Passenger Eddie Mainwaring is aware of the problem and hangs as far out of the chair as possible. Longman bounced Mainwaring off the wall and overturned the outfit. Dixon in the rear of the picture, missed the melee and went on to win.

neers, but a few 'comments' from Freddie convinced them to let him try a practice lap demonstration. He recorded a safe circuit at a respectable time and even had his passenger, Walter Denny, release the lever suddenly at 70 mph to see how this would affect the handling of the machine. He found that the sidecar only sank gently to its 'low' position and didn't affect the steering of the outfit at all. The scrutineers were convinced and allowed him to use the outfit.

Most of the sidecar competitors were converted solo riders and they found the adjustment hard. But not Freddie. He was reported as rounding Ramsey Hairpin, cigarette in mouth, skidding the outfit round to help his cornering speed. He reckoned he could get round the hairpin faster on his sidecar than he could on his solo machine. The sidecar was fitted on the left of Dixon's bike so the effect of the banking outfit was more pronounced on left hand corners. Freddie reckoned it allowed him to corner 10 or 15 mph faster.

The race, which was over three laps of the Mountain course, was expected to be a battle between Dixon and Harry Langman [Scott], and so it proved. Dixon started two minutes ahead of Langman on the roads and went at a good but safe speed on his opening lap. But Langman had lapped at 54.69 mph and had taken a substantial lead. Teams didn't have signalling stations in those days and Freddie was unaware of the position until, to Freddie's great surprise, Langman caught him on the road shortly after Ramsey on the second lap.

Dixon realised that Langman must have a lead of two minutes and increased his speed to draw away from the Scott. But at the end of the lap Dixon had to re-fuel, whereas Langman went straight through to start his last circuit. The race looked all over until Dixon arrived at Braddan Bridge where marshals were trying to clear away a crash. Freddie avoided the debris and spotted that the crashed machine was the Scott. Langman was not badly injured but was unable to continue. Dixon took things easier on the final lap and was coming home to an easy win when part of the sidecar frame broke at Hillberry and the chair leaned over so much that the handle-bars of the bike tangled with the sidecar body. With Walter Denny pushing the sidecar away from the bike by hand as they went through the last bends, Dixon got the outfit home to win. His race speed was 53.15 mph and he finished one minute thirty-eight seconds ahead of second place man Graham Walker on the Norton. It was an historic victory.

Freddie was also riding for the Indian team in the Senior race. The team was managed by Charles B Franklin, the Dubliner who had been second on an Indian in the 1911 Senior and was now a vice-president of the company. Dixon had fitted his own design of steering damper to the front forks of his machine. The race was held in bad weather with heavy rain and thick mist. Dixon led the race when a stretched valve meant a stop of three minutes. He got back up to third place but couldn't catch Manxman Tom Sheard [Douglas], [who had a clear advantage in the conditions], or second place man G. M. Black on a Norton. Dixon finished two minutes nineteen seconds down on the Manxman and thirty-six seconds behind Black at an average speed of exactly 55 mph.

Freddie went on to win that year's Belgian GP riding his Indian single. Travelling by rail to Dinant for the GP the train split in two when a coupling broke. The passengers were told they would have to stay put until a repair crew could be brought up on another train. Dixon decided he couldn't wait, bound up the broken coupling with spare motorcycle chains and the train continued on its way. Later, in Boulogne in September, he captured the World motorcycle speed record at a speed of 106.5 mph riding his 1198cc Harley-Davidson .

In 1924 Freddie moved from Indian to the Douglas factory. Once again he was entered in the Sidecar and Senior TTs. The sidecar outfit still had the banking mechanism but with refinements over the previous year. Freddie had also fitted an extra fuel tank in the sidecar tail, to avoid the need for a pit-stop. In practice, though, it was the Nortons of George Grinton and George Tucker which set the pace. The omens weren't good when Dixon also had to do some last minute repairs on the start line to a cracked frame lug.

Freddie set off to prove all the pundits wrong. Starting first on the roads he was at Ramsey before anyone else reached Sulby and at the end of the lap he led by sixteen seconds from Grinton [Norton]. Grinton fell back on the next lap whilst Freddie set the fastest lap of the race at 53.24 mph to lead by nearly three minutes from Tucker [Norton]. But this time it was Freddie's turn to hit trouble on the last lap. Dixon retired between Ballacraine and Sulby with piston trouble. Tucker won by over half an hour from Harry Reed [DOT]. Only five machines finished from the ten starters.

In practice for the Senior Freddie had only been tenth fastest as the Douglas camp suffered a variety of problems. Piston problems had put Freddie out of the Sidecar race and it was feared that he might have similar problems in the Senior TT.

Freddie determined again to show the prophets wrong. He led the race for the first four laps, setting a record lap at 63.75 mph. On the fourth lap Freddie was leading from Alec Bennett [Norton] when he fell at Governor's Bridge . Freddie had bent the machine's number plate and screen but there was no more serious damage and he remounted to ride to the Grandstand and make his scheduled refuelling stop.

A stop on the next lap to change a plug lost Freddie the lead and he fell further back when Bennett passed him on the roads on the last circuit. Freddie finished second on the roads and third on time, sitting bolt upright on the machine and with a wry smile on his face at his own misfortune - and luck. His front piston had broken on the last lap and eventually he had to stop at Signpost. Most of the piston went out as powder through the exhaust pipe and he carried on to the Grandstand on the rear cylinder only. When his bike was taken away for measuring [standard practice with the first three machines], Freddie said he thought the front piston would take some measuring as he didn't think it was there. He was right. A number of aluminium balls were lying in the crankcase. The rest of the piston had escaped through the exhaust.

By 1925 Freddie was working full time at Douglas on the preparation of their racing machines. So he must have been doubly disappointed at his results in that year's TT.

There were eighteen entries in the Sidecar race which was expected to be another Norton/Douglas battle. Freddie led at the end of the first lap from his team-mate Fred Hatton, with Len Parker [also on a Douglas] third. On his second circuit Freddie set a record lap at 57.18 mph and led from Parker and Bert Taylor [Norton]. Then it happened again. Ahead on the last lap Freddie retired, leaving Parker to give Douglas a win from Taylor and Grinton [Nortons]. Freddie had no chance to change his luck. It was the last Sidecar TT for twenty-nine years.

That year, Freddie competed in the Junior for the first time. He led that too on the first lap, albeit by just one second from Wal Handley [Rex Acme]. But he retired on the next lap. Things were little better in the Senior. Of the Douglas team of seven riders, six retired, including Freddie. Their highest placing was nineteenth.

If 1925 had been a disappointing year, 1926 got off to a good start. In January Freddie married a Middlesbrough girl, Margaret Thew.

The 1926 TT races were a godsend to an Isle of Man tourist industry severely hit by the U.K. General Strike. Despite the economic situation all the major British factories were represented and Freddie was again riding for the Douglas concern. His team-mates included Jim Whalley and Vic Anstice. The motorcycle press reported that Dixon had spent the last few months modifying the Douglas engines and redesigning any parts which had given trouble in the past.

In practice Freddie thrilled the spectators and commentators alike with his exciting riding style. But despite Dixon's winter efforts reliability still seemed to be a problem. The Douglas team did some fast laps but also some very slow, trouble-hit ones.

For the Junior race the rumour was that Dixon, riding, as usual, without goggles or gloves, had a machine so fast even he couldn't use all the available speed. Sadly, it wasn't true.

All the Douglas machines were reluctant to start at all and their riders had to push with all their strength to get the machines to fire. At the end of the opening lap Dixon was in fourth place behind Handley, Simpson and Bennett. Though the lead changed ahead of him Freddie could make no impression on the first three and by the fourth lap, was over five minutes behind leader Alec Bennett.

Fans suggested that Freddie was just biding his time; he would come through the field Alec Bennett-style. On lap five Dixon did get up to third place, but only because Handley had dropped back. Reports from around the course confirmed that Freddie was really trying, but so was Jimmy Simpson whilst Bennett was in a class of his own. Then Walter Handley came storming back and on the last lap overtook Freddie to take third place. Dixon had to settle for fourth at an average of 63.25 mph, thirty seconds behind Handley and thirteen minutes behind winner Bennett. He was the only works Douglas to finish.

In the Senior Freddie had last minute problems. In a final try-out of his machine a broken valve wrecked the cylinder. Freddie and the mechanics had to work all night to repair the damage. Needless to say, Freddie was late for the pre-race weigh-in and was fined £3 for late arrival. An official asked Freddie 'What would you have done to the bike if you'd another day to spare?' 'I've done everything I know except pray' replied Freddie, 'and I'm doing that now'. His prayers weren't answered. He retired at Ballig on the first lap with engine trouble.

The rest of the Douglas team fared no better. Disillusioned with his poor results, Freddie left Douglas at the end of the season and went to join J. A. Prestwich, makers of the JAP engines.

The change was a successful one. JAP didn't have a road racing team so Freddie agreed to ride the JAP engined HRD machines designed and built by H. R. Davies. Freddie was part of a three man team with Howard Davies himself and C. P. Wood.

As usual, Dixon modified his machines, including adding a foot controlled clutch of his own design. The press reported, however, that to

1927: Freddie receives the plaudits of his female fan club after winning the Junior TT on the HRD.

everyone's surprise, Freddie Dixon's HRD looked very like an HRD. Even the word Indian written in bold letters on the footboards failed to convince anyone. Freddie also attached a backrest to the saddle as he had begun to suffer from back trouble. He rode without goggles and wore socks and shoes rather than the thick riding boots worn by other riders for protection. The others said it was because Freddie was already made of rubber and steel.

In practice Dixon was up to his usual tricks. He came down Bray Hill on one lap snaking about all over the place but seemingly quite happy himself. His team boss seemed happy too. One early morning session Howard Davies stopped at Creg-ny-Baa for a welcome cup of tea. Whilst he was there along came Freddie approaching the corner too fast and narrowly missing the protective bolsters on the exit - much to the amusement of Howard Davies.

Freddie's Junior bike had been misfiring badly on his last practice lap and at the start of the race it looked like another retirement for Dixon. His JAP engine seemed to be tightening up in the early miles of the lap but, after he eased up for a bit, the engine came back strongly. By the end of the lap he was in second place, albeit nearly a minute behind Wal Handley [Rex Acme].

For the next two laps Dixon kept pace with Handley but was unable to close a gap of around eighty seconds. Dixon pitted at the end of lap three and the gap went up to two minutes fifty seconds but Handley had to pit the following lap and the gap was down again to one minute forty-four seconds. Freddie continued to ride his machine as fast as he could but on the penultimate lap Handley pulled still further ahead and, going into the last lap, had a lead of over two and a half minutes. It looked like an easy win. But this time fate was on Freddie's side. The indicators on the scoreboard showed Dixon had overtaken Handley half way round the final circuit and as Handley retired Dixon cruised home to win his second TT.

Freddie's winning speed of 67.19 mph was a race record

and he finished a comfortable eight and a half minutes ahead of Harold Willis on the Velocette. Apart from the trouble at the start, and a broadside skid at Kirk Michael, it had been a trouble free ride. The other HRD riders had been less successful and both had retired. At the Prize Presentation Freddie was chaired to the stage by fans to the tune of `Why was he born so beautiful... He paid a warm tribute to Wal Handley.

Conditions for the Senior race were dry but with mist on the Mountain. As Freddie started off the band at the Grandstand broke into 'Why was he born so beautiful' to remind him of his Junior triumph. At the end of the first lap Freddie was second, fifty-three seconds behind Stanley Woods [Norton]. Freddie's second lap was slower than his first and he was now well down on Stanley and having a job to hold off Jimmy Simpson in third. Then on the third lap spectators came back from Bray Hill with white faces. Trying desperately to catch Woods and stay ahead of Simpson, Freddie had tried to overtake another rider as he came down the hill at over 90 mph. Dixon had taken to the gutter, hit a bump, the machine had leapt several feet in the air and had almost reared up too far to be caught. But caught it Freddie had and passed the other rider as if the latter was standing still.

On the next lap, however, Freddie slowed dramatically with a lap time of forty minutes. The gear lever support had broken and the gear change linkage came adrift. Dixon rode on changing gear as best he could. By the penultimate lap he was down to ninth but a combination of continuing effort from Freddie and the retirement of others brought him up to sixth place at the finish. He was the only HRD to finish.

For 1928, Rex Judd persuaded Freddie to return to the Douglas factory. Freddie worked on the new twin-cam engines for the TT. For the racing period itself he was in charge of the Douglas team. The responsibility seemed to weigh him down a little and he was reported to be far from the old carefree Freddie.

1934: Freddie Dixon turns back up Bray Hill in his Riley during the Mannin Veg race. Note the traffic lights, soon to be reinstalled at this point.

In the Junior Freddie hit trouble early on, first with his shock absorber and then with a broken throttle wire. His first lap took nearly forty-six minutes and his second lap over an hour. Thereafter he lapped at a consistent thirty-four-thirty-five minutes to finish in eighteenth - the first Douglas to finish.

Freddie fancied his chances in the Senior event. But the race was held in poor conditions with wet roads, mist and fog. There were a lot of greasy patches on the roads round the course, including one at the Gooseneck.

Its first victim was Oliver Langton [Scott] followed by Jimmy Shaw [Norton]. Then Freddie, trying to avoid the debris, became the Gooseneck's third victim when he also skidded and fell. The loudspeaker at the Grandstand reported that Freddie was resting for a few minutes and was discussing the race with Jimmy Shaw. But Langton confirmed afterwards that Dixon's crash was a spectacular one with Freddie doing several somersaults up the road. Even the Iron Man had been shaken by the spill and had broken his wrist and dam-

aged his thumb. Whether because of the crash or because he simply wanted to move on to a new challenge, it was Freddie Dixon's last motorcycle TT. He had competed in seventeen races and finished in nine. He had won on two wheels and three, finished second once and third twice. Now his interests turned to cars.

Freddie stayed with Douglas' racing and design department for another two years, and several of the company's patents during that time bear Freddie's name. There were rumours of a TT comeback in 1930 but it never materialised. After leaving Douglas Freddie tried to design his own water-cooled four cylinder machine but the Depression meant there was no capital to develop the bike. However, in 1938 Brough Superior, with Dixon's agreement, based their proposed 'Golden Dream' on Freddie's four cylinder design. The bike was the sensation of the London Motorcycle Show but the war intervened before it was put into production.

In 1932 he entered the Ulster TT car races. The race was a handicap event over thirty laps of the twelve point six mile course at Ards near Belfast. Dixon had bought a black 'Brooklands' four-cylinder 1.1 litre Riley with a distinctive long 'tail'. Freddie led for most of the race but, with three laps to go, was passed by Whitcroft in a factory Riley. Freddie narrowed the gap again but tried to take a corner too fast, hit a kerb and sailed over a hedge, landing on all four wheels in a rhubarb patch. A wheel was too damaged for the car to continue.

The following year Freddie finished fourth but was disqualified for having a defective exhaust, despite mechanic Len Ainsley having held it together with towels for the last few laps. Freddie's comments on the decision are not recorded.

Dixon raced Rileys for a number of years, making various modifications needless to say, including always having one carburettor for each cylinder. The modifications worked for he was often faster than the works models. He also drove for MG but the arrangement didn't last - they wouldn't let him set the car up himself.

In 1933, Miss Rita Don drove the Riley in a Ladies' Race at Brooklands, with Dixon as mechanic and passenger. Freddie is supposed to have 'helped' his driver by keeping the hand throttle wide open and prodding Miss Don with a hat pin if she braked too early. Miss Don won by a large margin.

Injuries from a crash at Donington put Freddie out of the 1934 TT, but the following year Freddie was back with a vengeance. Driving his own 1.5 Litre Riley he soon drew away from the factory models and won the race by a comfortable seventy-three seconds. Eddie Hall was second in a Bentley and Earl Howe third in a Bugatti. Afterwards Freddie was said to be 'one big grin'. Just to prove it was no fluke Dixon won the TT again the following year with fellow TT winner Charlie Dodson as his co-driver. Dodson had won the 1934 car TT in his M.G. becoming the first man to win TTs on two and four wheels.

Altogether Freddie's racing successes included the 1934 BRDC 500 Mile races, the 1935 British Empire Trophy, two TT wins and a third place in the 1934 Le Mans 24 Hour Race. He also won the 1933 Mannin Beg race in the Isle of Man and was the only driver to lap Brooklands at over 130 mph in a car of under 2 litres. He also bought a Sunbeam car named 'Silver Bullet' with the intention of trying for the World Land Speed Record but decide eventually that the car wasn't up to it.

Freddie hadn't entirely lost his old ways and he often practised his racing driving in his road cars on the public highway. This led to serious problems and in 1935 he spent a short time in Durham Prison as a result of a motoring offence.

After the war, Freddie became mechanic and engineer to racing driver Tony Rolt, helping to prepare Rolt's ERAs. Freddie died suddenly on the fifth November 1956 at his home in Reigate. He was sixty-four. At his request his ashes were scattered over the Home Banking of his beloved Brooklands.

The TT has always attracted great riders, and Freddie Dixon certainly ranks amongst them. But, more than any other race perhaps, the TT has also attracted great characters. It is the mixture of the two that is part of the TT's attraction and makes it something uniquely memorable and special. There have been no greater TT characters than Freddie Dixon and he richly deserves his place in TT history.

Chairmen

They have to be a little mad. Like football goalkeepers, sidecar racers, and particularly passengers have a reputation for being a little touched.

Watching the Sidecar races was one of the greatest thrills of my early TTs. It was tremendous to see these heavy, powerful machines sliding around corners [the proper term was 'drifting', my father told me], the passenger leaning out, or sometimes hanging on, to keep the machine on the road and themselves on the machine.

Sidecar racing in the TT has had a chequered history. It started in 1923 with the race won by Freddie Dixon on his banking sidecar outfit. But dwindling entries made for a poor spectacle round the Mountain course and the class was dropped after 1925. It returned in 1954, thanks mainly to the lobbying of Eric Oliver, four times World Champion in the Sidecar class, a frequent solo competitor in the TT, and a very determined character.

The return of sidecars to the TT, however was to the 10.79 mile Clypse course rather than the full Mountain course. It was just as exciting, nevertheless, to see such riders as Oliver, Cyril Smith, Willi Noll, Fritz Hillebrand, Walter Schneider and Pip Harris throw their machines around the tight corners at the Manx Arms, the Nursery Bends and Signpost Corner in my home Village of Onchan. There was a wide variety in the entry - more so even than in the solo classes. There were a few 'works' entries, the immaculate white faired BMWs and the beautifully prepared 'Watsonian' outfits, but, down the field, there were a number of distinctly 'home-made' outfits. They often struggled to finish but gave their crews and spectators plenty of thrills along the way.

In 1960 the Sidecar race returned to the Mountain course after an absence of thirty-five years. With its return we were privileged to see a series of battles over the next six years between two of the greatest ever sidecar racers - Max Deubel and Fritz Scheidegger.

-----oOo-----

Fritz Scheidegger was born in 1930 in Courtelary, Switzerland. A garage owner, he was Swiss 350 and 500 solo Champion in 1957 before turning to sidecar racing. He rode with a left-hand 'chair' rather than the right-hand outfits of the German riders.

1954: First lap, and the field pile into Parkfield Corner on the first lap. Eric Oliver (Norton) is already ahead of the field, followed by Pip Harris (Norton) and Fritz Hillebrand (BMW).

Max Deubel was born in Mulhenau, Germany in 1935. He was the most consistent sidecar rider of the 1960s, winning the World Championship four years in succession from 1961-1964.

Scheidegger made his International debut in 1957 when, with German passenger Horst Burckhardt he finished fourth in the Italian GP at Monza. Deubel's first major sidecar races came the year after in 1958.

Scheidegger was the first to make his TT debut. With Burckhardt as passenger he won the 1959 French GP; then came to compete in the Sidecar TT over the Clypse course. He finished a fine third on his debut, averaging 69.42 mph and finishing behind Schneider and fellow Swiss driver Florian Camathias. Scheidegger won the Overseas Newcomer's trophy for the TT meeting and the Ray B. Westover trophy for the best overall TT newcomer.

In the remaining GPs that year Deubel and his passenger Emile Horner finished third in the West German GP with Scheidegger in fifth place. Scheidegger finished third in the Belgian GP and third in the World Championship overall, behind Walter Schneider and Florian Camathias.

The French GP at Clermont-Ferrand was the opening side-car GP of 1960. Scheidegger finished second to Helmut Fath with Deubel not far behind in fourth. Then both prepared to make their debuts over the Mountain course.

It was not a happy debut for Deubel. He crashed at Brandish in practice and, in the race, got no further than Governor's Bridge on the first lap, where he retired with engine trouble. Scheidegger looked likely fare a little better after managing fifth place on the practice leader board.

There were thirty starters for the race itself. Fath and 'Pip' Harris set off first together on the roads, followed by Scheidegger and Camathias. The latter lapped at 84.53 mph and led Fath at the end of lap one by seven point six seconds. Scheidegger, lapping at 82.75 mph, was twenty-seven seconds further back in third place with Harris a further eight seconds off.

On the second circuit Fath set a lap record of 85.82 mph and reduced Camathias' lead to six seconds, whilst Harris got one point four seconds ahead of Scheidegger. Then the last lap brought more trouble for the two Swiss. Camathias' engine seized at Sulby and again at the Guthrie Memorial and he coasted home to finish fifth. Scheidegger also hit mechanical trouble. The BMW's drive shaft coupling broke and he toured in to finish eleventh at an average of 72.28 mph.

Pip Harris finished second in the TT and won the following Dutch GP on his BMW. Scheidegger was third and Deubel sixth. In the Belgian round Scheidegger finished second to Fath, and the order was repeated in the West German GP at Solitude where Deubel finished fourth. Fath won the Championship with Scheidegger again in second place.

Both Deubel and Scheidegger had done well enough in 1960 to attract BMW works support for the 1961 season. At the opening GP in Spain it was the old familiar story as Fath won from Scheidegger. But at the West German GP at Hockenheim Deubel and his passenger Emil Horner won from Scheidegger and Burckhardt. The positions were reversed at Clermont Ferrand so the two came to the TT battling hard for the World Championship, with Scheidegger in the lead.

Both were flying in practice, with Scheidegger lapping within four seconds of Fath's lap record and Deubel only a further four seconds back. There were thirty-two starters for the race itself which was held in ideal conditions. Scheidegger, Deubel and Otto Kolle formed the BMW works team. Scheidegger started first on the roads with Charlie Freeman [Norton]. Deubel started number three, ten seconds behind.

At Sulby Scheidegger was still ahead on the roads but he and Deubel were together at the Mountain Box. At Creg-ny-Baa Scheidegger was ten yards ahead on the roads, and by the Grandstand he had increased the gap to twenty yards but he was eight point eight seconds behind the German on corrected time. Scheidegger had broken the lap record from a stand-

1963: Fritz Scheidegger and Johnny Robinson slide their BMW round Sulby Bridge.

ing start at a speed of 86.71 mph. But Deubel had gone even quicker at an amazing 87.20 mph.

On the next circuit Deubel passed Scheidegger on the roads and was 100 yards ahead by Sulby. At the end of the lap Scheidegger had broken Deubel's new record and lapped at 87.45 mph. But Deubel had gone faster still - 87.97 mph. He led by eight seconds on the roads and by twenty-eight seconds on corrected time. Pip Harris, averaging a respectable 85.25 mph was third, nearly a minute back on Scheidegger.

Despite their fantastic speeds, both Scheidegger and Deubel negotiated the last lap safely and Deubel came in to win at a record average of 87.65 mph, nearly 2 mph faster than the previous lap record. Scheidegger finished second, thirty-three seconds behind at 87.03 mph, and Harris third over a minute and half behind Scheidegger. Kolle retired at Cruickshank's Corner with engine trouble, so BMW failed to win the Manufacturers' Team Prize.

Deubel reported that his engine had misfired briefly on the Mountain on the last lap. Otherwise he'd had no problems. Scheidegger complained that his bike had been badly under-geared for the day but otherwise he'd had a trouble-free ride. Both got warm ovations at the Prize giving.

The TT result left Scheidegger on twenty-six points in the World Championship to Deubel's twenty-two. But at the following Dutch GP at Assen Scheidegger retired early on whilst Deubel went on to win. Deubel had thirty points to Scheidegger's twenty-six. The championship all came down to the last GP at Spa in Belgium. Scheidegger won the race. But Deubel knew he only had to finish second. He did so and won the Championship by thirty-six points to Scheidegger's thirty-four.

The battle for the championship had been a tremendous

one and everyone looked forward to a repeat in 1962. Unfortunately it wasn't to be. Scheidegger missed the first three GPs, by which time Deubel had taken a healthy lead.

Deubel won the opening GP rounds at Barcelona and Clermont-Ferrand, and came to the TT a hot favourite. There were twenty-seven starters and, in the absence of Scheidegger, Burckhardt passengered Florian Camathias. Camathias had been fastest in practice lapping at nearly 90 mph. Deubel and Chris Vincent [BSA] led the field away followed ten seconds later by Camathias and Kolle.

By Sulby Deubel was twenty seconds ahead of Camathias on the roads and thus ten seconds ahead on time. The lead was up to fifteen seconds by Ramsey and by the end of the lap it was sixteen seconds. Deubel had set a new lap record from a standing start at 90.70 mph, the first 90 mph sidecar lap. Vincent was in third place, but over a minute and a half behind Camathias.

At Ramsey on the next lap Vincent was second on the roads and in the race. Camathias had crashed at Kerroo Mooar. He suffered abrasions and bruises and Burckhardt had a broken leg. Deubel lapped at 90.50 mph and, by the end of lap two led Vincent by almost three minutes. Kolle was up to third but forty-eight seconds down on the BSA. It looked like an easy victory for Deubel but, to the unfortunate but understandable cheers of the crowd it was announced that, at Kirk Michael, Vincent led on the roads and on time. Deubel had retired at Ballig with engine trouble.

Vincent won at an average speed of 83.57 mph, the first sidecar win on a British machine since Oliver in 1954. Kolle finished thirty-four seconds behind in second, with Colin Seeley on a Matchless third.

Scheidegger returned for the Dutch GP, he and new passenger, Englishman John Robinson, winning the race from Deubel. Camathias won the Belgian GP from Scheidegger and Deubel but Max won the West German GP at Solitude, and took the World Championship, from Camathias and Scheidegger.

1963 got off to a good start for Deubel with a win in the Spanish GP. For once Deubel didn't win the West German round [Camathias winning from the German], and the French round was cancelled because of fog. So Scheidegger was well behind in the Championship as they came to the 1963 TT.

Camathias, having one of his frequent difficult times with the BMW factory, was riding an FCS - a BMW engined machine in a special low frame of Camathias' design. He wasn't allowed to use the really low model in the TT, the scrutineers feeling there was insufficient ground clearance for the bumps of the Mountain course. So he had to use a more conventional outfit. It made no difference. Camathias took the lead on the second lap and went on to win by thirty-eight seconds from Scheidegger. The weather slowed speeds and engine problems slowed Deubel who could manage no better than eighth place. British fans, lamenting that there was no repeat of a British win, could take some comfort from the fact that the Matchless trio of Colin Seeley [sixth], Owen Greenwood [seventh] and A. J. Thurgood [twenty-third] took the Manufacturers' Prize.

Deubel made up for any TT disappointment by winning the Dutch GP from Scheidegger and finishing second to him in the Belgian GP to take his third World Championship in a row. Camathias finished second and Scheidegger third.

Barcelona opened the 1964 season, but both Scheidegger and Deubel were out of luck. Scheidegger retired whilst Deubel could manage no better than fourth. It was back to normal at the French GP where Scheidegger won from Deubel.

For 1964, Gilera had loaned Camathias a four cylinder engine for his sidecar outfit. It was fast and I can testify that it was certainly the best sounding TT sidecar outfit ever. Conditions were not ideal for the race and it seemed unlikely that the lap record would be broken. Deubel set the fastest opening lap and led, but only by five point six seconds from Camathias. Scheidegger was third a further six point four seconds back, with Colin Seeley on the FCS in fourth place.

1964: Max Deubel and Emil Horner at Bedstead Corner in practice; this was Deubel's second TT win.

Scheidegger retired on the next lap whilst Deubel set the fastest lap of the race [89.63 mph] to extend his lead on Camathias. Then, on the last lap, the Gilera engine went off song and Camathias had to push in to finish fifteenth. Deubel won at a record race speed of 89.12 mph and by just over two minutes from Seeley on the FCS. Goerg Auerbacher [BMW] was third, two minutes down on Seeley.

The following Dutch GP saw Seeley win from Chris Vincent [BMW] with Scheidegger and Deubel back in third and fourth respectively. Things were back to normal at Spa, though, where Deubel won from Scheidegger, and although Scheidegger turned the tables at Deubel's own West German

GP, Deubel had won his fourth successive World Championship.

1965 saw Deubel chasing his fifth Championship and Scheidegger determined to improve on his second place. It promised to be a great battle and this time it didn't disappoint.

Scheidegger won the West German round at Nurburgring but Deubel won in Spain. Camathias won the French round with Scheidegger second and Deubel third. Scheidegger had twenty points to Deubel's twelve as they came to the TT.

Deubel responded magnificently. Camathias [BMW] led from Scheidegger at Ramsey on lap one but then retired with clutch and gearbox trouble. At the end of the opening lap

Scheidegger led from Deubel. But on the next circuit Deubel set a new lap record of 91.80 mph and took over the lead on time. On the final lap Deubel almost caught Scheidegger on the roads and came home to finish fourteen seconds in the lead at a record average of 90.57 mph - the first 90 mph race average. Auerbacher was third and Heinz Luthringhauser fourth.

Scheidegger now had twenty-six points and Deubel twenty. But Scheidegger was not to be denied that year. He won all three of the further GPs at Assen, Spa and Monza and took the title easily from Deubel in second place.

1966 saw some more terrific races as Deubel strove to regain his title and Scheidegger to retain his. But there was no better race that year than the TT - and none more controversial.

A seamen's strike postponed the TT until the end of August. By that time Scheidegger had already won the West German, French, Dutch and Belgian GPs and secured his second World Title. But Deubel, who had decided to retire at the end of the season, was anxious to make it three TT wins in succession.

The 1954 Senior remains the most controversial TT, but the 1966 Sidecar race, known as the 'Tiger in the Tank' TT, certainly runs it close. Sadly, the controversy overshadowed one of the greatest ever TT races.

Deubel set the early pace lapping at 91.5 mph to lead by eleven point six seconds at the end of lap one. Scheidegger was second, thirteen seconds ahead of Auerbacher. On the next lap Deubel went even faster and increased his lead to fifteen seconds. Auerbacher had a leaking petrol tank and called at the pits for a refuel only to discover this wasn't allowed under the race regulations. He set off again in fourth place behind Colin Seeley [BMW].

Then the real drama started. At Union Mills on the last lap Deubel's engine started to seize. He managed to get the bike to restart but, having lost a lot of oil, he had to try and coax it home. Meanwhile Scheidegger was catching up all the time.

By Ramsey the lead was down to nine seconds. By the Bungalow it was down to five. At Signpost Corner they were almost together on time - then potential disaster for Scheidegger. The gearbox burst at Governor's Bridge - but the engine kept going. He flashed past the flag flat out - unlike Deubel who eased back as he approached the flag; and that was the difference. Scheidegger won the race by just point eight of a second! Auerbacher caught Seeley at Ramsey and finished third, despite running out of fuel as he came up the finishing straight.

Then the controversy started. The TT regulations required competitors who weren't contracted to a particular petrol company to use the [Shell] fuel provided by the organisers. Scheidegger claimed he'd been refused petrol from the refuelling tanker. So he'd gone down to the nearest filling station and filled up with Esso. He declared this to the Scrutineers before the race and no objections were raised. There was no question of the 'wrong' fuel having given him any advantage. But the International Jury were adamant. Scheidegger had broken the rules and had to be disqualified. It took an appeal and another three months before the decision was overturned and the race awarded to Scheidegger.

Deubel retired as planned at the end of 1966. He later became West Germany's representative on the FIM Road Race Committee. In 1994 he returned to the Isle of Man and led the sidecar section of the Classic Parade on a BMW. He was followed by an old rival, Heinz Luthringhauser, also on a BMW.

Unfortunately, the 'Tiger in the Tank' TT had a tragic consequence for Fritz Scheidegger. He had decided to retire from racing in protest if his appeal was not upheld. When it was, he decided to race for one more season. At the Easter Sunday Meeting at Mallory Park in 1967 the rear brake arm of his machine broke and sheared the hydraulics as he approached the Hairpin. He crashed into the wall. John Robinson, his passenger, was seriously injured. Scheidegger himself died from his injuries.

The Kiwi Flyer

Hugh Anderson was born in New Zealand in 1936. One of the first to adopt the 'knee out' style of riding, he was a dedicated, skilled and forceful rider who kept himself to himself and attracted much less attention than some of his more flamboyant contemporaries. I think that was why he was one of my favourites. He seemed unfussy, he just got on with the job of winning.

Anderson won only two TTs but was World Champion four times in a period of fierce competition between the works teams of Honda, Suzuki, Yamaha and, in the 50cc class, Kreidler.

-----oOo-----

His first season in Europe was in 1960 and that was also his TT debut. Anderson entered for the Senior and Junior on Norton and AJS machines respectively. Wisely, he started cautiously in practice and lapped around twenty-nine or thirty minutes. But he was a quick learner, and by the end of the week his lap times were down to twenty-five and twenty-four minutes. He ended up sixth on the Junior practice leader board just behind Mike Hailwood on his AJS.

There were eighty starters for the Junior race and, for the first time, these were seeded with the fastest men at the front. The ACU clearly knew very little about Hugh Anderson for he was down to start No 74. This gave Anderson a big disadvantage, for he had to spend the first lap making his way past slower riders. By the second lap, however, he was up to eighth place behind Bob Anderson [Norton] and ahead of TT regulars like Ralph Rensen, Mike Hailwood and Syd Mizen. It wasn't to last, though, and on the next lap Anderson retired at Bishopscourt with engine trouble.

In the Senior Anderson was also out of luck. His first lap was a respectable 92.40 mph but he hit trouble on the next circuit and was reported touring in from the Mountain to retire. Still he did enough in these races and in later races in Europe to show his potential and attract the attention of the Suzuki Factory.

1960 had also been Suzuki's debut in the TT. They entered a team of Japanese riders in the Lightweight 125cc class. Confusingly, the bikes were entered as Colledas - the model name. The machines were well outpaced and the riders hampered by their lack of experience. For 1961 Suzuki decided they needed the help of some more experienced riders. They signed Paddy Driver, Frank Perris, Hugh Anderson and, for the TT only, Alistair King. They also produced a 250 twin for the larger Lightweight class with maximum revs of 11, 000 rpm but a very narrow power band.

In TT practice the 125 Suzukis were plagued with problems. In the first session, Anderson's clutch failed to free and the bikes had piston problems throughout the week. Suzuki had two works teams for the 125 TT. One consisted of King, Driver and Anderson [Perris was unavailable for the TT]; the other of Japanese riders Mitsuo Itoh, Masuda and Ichino. In view of the poor showing of the machines in practice, it was decided to let the Japanese riders compete but to withdraw the other team. All the bikes broke down in the race and none of them finished. Itoh went out on the first lap, Masuda on the second and Ichino on the last lap.

There had been similar problems in practice with the 250 but it was agreed to still continue with the original entries. In fairness, Suzuki were not the only ones with problems. After practice difficulties, Yamaha had to withdraw Peter Pawson and Tony Godfrey whilst MZ withdrew Ernst Degner and Alan Shepherd.

Alastair King retired at the end of the first lap of the race. Hondas filled the first nine places except for Hocking in second on the MV. But Anderson was ninth behind Fumio Itoh

1962: Mike Duff (AJS) leads Phil Read (Norton) and Hugh Anderson (AJS) at Whitegates, Ramsey. All three riders found greater fame when they transferred their allegiances to ride the lightweight Japanese machines.

[Yamaha] and ahead of team-mate Paddy Driver. The next two laps saw Driver retire at the Mountain Box with engine trouble and Anderson drop to eleventh behind Tommy Robb [GMS] and Gilberto Milani [Aermacchi]. Then at the end of the third lap came further problems for Anderson. Whilst making his pit-stop for refuelling his mechanic pulled the filler hose out while still pouring and drenched Anderson with petrol. As well as giving Anderson an uncomfortable ride, the resultant delay meant the pit-stop took sixty-two seconds.

The delay put Anderson down to thirteenth place behind Arthur Wheeler [Guzzi] and Dan Shorey [NSU]. However, retirements on the last lap put him up to tenth, twenty-nine seconds behind Peter Chatterton [NSU]. Anderson's race average was 82.53 mph and he finished twenty-two minutes behind winner Mike Hailwood. Anderson was six and a half

minutes ahead of Ichino in twelfth, the only other Suzuki finisher.

Anderson rode his own Norton and AJS in the Senior and Junior. In the Junior he finished just off the leader board in seventh, four point four seconds behind Roy Ingram [Norton but nearly a minute ahead of Ellis Boyce [AJS]. In the Senior he was a retirement again.

It was clear to Suzuki that if they were going to improve the performance of their bikes they were going to need some help. For a while they negotiated with Dr Joe Ehrlich, developer of the EMC. In the end, though, Suzuki opted for a more daring strategy. They helped Ernst Degner defect from East Germany.

Suzuki's racing manager, Jimmy Maysumiya, and MZ star Ernst Degner had become friends through their contacts on the Grand Prix Circuit. Degner had revealed his desire for his family and himself to leave the East. Suzuki and Maysumiya agreed to help. The defection took place after the Swedish GP and robbed Degner of his chance of the 125cc World Championship, for the FIM would not allow him to race at the last GP at Buenos Aires on anything other than an MZ.

Degner was a talented engineer as well as rider and set about redesigning the Suzuki works bikes. But the new 125s were not ready in time for the 1962 TT. Suzuki had entered a team of Degner, Anderson and Perris in the Lightweight 250 race but all were non-starters. Practice for the 125 race was much the same as the previous year. The bikes were plagued with seizures and, whilst Degner was able to rebuild his machine himself, Anderson and Perris had to struggle on with what the factory produced.

In the 125 race itself Perris got no further than Ballaugh on the first lap. Anderson's machine was reluctant to start, but once underway made it as far as the Mountain before giving up. Honda took the first five places in the race with Degner in eighth the only Suzuki rider to finish.

Anderson rode an AMC prepared AJS in the Junior TT in perfect weather conditions. By the end of lap two he was in ninth place behind Mike Duff [AJS] and Phil Read [Norton]. By the fourth lap Anderson was sixth and he Read and Duff were together on the roads giving spectators around the course the excitement of a real dice to watch. Anderson finished in sixth spot, one minute behind Duff on time but 48 seconds ahead of Read.

Anderson had been fifth on the practice leader board for the Senior, sandwiched between Bob McIntyre [Norton] and Alistair King [Matchless]. AMC had entered a Matchless team for the race, consisting of Anderson, Alan Shepherd and Mike Duff. But Anderson went out at Quarry Bends on lap two with engine trouble and Shepherd retired on the same lap. Duff was running well for a while, but retired on the fourth circuit.

At least the final race day had brought Suzuki some joy.

Ernst Degner won the first ever 50cc TT with Itoh fifth, Ichino sixth and Suzuki winning the Manufacturers' prize.

In the rest of the season Anderson could manage no better than a fifth in Ulster and a sixth in the French GP on the 125. But the season ended on a more promising note. Degner won the inaugural 50cc World Championship and Anderson won the 125 and 50cc Argentine GPs. Perhaps 1963 would be better.

Suzuki wisely decided to abandon the development of their 250cc machine for the time being and to concentrate their efforts for 1963 on the 50cc and 125 machines. The new 125cc disc valve machine proved virtually unbeatable that year and gave Suzuki a 1-2-3 clean sweep in the Lightweight 125 TT. Anderson smashed the lap record with a fastest lap of 91.32 mph but eased off towards the end of the race and his race speed of 89.27 mph was slower than Taveri's the previous year. Anderson finished one minute twenty seconds ahead of team-mate Perris with Degner third a further six point six seconds back. Taveri in fourth place was the first Honda home followed by new recruit to the Suzuki team Bernt Schneider.

Anderson went on that season to win the French, Dutch, German, Ulster and Finnish 125 GPs and to win his first World Championship. Honda gave Suzuki some close races and Taveri and Redman finished second and third in the Championship. But Perris, Degner and Schneider won a GP each to reinforce the superiority of the 125 Suzuki.

In the 50cc race, Suzuki scored an historic victory. Ernst Degner led the race for the first two laps, setting a new lap record of 79.10 mph. But he broke down on the last circuit. This let in Mitsuo Itoh for the first TT win by a Japanese rider [and the only one to date]. Anderson finished second twenty-six point eight seconds behind Itoh, and only four point six seconds ahead of Hans Georg Anscheidt on the amazing fifteen-geared Kreidler. Anderson went on to take second place in the Spanish, Dutch and Japanese 50cc GPs, first in the Argentine round and to win his second World Championship of the year by thirty-four points to Anscheidt's thirty-two. It had been a great season for the New Zealander.

Honda were quick to respond to the Suzuki dominance in the 125 class and for 1964 produced a new 125 4-cylinder 8-speed machine that proved more than a match for the already aging Suzukis. The Lightweight 125cc was a disaster for Suzuki with all three machines retiring after trying to stay with the Hondas. Taveri won from Redman and Bryans and set a new lap record of 93.53 mph. Anderson continued to chase the Hondas hard all year and managed wins in East Germany and Ulster. But Taveri won the Championship, with

forty-six points to Redman's thirty-six and Anderson's thirty-four.

In the 50cc, it was a different story. The single cylinder Honda was no match for the Suzuki single and the main challenge was expected to come from Kreidler, poor Anscheidt still making more gear changes than any bike in TT history.

Anderson broke the lap record from a standing start at 79.69 mph and led Itoh by eight point four seconds. Anscheidt was point eight of a second back in third and Koshino [Suzuki] only point eight of a second further back in fourth. All four riders had broken the old lap record. On the second lap Anderson passed Anscheidt and became first on the roads as well as on time. The New Zealander upped the lap record to 81.10 mph, the first 80 mph lap on a 50cc machine. Anscheidt had moved up to second, but thirty-six seconds behind Anderson, with Koshino third only one second further back. Itoh dropped to fourth.

On the last lap Ralph Bryans finally got the Honda moving and raced through to take second place as others slowed. But Anderson, setting a record race average of 80.64 mph, was fifty-nine seconds ahead at the finish. Morishita [Suzuki] was third with Anscheidt slowing to fourth and Itoh in fifth. The Suzuki team took the Manufacturers' prize.

Later in the season Honda introduced their new 50cc twin cylinder, ten speed machine running at 20, 000rpm and developing 13 bhp, with a reputed top speed of over 100 mph. But it wasn't enough and with four GP wins and a second, Anderson took his third World Championship, with thirty-eight points to Bryans' thirty.

It was Suzuki's turn to come up with new

1966: Hugh Anderson (Suzuki) leaves Ramsey Hairpin on his way to third place in the 50cc race, behind the Hondas of Ralph Bryans and Luigi Taveri.

machines in 1965. They followed Honda's lead in making the 50cc model a twin but as a two stroke rather than a four. The bike had a twelve speed gearbox and revved up to 16,500 rpm. The 125cc twin was now water-cooled and had a nine speed gearbox whilst more work had been done on the fast but unreliable 250-4 machine, nicknamed 'Whispering Death' by its riders for its habit of seizing without warning.

In the 125cc the Suzukis were well behind the Hondas and Yamahas. Anderson could manage no better than tenth on the first lap and ninth on the second, behind team-mate Katayama. On the last lap, though, Anderson showed the potential of the new Suzuki by setting the fastest lap at a record 96.02 mph, managing to get ahead of Bryans [Honda], Ivy [Yamaha] and Degner [Suzuki] to finish fifth. But he was well down on winner Read [Yamaha].

The potential shown by the Suzuki in the TT was more than borne out by the results in the other GPs. Anderson won seven rounds and Perris two. Towards the end of the season there were team orders that Perris should follow Anderson, leading to some friction within the team. But the two riders managed to remain friends as Anderson took his fourth World title by fifty-six points to Perris' forty-four. Derek Woodman on the MZ was third in the championship and, apart from Taveri's second place in the TT Honda couldn't manage a top three place all season until the final Japanese GP.

It was a different tale in the 50cc class. The 50cc TT was held in wet conditions. Itoh led on lap one by twelve point two seconds from Taveri [Honda] with Anderson six point eight seconds back in third. By the end of the second lap Taveri led Anderson by twenty-seven seconds whilst plug trouble put Itoh down to third. Itoh retired at Greeba on the last circuit and Taveri came home an easy winner by fifty-three seconds from Anderson, who averaged 78.85 mph. Degner was third and there were only seven finishers altogether.

Anderson won the Spanish 50cc GP but it was his only success in the class that year. Ralph Bryans won the Championship by thirty-six points to the thirty-two of Taveri and Anderson.

The Lightweight classes of 1966 saw some of the most exotic machinery in the history of motorcycling. In the 50cc class Suzuki had their two-stroke twin now fitted with a fourteen speed gear box and producing over 16bhp. Honda had a four-stroke twin and were known to have tested a 50cc three cylinder bike. In the 125cc class Honda had produced a fantastic five cylinder four-stroke bike and Yamaha had a 4 cylinder two-stroke machine. In the 250 class Yamaha and Suzuki had fours whilst Honda had the fabulous 250 six.

For the 125cc Yamaha decided to race their twins rather than the four-cylinder bikes. Suzuki had prepared a new short-stroke engine for Anderson, while Honda relied on the new five cylinder. But when the race was delayed because of bad weather, this upset the carburation of the Honda models. When the race finally got underway it was the Yamaha pair of Read and Ivy who made the running. After the opening lap Read led Ivy by twelve point two seconds with Anderson in third, Duff [Yamaha] fourth and Perris [Suzuki] fifth.

On the second circuit Ivy set a new lap record of 98.55 mph to not only catch but lead his Yamaha colleague by six point two seconds. Read was just over eleven seconds ahead of Anderson whilst Duff was twenty-one seconds behind in fourth. Just to show it had been no freak, Ivy lapped at 98.55 mph again on his last lap whilst Read eased off and was almost caught by Anderson. Ivy set a record race speed of 97.16 mph, faster than the old lap record, and won by thirty-one point four seconds. Read was just six seconds ahead of Anderson who averaged 96.82 mph, also faster than his old lap record. Duff was nearly a minute back in fourth and Perris in fifth. Mike Hailwood was the first Honda home in sixth. But Taveri went on to take the World Championship with Ivy second.

There were only seventeen starters in the 50cc race which was made a mass start rather than time trial event. Hans-Georg Anscheidt had transferred from Kreidler to Suzuki and the race was expected to be a straight Suzuki/Honda battle. There were no carburation troubles for Honda this time as Taveri and Bryans got away first and led at Braddan Bridge. By Ballacraine Anderson had caught up the two Hondas and he outbraked and passed them going into the corner. Then at Sarah's Cottage Bryans got ahead again and, in trying to stay with the Hondas the pistons of Anderson's bike tightened at Baarregarrow and again at Rhencullen. The engine freed again each time but the edge had been taken off the Suzuki's performance and the Hondas had got well ahead.

Bryans lapped at 85.15 mph, 4 mph faster than the old lap record, and led Taveri by five point eight seconds. Katayama [Suzuki] was twenty-one point six seconds back in third, with Anscheidt fourth, Anderson fifth and Degner sixth. All the

first six had beaten the old lap record.

The second lap was a disaster for Suzuki. Anscheidt's engine locked up solid as he was going down Bray Hill. Fortunately he managed to pull in the clutch in time. Katayama retired with a holed piston whilst Degner hit plug trouble. The Hondas, however, just kept on going. Bryans did have an anxious moment when his plug covers split on the last lap, but he jammed them on tight again and won by fifty-one seconds at a record speed of 85.66 mph. Anderson 'limped' home to finish third, over a minute and a half behind Taveri but with a race average of 83.14 mph, still well ahead of his old lap record. Degner was fourth, well down on Anderson. Anscheidt had the consolation of taking the World Championship from Bryans and Taveri.

The end of 1966 was a watershed for the Suzuki team. Perris and Degner both decided to retire at the end of the season. Anderson had been showing an increasing interest in moto cross and, at the end of the season, he too decided to retire announcing to the surprise of most that road racing had become too dangerous.

After a spell in moto cross, Anderson settled in Assen where he ran a motorcycle business. In 1982 he returned to the Island and rode an AJS 7R in the Classic Parade. More recently he returned to the Isle of Man to ride in the 1985 Senior Classic race in the Manx Grand Prix meeting. He appeared, raced and left without fuss.

1985: Hugh Anderson (Matchless) readies his Matchless for the Senior Classic race.

Campionissimi

It's the most exciting point on the course. The machines come hurtling down Bray Hill. The bravest and most skillful riders aim as close as they dare to the pavement at the bottom; going as fast as they dare. At the base of the hill the suspension bottoms. Then it's uphill again until you hit the top of the ridge, where the front wheel rears up and the rider fights to get it down again quickly before the bike starts to wobble and weave too much. It's not a place for the faint hearted. It's the scene of one of the most famous of all TT pictures. The MV's front wheel is way in the air as the bike and it's rider crest the ridge, so high you'd think the rider could never get the bike back under control. But you can see from his expression that, amazingly, everything is under control. It's called 'Ago's Leap'.

During 1985-1987 I worked for the Island's Tourist Board. For me, the job had one main attraction. Through it, I was involved, in a small way, with the organisation and future of the TT races. It also gave me a chance to meet many outstanding current and former riders - Geoff Duke, Stanley Woods, Max Deubel, Mick Boddice, Joey Dunlop, Mick Grant and Mitsuo Itoh.

In 1987, It also gave me the opportunity to meet the most successful rider in motorcycling history, and one of my greatest early TT heroes, Giacomo Agostini.

It may seem strange that someone so committed to the TT should have adopted as one of his heroes the man who, perhaps more than anyone else, was responsible for the TT losing its World Championship status. I felt that way myself in 1976. Like most TT fans, most Manxmen, my pride was hurt at the loss of World Championship status and the thought that we would no longer see the cream of the world's riders competing over its greatest course. I shared the largely unspoken fear that it might mean the end of the TT. We should have had more faith.

Over the years, I've come to see that the decision was right; Indeed, that the TT has survived because of it. It has remained the greatest road race in the world and the fact that the riders who take part in it are largely a different breed from their GP colleagues adds to, rather than subtracts from, the TTs uniqueness and attraction.

In a brief conversation I asked Agostini who had been his favourite rider when a young man. His reply didn't surprise me. His hero had been Carlo Ubbiali.

It's astonishing that these two men, born within twenty-five miles of other near Bergamo in Northern Italy should have won between them twenty-four World Championships, one hundred and sixty one Grand Prix races and fifteen TTs. They are very different and very similar.

If you were setting out to design a motorcycle World

1951: Carlo Ubbiali at Braddan Bridge. He finished runner-up to Mondial team mate Cromie McCandless.

Champion, or a Champion of any sport for that matter, the model would turn out to be very like Giacomo Agostini. He was an immensely skillful rider, and a courageous one who was often at his best under adversity. He was ambitious and determined but a good sportsman. He was a great stylist with the champion's ability to make it all look easy, but also to raise his effort when required.

Ubbiali was highly competitive with nerves of steel, very necessary for the often close racing of the smaller classes. Both were good tacticians with a race plan worked out beforehand but the flexibility to change this if circumstances required.

Agostini had a 'playboy' image but he understood the technical side of racing very well. He and Ubbiali were very good at setting up machines and getting the best out of their bikes whilst still keeping them going. Ago had film star good looks, star quality, great charm, and was very popular with fans and, particularly, with the ladies. Ubbiali was a proud man, generally quiet and reserved, often isolated by only speaking Italian. This was sometimes taken for arrogance. Agostini speaks several languages and is articulate in all of them. He understood the needs of the media and sponsors and always handled both well.

They were both ultra-professionals and understood the value of preparation and testing. Ago kept meticulous records of his testing sessions and both came to races with everything as well planned as they could possibly make it. Neither were paragons but, most of the time, they kept any latin temperament in check. They were cool and calm competitors.

Ubbiali won nine World Championships between 1951 and 1960, but was often overshadowed by the feats of Duke and Surtees in the bigger classes. This was ironic given that whilst Surtees and Hartle had themselves and the circuits to contend with, Ubbiali often had fierce competition in the smaller classes. His record of World Championships has only been equalled by Mike Hailwood, only beaten by Angel Nieto and Agostini.

Agostini won fifteen world titles, but it was often said that these were won against little opposition. People forgot that he won the 1966 and 1967 500 titles against Mike Hailwood on the Honda, the 350 titles in 1971 and 1972 against Saarinen on the Yamaha and the 1975 500cc title against Read and the MV.

Italy has always had a close connection with the TT races. Italians were amongst the first foreign machines and foreign riders to compete in the Isle of Man. In the 1920s firms such as Garelli, Bianchi and Guzzi were enlivening the TT scene with riders such as Achille Varzi, Tazio Nuvolari and Pietro Ghersi. Stanley Woods gave Guzzi a Lightweight and Senior double in 1935 whilst Omobono Tenni won the Lightweight in 1937. In the 1950s MV, Gilera, Guzzi, Mondial and Morini thrilled TT supporters, as did riders like Dario Agostini, Ambrosini, Lorenzetti, Masetti, Milani and Provini. But head and shoulders above the rest, in the TT and the GPs, were Carlo Ubbiali and Giacomo Agostini - truly Campionissimi, Champions of Champions.

-----oOo-----

Carlo Ubbiali was born in Bergamo Italy on the second September 1929. He trained as a mechanic and started racing in 1948, initially on an old DKW until MV offered him a machine for local Italian meetings. He was short [5ft 3 inches] and slight but very strong, the ideal combination for a Lightweight rider. He was also a skillful trials rider and won a gold medal for Italy in the 1949 International Six Days' Trial in Wales.

Ubbiali soon came to prominence in Italian National races and was signed by the Milan based Mondial factory to ride for them in the 125cc class in 1950.

Mondial had been founded in 1929 by Massimo Boselli. But it had only just turned to making motorcycles. In 1949 the company produced single cylinder four-stroke 125 and 250cc machines. It was on the former that the racing machine was based. Designed by Alfonso Drusiani the machines were beautifully finished and prepared and proved to be as fast as they were attractive. There was no 125cc class at the TT that year, indeed there were only three 125cc GPs altogether. Ubbiali retired at the Dutch GP which was won by his team-mate Bruno Ruffo. Then, at the Ulster, there followed one of the most bizarre GP events of all time

There had been eleven entries for the 125cc Ulster GP, all from Italian riders and factories. But at the meeting itself only three riders turned up - the works Mondial team of Ruffo, Leoni and Ubbiali. Amazingly the race went ahead and Leoni broke down, leaving Ubbiali and Ruffo to fight it out. Ubbiali eventually won at 77.46 mph and so scored his first GP win, in very unusual circum-

1957: Carlo uses every inch of road (and pavement) leaving Parkfield Corner on the Clypse Course.

stances. At the following Italian GP at Monza there was a little more opposition from Morini and MV. Leoni won from Ubbiali but Ruffo took the World Championship.

For 1951 the 125 Championship as extended to five GPs, including the first ever Lightweight 125 TT. At the Spanish GP, the first of the rounds, Ubbiali finished second to team-mate Leoni. Then it was on to the Isle of Man.

The Lightweight 125 was held over two laps of the Mountain course. The race was held concurrently with the Lightweight 250 race with the 250s being set off first. The theory was that the larger bikes would thus be spared the difficulties of having to pass the slower 125s. In fact, the faster 125s, and especially the Mondial's, proved significantly faster than some of the older British 250s and caught many of the

bigger bikes to the embarrassment of their riders.

For the TT, Mondial had lent a machine to Cromie McCandless. With the combination of the Mondial's speed and his knowledge of the course, McCandless led from start to finish, with a fastest lap of 75.34 mph and a race speed of 74.85 mph. Ubbiali, averaging 74.38 mph, was twenty-two seconds back in second but nearly two and a half minutes ahead of Leoni and Nello Pagani in third and fourth. The four Mondial's were so much quicker than anyone else they were the only riders to gain Silver replicas. Mondial, however, hadn't entered for the Manufacturers' team prize, however, so that went to D.O.T. with Hardy, Horn and Newman in seventh, eleventh and twelfth places.

In the remaining World Championship rounds Ubbiali

again retired in the Dutch GP but won the Italian round and took the World Championship with twenty points to Leoni's twelve.

Mondial's main rival, MV Agusta, produced a new 125 machine for 1952 and the Championship was much more closely fought. Les Graham was originally to have ridden the new MV but decided instead to ride a 250 Velocette in the Lightweight 250 TT, again run concurrently with the 125 race. So MV recruited Cecil Sandford, and later Bill Lomas, to ride their machines.

For 1952 the Lightweight 125 had been extended to three laps of the Mountain course and was a mass start race rather than the traditional time trial. Sandford lapped consistently at around forty seconds a lap faster than Ubbiali and won by a margin of one minute forty seconds at a record race speed of 75.54 mph. Ubbiali's average speed, at 74.16 mph, was almost identical to his speed of the year before and he was two and a half minutes ahead of third man Len Parry [Mondial]. McCandless on the Mondial was fourth with Copeta on another MV in fifth. This time Mondial did win the Manufacturers' Team Prize.

It was a similar story in the remaining GPs. In the Dutch Ubbiali finally managed to finish a race,

1958: The winning trio at the conclusion of the Lightweight 250 race. From left: Tarquinio Provini (MV) 2nd, Carlo (winner) and Mike Hailwood (NSU) third.

but in second place to Sandford on the MV. In the German round it was Werner Haas on an NSU who headed Ubbiali, whilst in Ulster Ubbiali came off on the third lap trying to stay with the MVs of Sandford and Lomas. In the Italian round Ubbiali got the better of the MVs only to be beaten by Emilio Mendogni on the Morini. It was a crucial result and Ubbiali had to settle for second in the Championship with twenty-four points to Cecil Sandford's twenty-eight. MV had won their first World Championship.

Ubbiali could see that the Mondial's would no longer be competitive with the MVs, so, when he was offered the chance to join the MV team for 1953 he happily accepted. But the previous year's result in Germany had shown where the main opposition was now going to come from. The season was dominated by Haas and the NSU.

In the 1953 TT, however, Les Graham also rode the small MV and, with it, took his only TT victory. Ubbiali had been lying second when the oil pipe broke on the last lap and he was forced to retire. Haas finished second forty-one seconds down on Graham with Sandford on the MV just two seconds further back in third. With production versions of the MV 125 also available to private owners MVs filled eight of the first ten positions in the race. The factory won the Manufacturers' team Prize with Graham, Sandford and Copeta [fourth], whilst the MV mounted trio of Sandford, Bill Webster [sixth] and Fron Purslow [tenth] won the Club Team award for Nantwich & D.M.C. Tragically Graham was killed later in the week riding the 500 MV.

In the rest of the 125cc GPs it was Haas and the NSU who dominated. Ubbiali did manage to embarrass NSU by winning the West German 125 class, but Haas won the Championship by thirty points to Sandford's twenty and Ubbiali's eighteen points.

NSU dominated the 125 class again in 1954, this time with Rupert Hollaus as their main rider. In the Isle of Man the Lightweight 125 event had been moved to the new Clypse course. The race, over ten laps, was a furious and fast wheel to wheel battle throughout between Ubbiali on the MV and Hollaus on the NSU. Ubbiali was just in front for most of the race, but in the final stages Hollaus drew ahead to win by just four seconds. Haas, who had won the 250 race for NSU, crashed trying to catch the leading pair and Sandford [MV] finished third. Such was the speed of the first two, however, that Sandford was nearly four and a half minutes behind Ubbiali. Baltisberger on the third NSU was fourth.

Sadly Hollaus was killed later in the season in practice for the Italian GP. But by then he had already won the World Championship with thirty-two points to Ubbiali's eventual eighteen points.

NSU's withdrawal from racing at the end of 1954 left MV in a strong position for the 1955 season. In the opening 125 GP in Spain Ubbiali was third behind MV's new Swiss recruit Luigi Taveri and Romolo Ferri on a Mondial. But Carlo dominated the rest of the season.

The Lightweight 125 had been reduced in length to nine laps of the Clypse course. Ubbiali and the other works MVs rode with full 'dustbin' fairings which they had used at Monza for a number of years. It was Taveri's TT debut but it didn't take him long to feel at home. He led the 125 race for the early laps, but Ubbiali, with a new lap record of 71.65 mph gradually caught his team-mate and, on the sixth lap took the lead, albeit only just ahead of Taveri. The Swiss rider got ahead again on the last lap but Ubbiali repassed him at Cregny-Baa and came home to win by two seconds or just a few yards. Despite the lack of NSU opposition Ubbiali's race speed of 69.97 mph was a new record, although also over a shorter distance. Lattanzi on a Mondial was third two minutes thirteen seconds behind the two MVs. Bill Lomas finished fourth on the other works MV and helped MV take the Manufacturers' prize.

Ubbiali won all the remaining 125 GP rounds and took his second World Championship with thirty-two points to Taveri's twenty-six and Venturi's sixteen points [also on an MV]. At the end of the season Ubbiali also had his first ride on a 250 MV. Actually it was a bored out 175cc machine with a capacity of 203cc. But it was good enough for Ubbiali to win the 250 Italian GP and to persuade MV to produce a full 250 for 1956.

1956 was Ubbiali's most successful year to date. He competed in both the 125 and 250 Championships, each run over six rounds but with only the rider's four best results to count.

The Lightweight 250 race, over nine laps of the Clypse was held on wet roads so speeds were down on the previous year. It was far from an easy race for Ubbiali. Sammy Miller [NSU] gave him a terrific battle for the first four laps and just led on the roads going in to the fifth circuit. Then Miller retired at Creg-ny-Baa and Taveri crashed at Governor's Bridge, leaving Ubbiali the clear winner by over two minutes from Roberto Colombo [MV]. Baltisberger [NSU] made the fastest lap of the race at 69.17 mph in an effort to catch the two MVs but he was twenty-two seconds behind Colombo at the end of the race. Kassner on the other NSU was fourth. Ubbiali's winning average was 67.05 mph, well down on the race record.

The Lightweight 125 followed in the afternoon, again over nine laps of the Clypse course. Taveri's crash in the 250 race put him out of the 125. Sandford [who had switched to the Mondial team], led for the first four laps but then retired leaving Ubbiali to win by over five minutes from Cama, Gonzalez and Sirera on a trio of Montesa's. Ubbiali set the fastest lap of the race at 70.75 mph and his race speed was 69.13 mph, thirty-eight seconds slower than his time of the previous year. Both events had turned into poor races in the end, but Ubbiali's feat of winning two TTs in a single day [the first time it had been done], should not be underrated.

Ubbiali went on to win five of the six 125cc GPs [he was beaten in the German by Romolo Ferri on a Gilera]. To this he added five 250 wins out of their six GPs. He was beaten only in the Ulster when the wind caught his 'dustbin' fairing and slammed the MV into a wall. Ubbiali was double World Champion for the first time with maximum possible points in both classes.

The promise shown in 1956 by the performances of Miller and Sandford came to fulfilment the following year. Mondial were definitely the team to beat in both the 125 and 250 classes, and they had a new exciting addition to their riding team - Tarquinio Provini, a rider of real talent. Ubbiali and MV had their work cut out.

The Lightweight TTs had been increased in distance again to ten laps of the Clypse course. In the 250 race Provini set the early pace with a record lap of 78 mph, but the race soon developed into a battle between the Mondial's of Miller and Sandford. Ubbiali was trying hard to stay with the three Mondial's when he retired at just under half distance. Provini soon followed and the race became a terrific dice between Miller and Sandford. Miller was in the lead on the last lap. But he crashed almost in sight of the finish when the gearbox seized. He pushed in to finish fifth. Sandford won by nearly two minutes from the MVs of Taveri and Colombo.

In the 125 Provini got off to a bad start. But he soon came through the field to take the lead in the race. Ubbiali, in fourth position, managed to get ahead of Miller and Taveri but couldn't catch the flying Provini who had set a new lap record

at 74.44 mph. Provini stayed ahead to win by thirty-four seconds at a record speed of 73.69 mph. Taveri in third was two minutes twelve seconds down on Ubbiali. Miller and Sandford were fourth and fifth with Colombo in sixth. The MV trio took the Manufacturers' prize.

Ubbiali crashed at the following Dutch GP and his injuries affected his riding for the rest of the season. Provini took the 125 World title by thirty points to Taveri and Ubbiali's twenty-two. In the 250 class Mondial's dominance was even greater, Sandford taking his second title from Provini and Miller.

Mondial's shock announcement at the end of 1957 that they were withdrawing from racing left MV in a strong position in the 250 class, especially as they promptly signed up Provini to ride for them. But in the 125 class MV faced strong opposition from the new desmodromic Ducati's ridden by Gandossi, Taveri [who had left MV] and Ferri. The Ducati's were faster than the MV and it would take all Ubbiali's riding skills to win back the 125 title.

It was said that there were no team orders between Ubbiali and Provini, and that was certainly borne out in the Lightweight. The race was again over ten laps of the Clypse course and it was expected that the MVs would take it easy early on and save any racing between them until the last couple of laps. Ubbiali led for the early laps until Provini caught him at the end of the fourth. Now, everyone thought, they would stay together until the last lap. Provini did nothing of the sort. Setting a new lap record of 79.90 mph Provini proceeded to draw away. It was obvious from the riding and the speeds that both men were trying hard. But it was Provini who came home first, eight point two seconds ahead of his 'team-mate' Ubbiali. Provini set a new race record of 76.89 mph with Ubbiali also over a minute inside the old record with a race speed of 76.77 mph. A young Mike Hailwood was a creditable third on an NSU, two and a half minutes back on Ubbiali.

In the 125 race Taveri took the early lead on the Ducati

with Provini and Ubbiali in hot pursuit. But when Provini crashed at the Nursery on lap four and Taveri retired at Cregny-Baa the race was effectively over as Ubbiali used all his riding skills to hold off Ferri on another Ducati. Ubbiali's winning margin was thirteen seconds with Dave Chadwick on another Ducati in third [despite two stops to adjust his gear lever]. Sammy Miller [Ducati] was fourth with the MZs of Degner and Fugner in fifth and sixth. Ubbiali set the fastest lap of the race at 74.13 mph but this and his race speed of 72.86 mph were down on the records of Provini the year before.

At the TT prizegiving Provini teased Ubbiali with the 250 trophy and it was obvious there was little love lost between the two Italians. Fortunately for MV the results soon settled the rivalry; Ubbiali did better on the 125 and Provini better in the 250 class. MV were outclassed by the Ducati's in the Belgian, Swedish and Italian 125 GPs, but Ubbiali won at the Dutch, German and Ulster rounds to take the title with a maximum thirty-two points to Gandossi's twenty-five and

Taveri's twenty. In the 250 class Ubbiali retired in the German and Swedish rounds and finished second to Provini in the Dutch GP. Provini won in Holland, Germany and Ulster to take the World Championship with thirty-two points to Fugner's twenty-five on the MZ and Ubbiali's sixteen points.

Battle resumed in 1959, with MV facing strong opposition from Morini, Ducati and MZ. But, once again, the biggest battle was inside the MV camp. This was the last year of the Clypse course with both 125 and 250 TTs being held over ten laps. In the 250 race Mike Hailwood, riding a Mondial, gave the MVs a real scare when he took the lead on the sixth lap and held it for the next two laps. Unfortunately he retired at Brandish Corner. Provini and Ubbiali were thus left to battle it out which they duly did in a tremendous scrap. Both became the only men to lap the Clypse course at over 80 mph as each strove to outdo the other. Provini set the lap record at 80.22 mph and finished a couple of wheel lengths in front after a tremendous battle. The winning margin of point four of a second was the smallest in TT history. Provini's race

1959: Carlo shows the pavement route to team mate Tarquinio Provini at Parkfield.

1960: Carlo rounds Signpost Corner.

win by seven point four seconds with a record race speed of 74.06 mph. Taveri was second, Hailwood third and Fugner fourth. Ubbiali managed to get back up to fifth, followed home by a team of newcomers to the TT. They were the first ever Hondas to compete in the Island and, even then, they won the Manufacturers' team prize.

If the T.T, had been a disappointment to Ubbiali, the rest of the season certainly wasn't. A young MZ rider called Gary Hocking won the 250 classes in Sweden and Ulster. But Ubbiali narrowly won the 125 World Championship with thirty points to Provini's twenty-eight and added the 250 title as well, with twenty-eight points to Provini's and Hocking's sixteen. Needless to say, Provini was not pleased with the result and he left MV at the end of the season to sign for Morini. Count Agusta shrewdly replaced him by signing Gary Hocking.

The 1960 Lightweight races returned to the Mountain course, and a time trial basis. The 125 race, over three laps, was held on the Monday morning of race week, the first race of the meeting. Taveri was back with MV so the main opposition was expected to be the East German MZs.

speed of 77.77 mph was another record - both standing to this day. Dave Chadwick on another MV was third but three and a half minutes behind the two Italians.

The MZ trio of Taveri, Fugner and Degner were expected to provide the main opposition in the 125 race. But once again it was Mike Hailwood, this time on a Ducati, who took an early lead. Taveri soon overtook him, however, and set a new lap record at 74.99 mph. Ubbiali was forced to make a long pit stop with engine trouble which put him well back, but Provini managed to catch and pass Taveri by the beginning of the last lap. With Taveri's bike slowing Provini went on to

Mike Hailwood [Ducati], and Gary Hocking [MV] got the race underway with Ubbiali starting twenty seconds behind them on time. By the end of the first lap Hocking was ahead on the roads, but Ubbiali was only eight seconds behind him, giving the Italian a lead on time of 12 seconds. Taveri was third, five point four seconds behind Hocking, with Eddie Crooks [MZ], Bob Anderson [MZ] and Kitano [Honda] making up the rest of the leader board.

Ubbiali had lapped at 85.02 mph on his opening lap and, on his second, went even faster at 86.13 mph - 7 mph faster than

Les Graham's 1953 lap record. At the end of the lap Hocking still led on the roads, but only by a couple of hundred yards. Ubbiali was seventeen point six seconds ahead on time with Taveri forty-nine seconds further back in third. Anderson was now fourth, Hempleman [MZ] fifth and Phillis [Honda] sixth. Ubbiali knew he only had to sit behind Hocking on the last lap to win, and that's exactly what he did. Hocking crossed the finishing line just a machine length ahead of his team-mate with Ubbiali winning by nineteen point eight seconds. His winning speed of 85.6 mph was a new race record. Taveri came home third, over a minute back, to give MV a 1-2-3. Hempleman got up to fourth place with Anderson fifth and Taniguchi [Honda] sixth. MV won the Manufacturers' team prize.

Ubbiali had suffered badly from cramp in the 125 race and there was some doubt whether he would start in the five-lap 250 race on the Monday afternoon. Perhaps the prospect of renewing his rivalry with Provini was sufficient incentive, but for whatever reason Ubbiali was determined to compete. Provini on the Morini was expected to be the main threat to the MVs.

The race was dominated by Gary Hocking on the MV. Provini was first away on the roads followed ten seconds later by Ubbiali and Taveri with Hocking a further ten seconds back at No 5. But by Sulby on the first lap Hocking was already first on the roads with Provini right behind him and Ubbiali not much further back. The positions on the roads were much the same at the Grandstand. Hocking's opening lap was 91.70 mph and he led Provini by twenty-two seconds on time with Ubbiali a further three point two seconds back in third after a 90.12 mph lap. Tom Phillis on a Honda was fourth and Hempleman [MZ] fifth.

On his second circuit Hocking went even faster, lapping at 93.96 mph. Ubbiali had raised his speed to 91.08 mph, but he was still six point four seconds behind Provini who was now forty-eight seconds down on Hocking. Phillis and Hempleman remained in fourth and fifth with Taveri now in

sixth. By the fourth lap, though, Hempleman had retired, joining the other MZ entries. Hocking had set another lap record at 94.29 mph but Ubbiali had gone even faster - 94.35 mph - in his determination to catch and overhaul Provini. Hocking led the race by just under a minute but Ubbiali was now just one point four seconds behind Provini's Morini. The stage was set for a last lap confrontation between the two great Italian rivals.

At Ballacraine it was clear Ubbiali was now ahead on time and was rapidly catching Provini on the roads. The two Italians gave the spectators and the BBC commentator at Sulby a real thrill as they passed either side of a slower rider at Sulby Bridge. Ubbiali had only to stay behind Provini to finish ahead of him on time, but Ubbiali wanted more. Hocking finished first to win the race - but then came Ubbiali, about a hundred yards ahead of Provini and eleven point two seconds ahead on time. Ubbiali's last lap had been a record 95.51 mph - over 5 mph faster than his opening lap. There was no cool and calculating Carlo that afternoon.

At the Prize presentations Ubbiali received his 125 Trophy and uttered just five words of Italian. He was very happy at his good fortune. Somehow you got the impression, however, that his second in the 250 had given him more pleasure. I hope so. It was to prove Ubbiali's last TT.

Ubbiali went on to retain the 125 World Championship with twenty four points to Hocking's eighteen. It was even closer in the 250 class. Hocking came to the final GP - the Italian - with twenty-eight points and with Ubbiali needing a win. Hocking took the lead but his gearbox seized. Ubbiali went on to win the race and the Championship, a double World Champion again.

At the end of 1960 MV decided not to support a works team in the 125 and 250 classes for the following season. Ubbiali was offered a lucrative contract with Honda but he decided instead to retire.

-----oOo-----

Giacomo Agostini was born in June 1942 in the village of Lovere, about twenty-five miles from Bergamo. The eldest of four brothers he was born into a wealthy family who were very much opposed to his motorcycle racing. But Agostini defied them and started racing in hill-climbs, then in road races on a Morini. In 1964 he won the Italian 250 championship and was signed by MV for the following season as a back-up rider to Mike Hailwood.

Ago made his TT debut in the 1965 Junior, riding the new MV 350-three cylinder. It was an impressive debut. The race itself was a battle between Hailwood [MV] and Honda team leader Jim Redman with Hailwood leading for the first three laps. Then Hailwood slowed and eventually retired. Redman led from Phil Read [Yamaha], with Ago in fourth place. Then the last lap retirement of Derek Woodman [MZ] let Ago up to a fine third place in his first TT.

In the Senior both Hailwood and Agostini rode the big 500 MV-4s. The race was started in the dry but there were still wet patches on parts of the course, particularly under the overhanging trees. Hailwood led Ago by twenty-eight seconds at the end of lap one but then came almost total disaster for the MV team. Agostini came off at Sarah's Cottage on the second lap and had to retire. Then Hailwood came off on the next lap at the very same spot. Fortunately Hailwood was able to remount his machine and, with the MV looking distinctly second hand, continue to the finish to take another win.

Ago's World Championship debut was equally impressive. He finished second to Hailwood in the 500cc Championship and nearly won the 350 title. In the last 350 round in Japan he was leading the race and would have won the Championship. Then a contact breaker spring broke and forced him to retire. He finished six points behind Jim Redman [Honda].

Ironically, Ago's success caused a problem for MV.

1965: Giacomo and Mike Hailwood share the sun before the Thursday afternoon practice. Hailwood's move to Honda set the scene for some unforgettable battles on the GP scene.

Fearing that he would receive less favourable treatment now that the team had an Italian star, Hailwood left MV at the end of the season and joined their main rivals Honda, who had just produced a new four-cylinder 500. Ago was left to carry the flag for MV and ride their new three-cylinder 500. For racing fans, however, it was all good news. The 1966 season saw the closest fought 500 GPs for years between the two best riders on the two best machines.

The 1966 TT was delayed to August/September by a seamen's strike. By then the 350 world title was pretty much settled. Honda had won in West Germany, France, Holland, Czechoslovakia, Finland and Ulster, whilst Ago had only managed a single win in East Germany. But the 500 Championship was still in the balance. Redman had won for Honda West Germany and Holland with Ago in second place each time. But Redman had crashed at the Belgian and was now effectively out of the Championship. Ago had won in Belgium and Finland but Hailwood was victorious in Czechoslovakia and Ulster where a win for Ago might have sealed the title. Instead it was all to ride for in the last two rounds - the TT and the Italian GP.

In the Junior, Ago had an easy win after Hailwood retired at Bishopscourt on the first lap. Ago set a new lap record at 103.09 mph and went on to win at an average of 100.87 mph, over ten minutes ahead of Peter Williams [AJS] and Chris Conn [Norton].

The Senior was a foretaste of things to come. Hailwood, riding No 2, started off with his usual tactic of a fast opening lap from a standing start to demoralise the opposition. His opening speed was 105.82 mph, the sort of speed that had been enough to see off the Gileras three years earlier. But Agostini was not intimidated. Although it was only his second year in the TT he lapped at 105.30 mph and was only six point two seconds behind the Honda star.

On his second lap Ago went even faster and lapped at 106.68 mph, faster than Hailwood's old lap record. But Hailwood went faster still. Despite the handling problems of

the Honda he used all his experience and skill to lap at 107.07 mph, a new lap record, and lead Agostini by ten point eight seconds. Gradually Hailwood managed to pull away. His third lap was 106.77 mph whilst Ago was averaging 105.94 mph. Both men pitted at the end of the third lap, Hailwood getting away just as Agostini [No. 6] was coming in. But the Italian was twenty-two seconds behind on time. On the fourth circuit it began to rain at Ramsey and both men began to slow. Hailwood increased his lead to fifty-five point six seconds at the end of the fourth, nearly two minutes at the end of the fifth, and won by over two and a half minutes at the end. Hailwood had averaged 103.11 mph to Agostini's 101.09 mph.

The TT result meant the 500 World Championship came down to the final round at Monza. If Hailwood won he could still add the 500 title to the 250 and 350 titles he had already won. But if Ago won he would take the title. In theory the fast Monza circuit should have favoured the faster Honda but the circuit was also bumpy. In the event buckled valves caused Hailwood to retire and Ago won the race and his first World Championship - the all important 500 title. It was only his second GP season and he had beaten the best of them all.

There were some great races in the 125 and 250 classes in 1967. But most peoples' interest was in the 500 class and the resumption of the battle between Hailwood and Agostini, Honda and MV. During the winter MV tried to improve the power output of their better handling new 500-3. Honda and Hailwood tried to improve the handling of their more powerful 500-4. So they could concentrate on the bigger classes Honda ceased their involvement in the 50cc and 125cc World Championships.

In the previous year Honda's fabulous 250 six-cylinder machine had proved faster than their 350-4. So for 1967 Hailwood raced a 297cc version of the six in the 350 GP rounds. It was light, fast and handled well and was Mike's favourite Honda. He won the opening 350 GP in West Germany. The Junior was the second round in the

Championship. Ago on the MV couldn't stay with the Honda. Hailwood set a new lap record of 107.73 mph from a standing start, beating the outright lap record for the course and more than 4 mph faster than the previous 350 record. Hailwood finished the six lap race at a record average of 104.68 mph, well ahead of the previous lap record, and three minutes ahead of Ago. Agostini had averaged 102.28 mph, well ahead of the old race record but nowhere near the flying Hailwood. Derek Woodman [MZ] was third, eight minutes behind the MV.

In the 500 World Championship the early honours had gone to Agostini with a win at Hockenheim. But Hailwood had led the race until near the end when he had been forced to retire with engine trouble. So the championship moved to the Isle of Man.

It was the greatest race I've ever seen, and that's the feeling of most people who were there to see it. It had everything. It was the Diamond Jubilee of the TT and the Senior was the Blue Riband of the meeting. It was a special and historic occasion. The race, we knew, would be a battle between the two best riders in the World, one of them then perhaps the greatest TT rider ever. Earlier in the week, Hailwood had beaten Stanley Woods' all time record of ten TT wins. If he won now he would repeat his feat of 1961 in winning three TTs in a week. The MV and Honda were the fastest racing machines in the World and, to us, this was the greatest course in the World. Agostini had set the fastest lap in practice at a fantastic 106.28 mph. But then had come Mike's incredible lap in the Junior - 107.73 mph. It must have demoralised Ago, but it was he, not Hailwood, who was the reigning World Champion. It was Ago's twenty-fifth birthday and there was no doubt what he wanted as a present.

The sense of anticipation before the race was tremendous. You just knew something special was going to happen. The weather conditions were perfect with warm sunshine to keep the crowds happy and the speeds high.

Hailwood started No 4. Ago started No 9, thirty seconds behind Hailwood on time. Both men got off to fast starts. No time to waste, down to it straight away as they headed to Bray Hill. Fans all around the course strained their ears to the radio commentary. We knew Hailwood's usual strategy. The quick first lap to demoralise the opposition. Then came the first shock. Ago led at Ballacraine by five seconds. Hailwood would soon pull it back by Ramsey. He didn't, Ago led by nine seconds. Mike would have got the signals by now, he'd be pulling the advantage back over the Mountain. He didn't. At the Bungalow Ago led by eleven seconds. Staring at the lights on the scoreboard. Hailwood at Signpost, then Agostini. Looking up the Glencrutchery Road. Today the sun really does glint on the fairing. Here's Mike. The Honda sounded great but Hailwood gave the 'thumbs down' to his pit. Here's Ago. MV sounds terrific. What's the time difference? Ago leads by eleven point eight seconds! What's the lap time? Here it is - 108.38 mph - gasps from the crowd, unbelievable!

Round the second lap. Can Mike respond? At Ballacraine the gap's reduced a little. Mike's favourite part of the course the fast run to Ballacraine. At Ballacraine the gap's reduced a little. By Ramsey it's ten seconds. Hailwood's clawing it back slowly. He is responding. Afterwards come reports from all around the course. Of Hailwood really on the limit, the big Honda bucking and bouncing over the bumps, of him using every inch of the road, riding like a demon, ten tenths, nothing in reserve, no margin for error. Bungalow still has Ago ahead by just under ten seconds. God, they must both be motoring! Grandstand again. Lights on. Hailwood screams through. No time for signals to the pit. Oil can hung out by the mechanic to remind the rider - fuel at the end of the lap. Will they have enough at these speeds? Ago goes through just as fast. God that MV sounds beautiful. What's the gap? Ago still leads by eight point six seconds, lapped at over 108 again but not as fast as the first lap. What's Hailwood's speed? 108.77 mph - unbelievable, incredible, surely they can't keep this up?

Third lap. Hailwood still whittling away at the lead. Both

still averaging over 108. Seven seconds at Ballacraine. He always likes that bit. But no-one's ever given Hailwood a race like this. Ramsey, and Ago's lead is down to five seconds. Can he respond? This isn't about demoralising anyone any more. This is real racing, flat out, everything on the line. God, keep them safe. Grandstand again. Pit-stops coming up. This is where it can be won or lost, says the commentator. Whole of the Grandstand look at the pits. Mechanics looking distinctly nervous. They know they can blow it here. They don't need reminding. Hailwood in first. Fuel hose in. Mike's shouting for something. What is it? Sounds like 'Hammer'. It is. He's hammering a loose twist grip.

1965: A jumping Giacomo at Ballaugh Bridge on the Junior MV.

Here's Ago into his pit, just two down from Hailwood. They've been so close on time throughout the race but this is the first time they'll have seen each other from the start. Ago's lead is down to two seconds but Mike must be losing time with this stop. Now he's away again. Crowd shouting him to go on, bike fires, scream from the big Honda engine. Away on the fourth lap. Pit stop's taken forty-eight seconds, about eighteen seconds too long. Now Ago's pushing off. Smooth stop, no problems, crowd shout for him too. We want the excitement to continue. MV fires, that beautiful full throated roar again. Only Pasolini's Benelli sounds better. Ago's stop was thirty seven seconds. So Mike's got it all to do again.

Ballacraine on the fourth lap. Both through safely. Ago leads by fifteen seconds. But Hailwood starts to make inroads again. A second by Ballaugh, a couple by Ramsey. Now they're here at the Grandstand again. Hailwood screams through. About twenty seconds later here comes Agostini. Flat over the tank, full speed, trying as hard as he can. Still eleven point seconds ahead of Hailwood.

Fifth lap, Ballacraine, Hailwood's knocked another few seconds off. By Ballaugh Mike's only a couple of seconds down. He's making his big effort. It's make or break. Ramsey - and Hailwood's ahead, by one second ! Well that's it. Mike's got him. Agostini's given him a terrific race but now that Hailwood's finally got ahead..... Well there's no-one better on this course than Hailwood. Experience will tell. Now he'll ride away from the MV........ Bungalow, Ago's back in front by two point five seconds. What a man. What a race. What a last lap it's going to be.

1967: The race of the decade; Giacomo Agostini (MV) (above) and Mike Hailwood (Honda) (right) pictured at Quarter Bridge.

Back to straining at the scoreboard lights. Hailwood's comes on. He's at Signpost. Where's Ago? Have they missed him? Here's Hailwood, flashing through to start his last lap. Then Peter Kneale's commentary. 'Here's dramatic news. Agostini is reported stopped on the Mountain with a broken chain. Rider OK.' A huge groan from the crowd, a huge sigh of relief from Hailwood as he gets the message from his signalling station at Ramsey. He's been getting signals from fans saying 'Ago out' but hasn't known whether to

believe them. Ago tours in to the Grandstand to a tremendous welcome. He admits later he cried all the way down the Mountain. So close....... so very close.

Hailwood slowed dramatically on his last lap once he knew the position. He won at a record average of 105.62 mph. His lap record of 108.77 mph was to stand for eight years until, many course improvements later, Mick Grant was finally to beat it on a 750 Kawasaki. Sportsman that he was, Mike was the first to pay tribute to Agostini's ride. Agostini, great

sportsman that he was, put away the crushing disappointment he must have felt and went to dinner with an attractive young lady.

In the 350 World Championship Hailwood went on to win the next rounds in Holland, East Germany and Czechoslovakia to clinch the title with a maximum forty points. Ago's only win in the class came at the Ulster GP. Mike took the 250 title as well, although chased to the wire by Yamaha's Phil Read and Bill Ivy.

In the 500 class, however, it was to and fro all season. Hailwood won in Holland, Czechoslovakia and Ulster, but

Ago took the Belgian, East German and Finnish rounds. Once again the decider was the Italian GP at Monza. Hailwood led the race with two laps to go when the gearbox seized and forced him to retire. Ago won the race and the Championship. After Hailwood won the Canadian GP both men finished with five GP wins but Ago had three second places to Hailwood's two. It could hardly have been closer, but Ago had retained his title against the toughest possible opposition.

At the end of 1967 came the shock news that Honda and Suzuki were to withdraw from GP racing. Honda's withdrawal left MV, once again, with little opposition in the 500 class. But, after some good early season results by Renzo Pasolini on the Benelli, MV were worried about the possible opposition in the 350 class. As back up for Ago at the TT therefore, they signed John Hartle to ride in the Senior and Junior. As we have seen it was not a happy return for Hartle.

MV's concerns about Pasolini seemed to be justified in practice when the Benelli lapped at 102.31 mph. But he never emerged as a serious challenger in either race. In the Junior Ago rode the new 350-3 and set a lap record of 106.77 mph on the very first lap to lead Pasolini by thirty-six seconds. Thereafter the opposition faded away and Ago won by two and a half minutes at a new race record of 104.78 mph. Pasolini finished second at a respectable 102.65 mph, faster than Ago's speed in finishing second to Hailwood the year before, and ten and a half minutes ahead of third man Bill Smith on a production Honda.

Agostini romped away with the Senior held in mixed weather conditions. His speed was well down on the previous year with a fastest lap of 104.91 mph and a race average of 101.63 mph. He finished eight and a half minutes ahead of the acrobatic Brian Ball [Seeley] who had a cornering style all of his own [one of the first to hang off the machine], with Barry Randle on the Ray Petty Norton in third place.

The World Championships were a similar story. Ago won the 350 title with a maximum thirty-two points to Pasolini's eighteen, and the 500 crown with a maximum forty-eight points to Jack Findlay's forty-four on his Matchless.

Ago had things all his own way at the 1969 TT In the Junior he found the notorious Sulby Straight so bumpy he called in the pits at the end of the first lap to check if there was something wrong with the MV's suspension or steering damper. Despite the unscheduled stop, and the bumps, he went on to win at the comfortable speed of 101.81 mph, with a fastest lap of 104 mph. He won by more than ten minutes from the brilliant Brian Steenson [Aermacchi] with Jack Findlay on a Francis Beart Aermacchi in third place, a further

minute back.

In the Senior it was another easy win. The organisers gave Ago a start number of eighteen in the hope that this might add some interest for spectators. But with a fastest lap of 106.77 mph Ago was soon ahead on the roads as well as on time and he cruised home at an average of 104.75 mph, eight and a half minutes ahead of Alan Barnett on the Kirby Metisse. Tom Dickie on the Gus Kuhn Seeley was third another thirty-two seconds back.

The method of scoring for the GPs changed in 1969 but it made no difference to the result in the 350 and 500 class. Agostini won the 350 title with the maximum of ninety points to Silvio Grassetti's fort-seven [on a mixture of Yamaha and Jawa rides], and the 500 class with a maximum of one hundred and five points to Gyula Marsovsky's forty-seven on the Linto.

Agostini's contract with MV ran out in 1969 and, after some initial trials with Ferrari in Formula 2 cars, there was some speculation he wouldn't renew it. But motorcycle racing remained his first love and MV remained the team he most wanted to ride for. 1970 promised some better opposition. In the 350 class, Benelli were back with Kel Carruthers and Pasolini in a renewed challenge, whilst in the 500 GPs Kawasaki were beginning to make progress with their machine, ridden by Ginger Molloy.

Agostini's response was a record breaking year, particularly in the TT. In the Junior the Benelli challenge soon disappeared with both Pasolini and Carruthers retiring. Ago set the fastest lap of 104.56 mph and came home at an average speed of 101.77 mph, just under five minutes ahead of Alan Barnett on the Aermacchi. Paul Smart on the Padgett Yamaha was third another one and a half minutes back. Ago raced away in the Senior too, with a fastest lap of 105.29 mph. Interest in the race was reduced to the battle for second, which saw a fine tussle between Peter Williams on the Tom Arter Matchless and Alan Barnett on the Seeley. Barnett was second for the first four laps but was then forced to retire. Williams took second place, five minutes behind Agostini, with Bill Smith third on a Kawasaki.

The two wins meant that Agostini was the only man in TT history to do three Senior/Junior doubles in consecutive years. The wins also placed MV above Norton in the number of all-time solo TT wins [although Norton kept the overall lead thanks to their sidecar wins]. Ago's performance in the GPs was even more spectacular. He completed his third 350/500 World Championship double and repeated the feat of earlier MV star John Surtees in winning all ten 350 GPs and all eleven 500 rounds. Agostini had now won 30 500cc GPs in succession. It was a remarkable tribute both to Ago's concentration and MV's reliability. At the end of the season Ago was approached by Benelli with a lucrative offer but he remained loyal to MV Agusta.

For once, 1971 did not prove an easy TT for Ago. In the 350 GPs he also had his hands full, with increasing opposition from a young Finnish rider called Jarno Saarinen on his 350 Yamaha.

The start of the Junior was delayed by bad weather but was still expected to be an Agostini benefit. Almost amazingly, however, the MV proved unreliable. Ago retired with engine trouble at Ramsey on the first lap. The announcement of his retirement was greeted [unfairly but understandably], with the biggest collective cheer in years in the Isle of Man. After a race in which Phil Read, Alan Barnett and Rod Gould all dropped out when in contention, the Junior was won by Tony Jeffries on a Yamsel to give him a TT double with his win in the earlier Formula 750 race.

The Senior was delayed a day by bad weather and, once again, Agostini hit trouble. He had to spend two minutes in the pits sorting out carburation troubles but still won by five and a half minutes from Peter Williams on the Arter Matchless and Frank Perris on a Suzuki. Ago's winning average was 102.59 mph.

Saarinen won two 350 GPs and Jeffries won the TT round, but Ago won the remaining six 350 GPs and the 350 World title yet again. With eight 500 GP wins he also took the 500 crown and so beat Mike Hailwood's and Ubbiali's total of nine World Championships.

1972 was to prove a sad year for Agostini and for the TT. Saarinen beat the MV in the first two 350 GPs of the season so MV produced a new 350 four-cylinder machine. Although Saarinen was not competing in the Isle of Man, MV decided to strengthen their team for the Island and Phil Read was signed to ride in the Junior Race whilst Alberto Pagani was to ride in the Senior. Read's race was a short one, dropping out on the second lap with engine trouble. Agostini cruised home to win at 102.03 mph and by four and a half minutes from the Yamaha's of Tony Rutter and Mick Grant.

The Senior Race was preceded by the Lightweight 125. Gilberto Parlotti on his Morbidelli was leading the World Championship in the class and was hoping to do well in the Isle of Man to further his chances of winning the title. The race was started in poor conditions with wet roads and mist on the Mountain. Parlotti, a close friend of Agostini and Pagani, was tragically killed when he crashed on the Mountain on the second lap.

Because of the weather, the start of the Senior race was delayed by two and a half hours and, during that time, the MV riders agonised over whether they should withdraw from the race. In the end they decided to race and Agostini won his tenth TT. Peter Williams led Pagani until Williams retired on the last lap, leaving Pagani to finish second, but far from happy.

After the race Agostini vowed he would never race in the Isle of Man again. He was supported by MV and his team-mate Read. Read later relented. Agostini never did.

Ago won the 350 and 500 Championships in 1972 to give him twelve World titles in all. But Saarinen had run him close for a while in the 350 class and for 1973 there were rumours that Yamaha were to also enter the 500 class. Sure enough Yamaha did produce a 500-4 cylinder two stroke for the early 1973 GPs. Saarinen made a fantastic debut on the new bike, winning the opening French and Austrian GPs, whilst Agostini crashed in one race and retired in the other. This left his team-mate Phil Read, who had been signed to help combat the Yamaha challenge, the best placed MV rider in the Championship. So, when MV produced their new 500-4 at the West German GP they gave the new bike to Read rather than Ago. To make things worse for Ago, Read won.

Tragedy followed at the Italian GP where, in the 250 race, Renzo Pasolini and Saarinen were both killed in the same incident. Yamaha withdrew their works machines from further GPs that year as a mark of respect for Saarinen, but the competition within the MV team was now as fierce as any with another factory. Agostini won the 350 title but Read won the 500 class, much to the chagrin of Agostini who felt MV should have treated him better as the number one rider. The season ended badly for Ago who also broke his leg in a crash at Misano in September.

In 1974, to the shock of the racing world, Ago signed for Yamaha rather than MV. Determined to win back his World title, Ago saw the two stroke as bound to take over in time and joining Yamaha as his only response now that MV had made Read their Number one rider. Ago had to adapt to the different riding technique needed for the two stroke machine. It was lighter than the MV and had no appreciable engine braking. So he had to rely much more on the brakes than he ever had on the MV. Ago soon showed he had mastered the Yamaha, however, by winning the Daytona 200 in the USA.

Ago went well in the 1974 350 GPs and effectively forced MV to withdraw from the class. Ago won the world title, his fourteenth, from fellow Yamaha riders Dieter Braun and Patrick Pons. But the 500 class was much more competitive. Read on the MV, Sheene on the Suzuki and Ago on the Yamaha were all in contention as the Championship came to the Swedish GP. In the race, Barry Sheene took an early lead but crashed and also brought Ago down. The crash kept Ago out of the race and the following Finish GP and Read went on to take the 500 World Title.

In 1975, however, Agostini proved that all the old skills were still there. He took the 500 World Championship by eighty-four points to Phil Read's seventy-six and finally gave a Japanese factory the 500 World crown.

Ironically, in 1976 both Yamaha and MV reduced their racing efforts. Ago ran his own team with a mixture of MV and Suzuki machinery. The 350 MV proved fast but unreliable and Ago soon abandoned it. In the 500 class his Suzuki had similar characteristics whilst the 500 MV, still reliable, was just not fast enough at most GPs. But at the West German GP at the Nurburgring the weather was poor and Agostini opted to ride the MV in preference to the Suzuki. To the delight of the assembled fans Agostini won on the beautifully sounding MV-4. It was MV's, and Agostini's last Grand Prix win.

At the end of the season Agostini announced his retirement as a rider. But, as a team-manager he remained heavily involved in the GP scene. His riders have included Eddie Lawson and Luca Cadalora and he was team manager of the Italian Cagiva concern. He is widely acknowledged as one of the shrewdest team managers around.

Agostini has not always been popular with British fans because of his opposition to the TT But, unlike some other TT critics, his stance has always been consistent. He has never called for racing on the Island to be banned, and he has always acknowledged the importance of the Island in motorcycling development and in his own career. His attitude has been simply that no-one should have to ride in the Isle of Man for World Championship points. That's a view we can agree on.

When we met briefly in 1987 he was still of the same opinion, but he hoped that sometime it would be possible for him to revisit the Island and ride a demonstration lap. I was glad he was able to do so in 1991, and that TT fans were able once again to hear the fabulous sound of the four cylinder MV - as ridden by a Champion of Champions.

The Irish Dasher

He was amazing. In 1957, aged fifty-four, he rode a Guzzi round the TT course as part of the TT Golden Jubilee celebrations. He lapped at 86 mph, almost as fast as he used to during his racing days twenty years earlier, and only 13 mph slower than the then course record.

In 1982, aged seventy-nine and with two replacement hips, he rode a 500 Velocette round the course as part of the Classic Parade. Despite clutch trouble he lapped at over 64 mph. His only problem came at the end of the lap when the gate to the finishers' enclosure was closed. With little in the way of brakes left he tried to use the defective clutch to give some engine braking, but only succeeded in stalling the engine. The gate was demolished. Rider and bike were fine.

For nearly thirty years he held the record number of ten TT wins. He won the Ulster GP seven times and many other GPs. Unfortunately there were no World Championships then. If there had been he'd have won them. Yet for all his success he remained the friendliest man you could ever hope to meet, likeable, modest, a real character, a lovely raconteur and a great TT supporter. He was also one of the greatest motorcycle riders the world has ever seen. His name was Stanley Woods.

There are nearly as many arguments about which was the greatest TT as there are about who was the greatest ever rider. Stanley Woods has a place of honour in both. In the end you can only compare what you saw. For my generation Mike Hailwood will always be the best rider, the 1967 Senior the greatest race. For those who watched racing in the 1930s, however, there is equally no doubt. Stanley Woods was the greatest rider. The 1935 Senior was the greatest race.

There have been many special TTs over the years. The Seniors of 1930 [Handley and the Rudge domination], 1937 [the Woods and Frith duel], 1938 [the Woods and Daniell battle], 1957 [Bob McIntyre and the magic ton], 1967 [Hailwood]

and Agostini], and 1992 [Fogarty and Hislop and the Norton win]. There's the 1934 Junior with Guthrie and Simpson, the 1959 Lightweight with Ubbiali and Provini, the 1966 Sidecar with Scheidegger and Deubel, and the 1967 Lightweight 125 with Stuart Graham and Phil Read. But the 1935 Senior had a more dramatic and more surprising finish than any other race in TT history.

It was an unauspicious start. On the traditional Friday race day the weather was bad and got worse as the morning progressed. The last straw was a Corporation bus coming past the Grandstand with its lights on at 11.30 a.m. There had been two deaths earlier in the week and the organisers were taking no chances. The race was postponed to the Saturday, the first time that had happened.

The decision proved fully justified as the weather on the Saturday was much better, with dry roads and sun at the Grandstand. Jimmy Guthrie on the works Norton was to start No 1 by virtue of his win the year before. Woods on the Italian Guzzi machine was to start No 30, giving a fifteen minute gap between Guthrie and him on the roads. Both men had signal stations around the course to tell them their positions. Nortons had theirs at Ramsey, linked by telephone to the Grandstand.

Woods had set the fastest lap in practice, breaking his own lap record. The Guzzi was rumoured to be faster than the Norton, but also thirstier. Stanley's tactics for the race were to bide his time and let Norton do the worrying.

At the end of lap one Woods was in third place, twenty-eight seconds behind leader Guthrie and just one second behind Walter Rusk on another works Norton. On the next circuit Woods got eleven seconds ahead of Rusk but was now forty-seven seconds behind Guthrie. At Ballacraine a group of Irishmen yelled with delight when Stanley passed them and offered to bet anyone that Stanley would win. There were no

1935: A study in styles. Stanley Woods (Guzzi) left and Jimmy Guthrie (Norton) right, at Governor's Bridge during their race-long battle.

takers. Stanley lapped at 84.14 mph and finished the lap fifty-six seconds behind Guthrie.

At the end of the third lap both leaders pitted. Guthrie took thirty-three seconds to refuel, Woods slightly less. Now, Stanley decided, was the time to make his presence felt. On the fourth lap he reduced Guthrie's lead to forty-two seconds. His compatriots at Ballacraine were offering even money on Stanley winning, still with no takers; and no wonder. On the fifth circuit Stanley set a new lap record of 85.66 mph and Guthrie's lead was now only twenty-eight seconds with two laps to go. The sprung frame of the Guzzi gave it much better roadholding on the fast parts of the course and Woods was using all his skill to pull back the deficit.

On the penultimate lap Rusk got the 'go easy' signal. He had come off twice trying to stay in reach of the flying Woods. But Guthrie was using all his considerable talents to stay ahead of his former team-mate. He succeeded in stopping the rot. The lead was kept at twenty-six seconds as Guthrie started his last lap and Norton were convinced that, unlike Guthrie, Woods would have to stop at the end of lap six to top up his fuel for the last lap. The Guzzi mechanics in Woods' pit could be seen getting ready for the fill-up.

Guthrie was approaching Ramsey. Twenty six seconds and the time for a pit-stop. Guthrie had plenty of time in hand. No sense in risking the motor blowing. Norton 'phoned their signal station in Ramsey to give Guthrie the 'go easy' signal.

Then flying down the finishing straight came Woods - and went straight through! Had he forgotten to stop? Was he gambling on having enough fuel? The Norton pit still looked unconcerned. The lead was still the same. Not even Woods was going to make that up on Guthrie in a single lap.

Jimmy Guthrie safely negotiated the Mountain for the last time and came home to finish. As instructed he had taken things a little easier on the last part of the lap and his time was nine seconds down on his previous lap. But everyone assumed that he had beaten Stanley. The public address announced him as the winner, he was cheered as such by the crowd and his supporters; the Island's Governor congratulated Jimmy on his win and, as Stanley Woods flashed by at the end of his race, Guthrie was led off to the microphone to be interviewed about his victory - only to be told that Woods had won by four seconds.

The non pit stop hadn't been a gamble but a shrewd tactical ploy which had worked brilliantly. Stanley had ridden the race of his life. He had pushed his machine beyond the limit, past the maximum revs and up to speeds of 120 mph on the faster stretches. His last lap speed had been a new record of 86.53 mph to snatch victory from the slowing Guthrie. The Guzzi still had fuel enough for another lap. Great sportsman that he was Guthrie was the first to congratulate Woods - once he got over the shock.

-----oOo-----

Stanley Woods was born in Dublin in 1903. He had a cheery, good humoured personality and was a good talker, though modest with it. He was an excellent all-rounder who rode and won in speedway, trials, scrambles, hill-climbs and sand racing. He was at his best, however as a road racer.

Stanley was a shrewd tactician and was the first rider to introduce his own signalling system on the TT course. He had a fine riding style [modelled on Alec Bennett's], and was a safe as well as fast rider. He used swimming and trials riding to make sure he was physically fit and often helped in the preparation of his machines to try to make sure they were equally fit to ride. Known by the motorcycle press as the 'Irish Dasher' he was originally a sales rep for Mackintosh's Toffee and rode in the TT in his annual holidays. Later he founded his own confectionery company making 'TT Toffee'.

He had learnt to ride a motorcycle at the age of thirteen on a neighbour's Indian Sidecar outfit. Later he bought his own 'Sun' and then a 9hp Indian. His first visit to the Isle of Man was in 1921 when he and some friends went to watch the Senior at Hillberry. With the confi-

dence of youth, Stanley and one particular friend felt they could do just as well, and resolved to enter the TT the following year. His friend was Paddy Johnston and they were both destined to prove that their's was no idle boast.

Before he could become a TT rider, however, Stanley needed a machine. With that lovely natural Irish combination of shrewdness, wit and nerve, he wrote to all the manufacturers who entered bikes in the 350 class saying he had a ride in the Senior but needed a bike for the Junior - could they help? Then he did the reverse with the Junior manufacturers. Perhaps because they were a comparatively new firm themselves [they had only been founded two years before], he got a reply from Cotton. When they inquired about his ability as a rider he referred them to the Cotton agent in Dublin, who just happened to be a certain Paddy Johnston.

Once in the Island, Stanley had to wait several days for the

1922: Stanley started his TT career on this Junior Cotton.

Cotton to arrive, they had been ridden to the Island, and his mount had seized a rocker on the way up. He was told to go to the Blackburne people and get the spares and fit them. Later, when the piston seized, he had to get the bits and then rebuild it himself.

His TT debut was in the Junior race and began with a series of problems. Like most riders of the day he carried spare spark plugs with him. These fell out as he pushed his machine away at the start and he had to go back for them, losing twenty seconds in the process. On the second lap he hit the kerb at Governor's Bridge and knocked the exhaust off the cylinder. But he was lying in fourth place, between the AJS's of H. R. Davies and Manxman Tim Sheard, as he came in for his pit stop. Then came the biggest disaster of all.

There was no requirement in those days for riders to switch off their engines as they came to their pits. Woods, along with many others, didn't do so. The mechanic spilt petrol in trying to refuel the bike and the next thing both Stanley and the Cotton were on fire. Firemen from the far side of the road, reacting automatically, started to bring their hoses across the roads only to be stopped by the shouts of the crowd who realised what might happen if another bike came through at racing speed. Stanley rolled on the ground to put out the fire on his leathers whilst marshals with Pyrene extinguishers put out the fire on the bike. It would have been enough to persuade most riders to retire but Stanley was determined to continue.

He got no further than Braddan Bridge on his next lap before the pushrod broke and he had to stop and repair it. Then at Greeba the rear brake failed. Stanley discovered he could go faster without it. There followed a couple of relatively uneventful laps before, on the last circuit, he went too fast into Ramsey Hairpin and slid off. He remounted to finish fifth. In future years Stanley would often claim that his winning rides had been problem free. Compared with his debut they probably were.

After his promising debut the year before there was no dif-

ficulty in persuading Cotton to let him have a machine for the 1923 Junior. In the race he got off to a slow start and at the end of the first lap was in fifth place behind Tommy de la Hay [Sunbeam]. Trying harder on his next lap he was off again at Ramsey Hairpin but with no damage to himself or machine. Skidding into his pit at the end of the lap he was in third place but seventy-eight seconds behind Bert le Vack [New Imperial] and well down on leader Jimmy Simpson [AJS]. This time there were no fireworks in the pits and Stanley was safely on his way.

Simpson retired on the next circuit but Woods was now over two minutes behind Le Vack. Stanley reduced the lead to seventy-four seconds on the fourth lap but was being caught himself by George Dance on a Sunbeam. Dance got passed the Cotton on time and then, as Le Vack retired took a lead of nearly two minutes with just one more lap to go. But Dance had been pushing the Sunbeam too hard and he too retired between Ballaugh and Ramsey, to give Stanley his first TT win in only his second meeting. He finished two and a half minutes ahead of Harris on the works AJS at a record speed of 55.74 mph.

Stanley said afterwards he hadn't expected to win though he thought he could make a good time. Apart from the incident at Ramsey he had a trouble free ride. After he passed Le Vack and Dance on the roads he knew he was certain of a top three place. He had taken things easy for the remainder of the last lap and was surprised to learn that he was the winner.

Woods' race average was faster than that year's Senior. To celebrate their success Cotton produced a new logo by extending the middle part of Cotton to give a high TT.

Stanley's first TT win didn't bring him luck. In the other races in 1923 he retired in the Lightweight on a Cotton and in the Senior on a Scott. For 1924 he was back on the Cotton in the Junior and was to ride the same bike in the Senior. He was third fastest in practice for the Junior but in the race got no further than Bray Hill on the opening lap before the flywheel burst.

Things were little better in the Senior. After brake trouble on the first lap he had to use his feet to stop the bike at his pit. He continued after adjusting the brakes, but then had a coming together with Joe Craig [Norton] at Governor's Bridge. Finally he hit tyre trouble on the fourth lap and toured round to retire.

Stanley fared no better in 1925. He retired in the Junior on a Royal Enfield and in the Lightweight on a New Imperial. There was one bright spot, however. Norton boss Bill Mansell had been impressed with Stanley's riding on the Enfield and marked him down as a possible target for Norton for 1926. Stanley had been offered the bikes for 1925, but considered his career as a toffee rep a more secure prospect at the time. But by 1926 things had gone a bit sour, the post Great War depression was just beginning to bite. Mansell's own impressions of Stanley Woods were confirmed by a recommendation from Norton's Dublin agent Dene Allen. So Stanley found himself part of a Norton race team with Alec Bennett, Jimmy Shaw and Joe Craig [later the team boss].

The 1926 Nortons were virtually production 490cc Model 18 push-rod machines with three-speed gearboxes. The bikes were fitted with pannier fuel tanks to cope with the extension of the Senior TT from six laps of the Mountain course to seven. Woods went well in practice but said afterwards that his race bike was not as fast as his practice machine.

Stanley got off to a good start and after the opening lap was lying second, twenty-three seconds behind Jimmy Simpson [AJS] but thirteen seconds ahead of Wal Handley [Rex Acme]. During the next lap

Simpson increased his advantage to over a minute and a half whilst AJS team-mate Charlie Hough took over third place, fifty seconds behind Stanley. The pace set by Simpson was suicidal and on the next circuit the AJS cried enough, leaving Stanley and the Norton in the lead.

Hough, now the main AJS hope, started to gain rapidly on Stanley. Woods' lead was down to twenty seconds at the end of the third lap and eleven seconds at the end of the fourth. But Stanley had been biding his time. By the start of his last lap Stanley had an advantage of thirty-nine seconds. Hough tried his best to cut the gap but overdid it and crashed between Sulby and Lezayre. Woods had a nasty moment when his

1925: Stanley's lightweight race mount was this JAP powered New Imperial.

engine misfired at the Creg but he kept going to win at a record race speed of 67.54 mph. He won by four minutes twenty seconds from Wal Handley who had come up into second place. Stanley was carried shoulder high past the Grandstand by his countrymen and supporters.

Apart from a back tyre that was too soft and caused a few skids early on it had been a trouble free ride. The celebrations afterwards had given him more bumps and bruises than the actual race.

Stanley's Senior victory was the third Irish win of the week. Alec Bennett, born in Ireland, had taken the Junior and Paddy Johnston had won the Lightweight on a Cotton. So the two friends had proved the truth of their youthful boast. They could do as well as the riders they'd watched. At the Prize giving Stanley was escorted to the stage preceded by an Irish Free State Flag which one of his compatriots [a Mr Murphy, naturally], presented to the Island's Governor as a souvenir.

1926: Stanley takes his Senior Norton round Ramsey Hairpin.

Norton gave Stanley a bonus of £500 and used his win extensively in their subsequent advertising.

By 1927 Stanley had abandoned his job as a toffee salesman and was working full time for Norton, riding for them in the season and acting as a sales agent out of season. That year's Nortons had a new frame and a new engine designed by Walter Moore. Stanley fitted a speedometer to his machine during one practice session and recorded a top speed of around 93 mph.

At the end of practice Alec Bennett, also Norton mounted, changed the clutch of his machine, suspecting it wouldn't last the race distance. He didn't mention his suspicions to Woods, whom he saw as his main rival for the Senior event.

In the race Stanley got off to a great start, breaking the lap record unofficially at a speed of 70.50 mph and leading from Freddie Dixon [HRD] and Jimmy Simpson [AJS]. Stanley's second lap was even faster, 70.99 mph, and he increased his lead over Freddie to over two minutes. After refuelling and a quick drink of cold tea Stanley set off again, well ahead of the field.

That remained the pattern of the race over the next couple of laps. As he came in for his pit-stop at the end of the fourth lap, Stanley was over four minutes ahead of Alec Bennett who was now in second place. For some unaccountable reason, however, the Norton pit told Stanley only that he was in the lead and had 'better keep going'. Stanley interpreted this as meaning he had better stick to his current pace rather than easing off for the last three laps. The clutch gave way on the Mountain on the fifth lap and Stanley toured in to retire. Bennett won the race. His experiences persuaded Stanley that he needed his own signalling stations around the course which could let him know his position and allow him to decide how to react accordingly.

Stanley had some consolation in Holland where he won the Dutch 500 TT despite never having seen the course before. He went on to also take the Belgian and Swiss 500 GPs.

Stanley left his job at the Norton factory to start his own

toffee business in Ireland but he continued in the Norton race team for 1928. For the first time Norton had produced a 350 racer for the Junior TT. It was essentially a scaled down version of the 500 and, like many scaled down 500s, the bike was heavy for its power output. Nevertheless Nortons had high hopes for the bike and had a team of five riders to compete in the Senior and Junior events. Bennett had left the team which now included Woods, Craig, Shaw, Matthews and a promising Scot called Jimmy Guthrie.

The 350 proved slow in practice with Stanley doing best in fifth fastest. The Nortons were certainly no match for the speedy Velocettes. In the race Stanley was lying seventh on the first lap but retired soon after with ignition timing problems. He was quickly followed by the remaining Nortons as all five bikes retired.

The Senior race was held in poor weather with the roads wet and greasy. Stanley was one of a number of riders to take a tumble on the first lap, sustaining minor damage to himself and his machine. After calling at his pit at the end of the lap to check the extent of the damage, Stanley set off to try and do the best he could in the circumstances. He charged through the field, twelfth at the end of lap two, seventh after lap three, up to fifth at the end of lap four. By lap six he was up to fourth place, but a misfire slowed him down again and eventually he finished a creditable fifth, the only 'works' Norton to finish. Post-TT he won the 350 Dutch TT and the 500 French GP.

For 1929, the Norton team comprised Stanley Woods, Tim Hunt, Jimmy Simpson [newly recruited from AJS], and Jimmy Guthrie. It would be difficult to think of a finer grouping of riders. Unfortunately the machines failed to match their riders talents. The Junior bikes were only slightly better than the year before. The machines were definitely more competitive [Simpson led from Woods at the end of lap one], but no more reliable. All four bikes retired.

Things weren't much better in the Senior . Stanley could manage no better than fifth for the first four laps. Given the

'go faster' signal he did his best to respond but crashed at Kirk Michael losing a couple of teeth and needing stitches in a cut lip. Hunt managed fourth place behind the Sunbeams of Dodson and Bennett and the Rudge of Tyrell-Smith, but all the other Nortons were retirements.

At the end of the season Walter Moore left Norton for NSU. Joe Craig took over the racing team and Arthur Carroll the job of trying to redesign the bikes for 1930. At first the new partnership appeared to make little difference. In practice for the TT it was obvious the Nortons were down on speed in both the Junior and Senior.

In the Junior race Stanley could manage no better than eleventh on the opening lap. Gradually he managed to work his way up to sixth at the end of the race, just twenty five seconds down on Williams on the Raleigh, but his average speed of 69.60 mph was little better than his winning speed four years before. Tim Hunt could only manage ninth whilst Simpson had retired on the third lap when the engine seized.

For Stanley the Senior was the same story. A misfire put him down to eleventh on the first lap. He managed to get up to eighth by the sixth lap only for the chain to come off forcing him to push in to retire. Hunt was another retirement but for once Jimmy Simpson kept going and finished third. As the season progressed, though, the efforts of Carroll and Craig began to bear fruit and Woods won the 500 French and Ulster GPs.

By 1931 the new Nortons were well and truly ready. After a brief spell at AJS Jimmy Guthrie was back in the Norton team who were well fancied in both the Junior and Senior.

In the Junior both Woods and Simpson unofficially broke the lap record on the opening lap. Freddie Hicks [AJS] chased the Norton pair and when he dropped out, Ernie Nott [Rudge] took up the chase. After a slow start due to plug trouble, Tim Hunt was also climbing rapidly through the field. On the fourth lap, Stanley was slowed by steering damper problems and, although still averaging 72.78 mph, dropped down to fifth place. When Simpson also slowed, Woods was

1932: Timekeeper Ebblewhite Senior gives Stanley the signal to start in the Junior TT.

two laps to make up the fifty-four seconds between him and Stanley, but in the end he failed by just five seconds and Norton had a 1-2-3.

Norton continued their domination in the Continental GPs and Woods won the 500 French, Belgian, Swiss and Ulster races and the 350 Dutch GP.

The 1932 Nortons were almost the same as the previous year's but there had been some efforts to reduce the weight of the bikes. On the other hand the TT machines carried a bigger fuel tank to try and ensure they only had to make one pit-stop per race. Nortons were expected to dominate the bigger classes again and the main danger was that their riders would retire through trying to race each other. So, controversially, Norton decided to introduce team orders. The riders could race amongst themselves for the first three laps. After that they had to hold their positions.

Under the new arrangements it would obviously be a big advantage for a rider to know his position relative to his team-mates. So Stanley set up his own private signalling system. He had two stations, one at Sulby Crossroads and the other at the top of Bray Hill. They were manned by his brother in law, Gordon Burney, and another trusted friend, Athol Harrison. Each timed the difference between Stanley and the other riders as they came through and telephoned this information to the other station who advised Stanley accordingly. It meant the information was half a lap out of date, but that was better than no information at all.

The Junior race was held in fine weather with dry roads. All Norton's orders and Stanley's preparations were academic. Stanley led from start to finish breaking the lap record on every lap except his fifth [which included his refuelling stop]. His fastest lap was 78.62 mph and he set a new race record of 77.16 mph, 3 mph faster than Hunt's speed the year before.

up to fourth but Stanley could manage no better than that, finishing three minutes down on Ernie Nott at an average of 71.39 mph. Tim Hunt, though, won the race for Norton and the factory trio of Hunt, Woods and Simpson [who eventually finished eighth] took the Manufacturers' Prize.

Nortons were dominant in the Senior race with the factory quartet soon taking the lead. The ill-fated Freddie Hicks [AJS] gave chase for a while and then Simpson crashed on the fourth lap leaving Hunt in the lead from Woods and Guthrie. Problems with a lost filler cap, which Stanley had to solve by stuffing his glove in the gap, dropped Woods down to third place. Ernie Nott [Rudge] made a great effort over the last

Wal Handley was second on the Rudge but two minutes ten seconds behind Woods, whilst Tyrell-Smith in third was a further six and a half minutes back. The other Nortons were less lucky; all of them retired.

The Senior was the first Royal TT and Woods and Hunt were hot favourites for the honours. Jimmy Simpson set the pace for the first two laps, lifting the lap record to 81.5 mph. But Stanley was only five seconds back on time as they went into the all-important third lap. Then Jimmy had clutch problems and Stanley took over the lead, gradually drawing further ahead of Simpson. Guthrie pipped Simpson for second on the last lap, but the Scot finished over two minutes behind his Irish team-mate. Stanley, who admitted to a couple of hairy moments during the early laps, set a new race record of 79.38 mph. He had joined Tim Hunt as the winner of a Junior/Senior double in the same year.

Stanley returned to Dublin in style, hiring a seaplane to take his party back to Ireland. At Dun Laoghaire he was welcomed by the Chairman of the Borough who expressed the pleasure all Ireland felt at the honour Stanley had brought to the Country. Then, with an escort of a hundred motorcyclists, Stanley was driven to the Mansion House in Dublin where the Lord Mayor of Dublin met him on the steps and hailed him as the World's Champion Motorcyclist. As if to underline the Lord Mayor's point, Stanley followed up his TT wins with victories in the 500 French, Belgian, Swiss and Ulster GPs and the 350 Dutch and Swiss races.

If there were any doubts left regarding Stanley's status as the 'King of the Roads' the 1933 TT must have finally dispelled them. In the Junior, he led once again from start to finish, although Tim Hunt put in a terrific effort on the last two laps and reduced Stanley's winning margin to just seven seconds. Guthrie was third after Simpson retired on the last lap. Woods set a new lap record of 79.22 mph and a new record race average of 78.08 mph. After the race a couple of UK newspapers were full of the reactions of Mrs Woods in the Grandstand. In fact, she was in Lyons in France. It was prob-

ably just as well as Stanley admitted afterwards he had almost lost the race when his attention was distracted on one corner by the waving of a group of attractive young ladies.

In the Senior, Stanley had strong opposition again from his Norton team-mates. Stanley's opening lap was 81.50 mph but he was only one second ahead of Jimmy Simpson with Guthrie in third. Hunt had another poor start, due to plug trouble. On the second circuit Jimmy S smashed the lap record but Stanley went even faster - 82.69 mph. Woods led by sixteen seconds Guthrie was third and Hunt was now up to fourth. Stanley increased the pressure still further on the next lap with a speed of 82.74 mph and by the fourth lap he was forty-six seconds ahead of Simpson. Jimmy managed to keep the gap static on the next circuit but, going in to his last lap, Stanley had an advantage of one minute thirty-nine seconds. There was an anxious moment when it was rumoured that Woods had dismounted at Glen Helen but it proved not to be true. Stanley romped home at an average speed of 81.04 mph, the first 80 mph race average speed. He finished one and a half minutes ahead of Simpson with Hunt third and Guthrie fourth.

Woods' win gave him a Senior/Junior double in consecutive years. Stanley modestly pointed out that but for Simpson's brake troubles and Hunt's loss of time at the start it might have been a different story. But the motorcycle press joined in the general adulation and confirmed Stanley as the World's greatest rider. All of which did not please some in Norton's Bracebridge Street headquarters. Norton were winning because they made the best machines not because they had the best rider. This cult of personality was not to be encouraged.

Stanley won the 350 and 500 Dutch GPs and the 500 class of the Swiss GP. But, strangely, Norton seemed less and less pleased. The crunch came at the Ulster GP. Stanley was ordered not to win his home Grand Prix, and was warned by Bill Mansell that, if he did, it would be Stanley's last ride for Norton. In the event, the retirement of other Norton runners meant Woods did win to Norton's relief. But the damage was done. Stanley left Norton at the end of the season.

Norton must have thought that Stanley would struggle without them. Nortons were better than any of the British competition. Stanley would have to chase for the minor places. No rider was bigger than Norton. It was a mistake they repeated 20 years later.

Stanley had other plans. Norton might be the fastest british bike. But what about the European manufacturers who were just starting to show an interest in the TT races? Stanley signed to ride a Guzzi in the Lightweight, so beginning a long association with the Italian company. He also reached agreement with the Swedish Husqvarna concern to ride one of their machines in the 500 class. Stanley was a superb test rider who had the ability to tell the mechanics exactly what was wrong with the machine and what needed changing. His ability and the resources and enthusiasm of the Continentals was soon to shatter the complacency of Norton and other British manufacturers.

Stanley had been due to ride an AJS in the Junior but, after testing he was unconvinced that the machine was raceworthy and declined to take the ride, George Rowley took over the machine instead. In the Lightweight Stanley had troubles early on but finished fourth behind the Rudge trio after a superb battle with Graham Walker. It was a promising start. But how would he get on in the Senior against the mighty Nortons?

At first it didn't look too promising. In loading the Husqvarnas at Gothenburg Docks for transport to the Isle of Man, a cable snapped and the bikes were dropped onto the quayside. They were rushed back to the factory for repair. In the Island the bad luck continued. Stanley's team-mate Ragnar Sunnqvist had appendicitis and was unable to ride. Then in practice, first man out, he was going through the blind left hander at Ballaspur when he came across a shepherd with a flock of sheep, he went through them and never hit one! Later that same lap, as he braked for Sulby the frame broke,

an experience that Stanley had encountered when testing the Husqvarna in Sweden earlier. But he did discover the Husqvarna was fast and light, with a rumoured top speed of 120 mph.

In the race, run in slow conditions, Stanley started No. 1 by virtue of his win the year before. He was never passed on the roads. After the first lap he had split the two Jimmys, with Guthrie leading and Simpson third. 'Jimmy S' got within fourteen seconds of Stanley on the second circuit but Stanley responded with the fastest lap of the race at 80.49 mph. By the fifth lap he was over a minute and a half behind Guthrie but two minutes ahead of Simpson. The rain returned and Stanley dropped the 'Husky' at Ramsey Hairpin but he remounted and continued without too much loss of time. As he went into the last lap Stanley was over three minutes behind Jimmy Guthrie but the same distance ahead of Simpson, and heading for a comfortable second place. Then he ran out of petrol at the Mountain Box and that was the end of his Senior race. Still, he had given Norton a scare, and the next year he was to do more than that.

1935 was another Woods year, and one which rocked the British motorcycle industry. Stanley had agreed to ride a Guzzi in both races. In practice for the Lightweight he and his fellow Guzzi rider Omobono Tenni had proved the fastest with the main opposition expected to come from the Rudges which had won the year before. Signor Carlo Guzzi came to the Island to watch the race.

It was drizzling as the riders set off. Woods still managed to lap at 73.68 mph, however, faster than the lap record, and led Ernie Nott [Rudge] by forty-three seconds. Tyrell-Smith [Rudge] was in third and Tenni fourth. By the second circuit the weather on the Mountain was terrible but Stanley still managed a new lap record at 74.19 mph. Tyrell-Smith was now up to second place but over a minute and a half down on Stanley, whilst there were only four seconds separating Tenni and Nott in third and fourth.

Visibility on the Mountain was now down to thirty yards in

places but Stanley was still averaging well over 70 mph. Tenni got ahead of Tyrell-Smith and Guzzi were in first and second position. Signor Guzzi must have been very pleased. But lap five was nearly a disaster for the Italian team. Tenni crashed at Creg-ny-Baa and had to retire. Then Stanley nearly dropped the other Guzzi at Governor's Bridge. He managed to correct the skid brilliantly and carried on in a comfortable lead.

This time there were no last lap problems and Stanley came home safely to the strains of the Italian National Anthem. It was the first TT win by a foreign machine since 1911 and the first ever TT win by an Italian machine. Woods had averaged 71.56 mph, only six seconds outside the race record, an amazing feat in the conditions. It was always said that Stanley could lap the TT course with his eyes shut. This race seemed to prove the point. Tyrell-Smith was second, nearly three minutes back, and Ernie Nott third a further four minutes back. To add to the victory the Leinster Club trio of Stanley, Tyrell-Smith and Stanley's brother in law Gordon Burney [eighth on a Guzzi] also won the Club Team Prize.

So to that memorable Senior and a dramatic second win for Guzzi and for Stanley Woods. Just to reinforce the message Stanley went on to win the 500 Swedish GP on a Husqvarna. Thanks to Stanley, the continentals had well and truly arrived.

He was back on a British machine for 1936. At the 1934 motorcycle show he had asked Peter Goodman about riding a 350 Velocette, but had been turned down. He approached them again for the 1935 TT, but again was turned down. It was Joe Craig who told Stanley the reason for Veloce's reluc-

1935: Stanley poses on the v-twin Guzzi that took him to victory in the Senior TT by 4 seconds from Jimmy Guthrie (Norton).

tance to take him on board, it was Wal Handley that would not have Stanley in the team. Coincidentally, it was Handley's injury in practice when he caught his hand in the chain, that allowed Stanley to try the machine, but for one lap only. That single lap was enough for Stanley to realise that, although it had a good engine, its steering, brakes and choice of gear ratios were bad by Norton and Moto Guzzi standards. He stated that if the faults can be corrected and that some sort of rear suspension could be fitted, he would consider riding for them in 1936. They came up with the machine that included all his suggestions and he then became Veloce's foremost team rider. He also had an agreement with Goodman that if they did develop a winner then a replica would be made avail-

1936: The DKW failed to last the pace. His white-over-alled mechanic of many years was Manxman Eric Brown.

able to the private rider, not just a look alike but a proper replica.

The 350 machine went well in practice, albeit down on speed on the Nortons. But it was rumoured Stanley was merely holding back and there was plenty of money on him at the bookies. Whilst the machines were lined up for the race the loudspeaker announcer speculated whether Stanley had any tactical tricks up his sleeve that year. From the grid Stanley just grinned and shook his head. It proved to be an accurate prediction. Woods got no further than Sulby on the first lap before he was forced to retire. As Velocette had hoped, however, Stanley proved an excellent test rider and his comments enabled Willis and the other designers to make significant subsequent improvements to the bike.

In the Lightweight race, Stanley was part of a team entered by the German DKW factory. With team-mates Geiss and Steinbach the DKWs were reckoned to be the fastest Lightweights on the Island; they were certainly the noisiest. In the race itself, though, all the DKWs were plagued by plug trouble. Stanley took an early lead lapping at 76.50 mph, and led Geiss by twenty-four seconds. Bob Foster on a New Imperial was in third ten seconds down on Geiss. On the second lap Geiss slowed with ignition problems and Foster came up to second with Jack Williams on another New Imperial up to third. On the next circuit it was Stanley's turn to have to stop and change a plug and Foster took the lead by twenty-five seconds.

Stanley set off again determined to try and regain his advantage. Riding like a man possessed, he gained over fifty seconds on the New Imperial to lead Foster by twenty-eight seconds. Foster responded magnificently and cut Stanley's lead again to fourteen seconds with two laps to go. Stanley gave the thumbs up to his pit as he went through to start his penultimate lap, but it was tempting fate. At the fifth milestone he had to stop once more to change a plug and Foster took the lead again by thirty-five seconds. The New Imperial pit was still worried by Stanley, for they gave Foster the 'go faster' signal as he started his last lap. But Stanley gave the thumbs down to the DKW pit as he went through and this time the signal was accurate. Stanley retired between the Waterworks and the Gooseneck and Foster went on to win a TT on his honeymoon. He had been married just before practice week. His New Imperial was the last British machine to win a Lightweight race for many years.

In the Senior TT Stanley rode Velocette's new rear-spring framed 499cc model. The advantages of a sprung frame had been proved by the Guzzi's performance the year before. The race was expected to be a renewal of the Woods/Guthrie battle of the previous year and the fans were not disappointed.

Guthrie took the early lead, breaking the lap record on the second lap and leading Woods by twenty-seven seconds. Norton new boy and Junior winner Freddie Frith was third and 'Crasher' White was fourth on another works Norton. Guthrie continued to lap at over 85 mph but gradually Stanley started to whittle away at his advantage. The gap came down to twenty-three seconds, then eighteen seconds. At the end of the fourth lap a worried Norton pit gave Guthrie the 'go faster' signal. Guthrie responded with a new lap record of 86.76 mph, extending his lead to thirty-one seconds. But Stanley responded in turn. A new lap record of 86.98 mph and the gap was down to twenty-two seconds. At the end of the sixth lap there was activity in the Norton pit. Guthrie came in for another refuelling stop. The stage was set for another great last lap struggle.

There was furious speculation amongst the crowd. The lead had been only twenty-two seconds and Guthrie's stop must have whittled most of that away. Guthrie was now thirty-nine years old and had crashed in practice. Would he have the stamina to match Woods? Would Stanley's new Velocette last the furious pace? Both men tried as hard as they could round the last lap, but Woods was slowed by a misfire. Stanley finished first on the roads and this year it was his turn to wait. Then Guthrie came flying through - he had beaten Stanley by eighteen seconds. Woods was amongst the first to say 'well done'.

Woods stayed with the Velocette team for 1937, though he agreed to ride a Guzzi in the Lightweight TT. The Junior was expected to be another Woods/Guthrie battle but, despite breaking the lap record on the second circuit Woods couldn't split the Norton 1-2-3 of Guthrie, Frith and White. By the fourth lap Stanley did manage to get ahead of White for third place but 'Crasher' came back on the last two laps to recover his position. Stanley finished with a race average inside the previous record but it was not enough. White finished thirty seconds ahead of Woods with Guthrie and Frith even further ahead.

In practice for the Lightweight the Guzzi proved easy to ride but down on speed compared with the DKW's of Ewald Kluge and Ernie Thomas. In the race Kluge took the early lead with Stanley in second, Tyrell-Smith [Excelsior] third, Tenni [Guzzi] fourth and Thomas fifth. On the second lap

Thomas broke the lap record at 76.54 mph, but the record lasted only seven seconds as Stanley came through to record 76.89 mph. Woods led by just one second from Kluge with Tyrell-Smith third, Thomas now fourth and Tenni fifth. On the third circuit it was Tenni's turn to break the lap record at 77.72 mph and move up to fourth, whilst team-mate Stanley increased his lead to nine seconds. Tenni was up to second on the next circuit, twenty-six seconds behind Stanley, with Kluge relegated to third. When the German retired on the next lap with a broken throttle wire Guzzi seemed set for a 1-2. But on the penultimate lap Ramsey reported that Stanley passed through misfiring and as he came through the Grandstand he gave the thumbs down signal to his pit. Tenni had taken over the lead by over a minute with Ginger Wood in third on an Excelsior. Stanley retired at Sulby on the last lap with broken valve springs and Tenni won from Wood and Thomas. At the prize presentations Signor Parodi of Guzzi apologised for not giving Stanley a better bike and said they hoped to do better the following year.

The 1937 Senior was described by the motorcycle press of the time as the most thrilling Senior ever held. The day got off to a noisy start when the new Steam Packet vessel Tynwald arrived at 6.00am on her maiden voyage to be saluted by sirens and rockets. In the warm up for the race Jock West on the supercharged BMW also added to the decibel levels, making as much noise as the rest of the field put together. The race was held in fine conditions with Guthrie starting No. 1, Woods No. 4 and Frith No. 24. Everyone expected a further Woods/Guthrie battle.

Guthrie took the early lead from Frith with Stanley in third and West back in fourth. Guthrie broke the lap record at 88.51mph to extend his second lap lead to twenty-six seconds but Stanley had got seven seconds ahead of Frith and the big two were once again at the head of the field. Jimmy Guthrie went even faster on the next lap and raised the record again to 89.85 mph. Leading Stanley by around fifty seconds. With three laps to go it looked like another Guthrie victory. But on the fifth lap he was forced to retire with engine trouble on the climb up the Mountain [at the spot where the Guthrie Memorial now stands], and Stanley Woods found himself leading the race.

Now Frith, only about ten seconds behind Stanley, got the 'go faster' signal from the Norton pit; and go faster he did. He picked up the ten seconds on a single lap and, as they started their last lap, Frith and Woods were dead level on time. With a ten minute starting difference between them on the roads the Grandstand crowd watched the clocks anxiously. Woods was at Kirk Michael. Woods was at Ramsey, Frith at Ballacraine. Woods had reached the Mountain, Frith Kirk Michael. Woods reached the Creg. At their speeds the ten minute starting difference was equivalent to the distance between Ramsey and the Finish. If Frith reached Ramsey as Stanley finished, the two would be equal. Sure enough, as Woods streaked over the line Frith's scoreboard indicator moved to R for Ramsey.

The crowd waited anxiously. Then came an announcement. 'Frith's through Hillberry but he scraped his footrest. He's carried on'. Next 'Frith's at Governor's Bridge'. Freddie crossed the line and the crowd waited expectantly. All eyes were on the Norton pit. One of the pit crew turned and gave the thumbs up to the crowd. Then came the official announcement. 'Frith has won by fifteen seconds'. Freddie had broken the lap record on the final lap with the first ever 90 mph lap of the course - 90.27 mph.

Afterwards Stanley admitted that he couldn't have done any more. He had even risked revving the Velocette to 7,000 instead of 6,500 rpm but it still wasn't enough to hold off the charging Norton. Velocette did have some consolation with their team of Woods, Mellors [fourth] and Les Archer [eighth] taking the Manufacturers' prize. The Birmingham M.C.C. team of Woods, Mellors and Jack Williams [tenth on a Norton] won the Club team award.

The 1938 Junior saw Stanley's assistance in improving the 350 Velocette well and truly pay off. Stanley was virtually unchallenged in the race and won by nearly four minutes, setting a new lap record of 85.30 mph in the process. His team-mate Ted Mellors was second but only by seven seconds from Freddie Frith on the first of the Nortons. Indeed, so fierce was their battle that Mellors nearly did eight laps, forgetting it was the last lap and getting to Creg-ny-Baa before he was finally flagged down.

Stanley was back on a Velocette for the Senior race, but once again he had to give second place to a new Norton star. The race was the most competitive for years with works teams from Norton and Velocette, a full BMW team of Gall, Meier and Jock West, and Bob Foster on the experimental AJS four-cylinder bike.

Stanley got off to a slow start and was twenty-five seconds behind Frith after the opening lap. Gradually Woods closed the gap to sixteen seconds and then, on the third lap, broke the lap record to take the lead by three seconds. On the next circuit Frith reduced Woods' lead to one second and Norton rider Harold Daniell equalled Woods' lap record to come within seven seconds of Frith. The stage was set for a great three man battle to the end. Stanley increased his lead to three seconds whilst Frith and Daniell were now equal in second place. On the penultimate lap Stanley equalled the lap record again - but it wasn't enough. Daniell had set a new record of 90.75 mph and taken the lead by five seconds. It was Frith and Woods' turn to be equal in second place.

It was all down to the last lap, and all round the course all three were reported as trying really hard. Frith was the first to finish on the roads, just breaking his old lap record. Then Daniell arrived, earlier than expected. He had broken the lap record again at 91 mph. 'If Stanley can beat that', he said 'good luck to him'. At the Grandstand it was announced that Woods had one minute in which to arrive to win. The seconds dragged by. Then Stanley roared past - fifteen seconds behind Daniell but two seconds ahead of Freddie Frith. Close, but not enough. Stanley had to settle for second again.

Understandably, the 1939 TT races were overshadowed by

the fear of war. Norton announced that they were too busy with MOD work to enter a full works team in the races, but they would loan machines to Frith and Daniell for the Senior and Junior. For Velocette the TT period brought its own bad news. Harold Willis, the popular and well respected Velocette boss, died from complications following a minor operation.

The Junior was a tussle between Norton, Velocette and Fleischmann on a fast DKW. Stanley was fourth at the end of the first circuit behind Frith, Fleischmann and Harold Daniell, but Harold fell on the next lap and let Stanley up to third place. Woods got ahead of Fleischmann on the next lap and set about reducing Frith's lead of thirteen seconds. He passed the Norton on time on the fourth lap and Frith retired on the next with engine trouble, leaving Stanley ahead of Daniell and Fleischmann [handicapped through having had to stop twice

1939: Stanley at Governors Bridge with the 500 Velocette that took him to fourth place in his last TT race.

for fuel]. Harold put in a terrific effort over the last two laps, reducing Stanley's lead from twenty-six seconds to just eight at the end. But it was Stanley's win and his tenth TT victory. Velocette won the Manufacturers' Prize and a Velocette trio of Stanley, Ted Mellors [fourth] and Ginger Wood [eighth] took the Team Prize for the Derby Club.

In the Lightweight TT Guzzi and Signor Parodi had kept their promise and provided Stanley with a faster bike. But the conditions for the race were bad and the Guzzi riders couldn't use their speed advantage. They also suffered from reliability problems. Stanley was second on lap one only eight sec-

onds behind his team-mate Tenni, but ignition problems put him down to eighth on the second lap. Stanley stormed back through the field as only he could. He was up to third by the fifth lap before retiring at Crosby with engine trouble.

The supercharged BMWs, with a rumoured top speed of 140mph [about 15 mph faster than the Nortons and Velocettes], were hot favourites for the Senior race. In practice, Stanley had tried the experimental supercharged Velocette twin, nicknamed the Roarer', but it was thought too untried to risk in the race. Tragedy had also struck BMW during the TT period when Austrian Karl Gall had been killed in practice after crashing at Ballaugh. BMW considered with-

1957: Stanley Woods pilots a work's Guzzi over Braddan Bridge on his 'Lap of Honour' during the Golden Jubilee meeting.

drawing from the race but, in the end, decided to compete.

The fastest of the BMW riders, Georg Meier, started No. 49, but even this disadvantage didn't stop him leading on the first lap. Stanley and Jock West tied initially for second place but gradually the two BMWs pulled away from the Velocette. A disastrous pit stop at the end of lap three, when it took Stanley three tries to get the bike to re-fire, put Woods down to fourth behind Freddie Frith. Whilst Stanley got ahead again into third, Freddie regained the position on the last lap, by just two seconds. Both he and Stanley were nearly three minutes down on Meier, however, and half a minute down on Jock West on the second BMW.

So ended Stanley's last TT It wasn't totally without silverware. Velocette won the Manufacturers' Prize and a Derby/Velocette trio of Woods, Mellors [seventh] and Whitworth [twelfth] won the Club team prize. But there was no disguising that the british bikes had been well and truly beaten. A more brutal and horrific struggle was to put an end to racing for the next eight years.

When the TT resumed in 1947 Stanley was back in the Island, but helping the Guzzi team not riding for it. When Freddie Frith fell off the 500 v-twin at Ballacraine in practice, Stanley was sorely tempted to ride, but, in the end, it was a temptation he resisted. He remained a good friend to the TT, a frequent visitor and, for a time, President of the TT Riders' Association who help injured riders and their families. When Mike Hailwood finally broke Stanley's record of ten TT wins, there to congratulate Mike was Stanley himself, as magnanimous as always, full of praise for Mike's achievement.

Stanley Woods died in July 1992, much mourned by racing fans everywhere. At the 1994 meeting, the Lieutenant Governor of the Isle of Man, on behalf of the TT Riders' Association, dedicated a clock at the TT Grandstand Scoreboard to the memory of Stanley Woods. It is a fitting tribute to the man who first introduced the signalling system to the TT and who will always be synonymous with the TT races. It is in memory, it says, of 'an outstanding motor cycle sportsman'. There is no one to whom that better applies than Stanley Woods - the Irish Dasher.

Yer Maun

We were all agreed; Bernie, Stan, Jeff, Tommy, Peter and the rest, the collective wisdom of the Scoreboard. We know our motorcycling, even if we do spend most of the race with our backs to it and our faces to the board.

We had watched him since 1976, been thrilled and disappointed with him, seen him in the bar afterwards more times than we could remember. We had heard him describe his victories in interviews so inarticulate they spoke volumes. An ordinary man to look at and listen to, down to earth, no side to him, a biker's biker - and the most successful rider the TT has ever seen.

It had to be the 125. That was our considered view. If he was going to do it, it would be in the 125. As he suspected, we weren't sure we wanted him to do it. We'd have preferred it in some ways if he'd retired after equalling Hailwood's record of fourteen wins. Hailwood's immortal but we'd have liked Mike's record to remain. We'd have liked the two of them to share the record. We'd have preferred him not to take any more risks. But that was his business. If it was going to be done, he was the only one we wanted to do it and we wanted it out of the way quickly. We didn't want him trying too hard chasing it.

It had to be the 125. He'd never liked riding production bikes so the Supersport 600 was out. Honda had given him an RC30 not the RVF so the Senior and Formula 1 were probably out. He had a chance in the Junior but so did half a dozen others, so it had to be the 125. He had won the 125 to equal the record. He could win it again to break it, brother Robert allowing. Robert had beaten him in 1991, lost to him in 1992. It would be between them again in 1993.

The 125s started after the Supersport 400 bikes. Robert was No. 64. Joey, a minute behind on the roads, was No. 69. Everyone around the course was willing him on. At the end of the first lap there was little between them. But by the sec-ond lap Joey led by fourteen seconds. They both came in to refuel. Robert filled up and was away quickly. Joey filled up quickly and then..... the bike spluttered as it crawled down the pit lane. 'Pick up please' we said. 'Don't let it end like this'. The bike fired but he must have lost some time.

Sure enough, the lead had been cut but Robert was still in second place. Joey drew away again, increased the lead to twelve seconds with half the last lap to go. Up the Mountain and then down again. An anxious time for the crowd, a worse one for Joey. Hoping it didn't run out of petrol, hoping nothing in the engine broke, praying he didn't do anything silly.

The light was on for No. 64. Robert came home to finish. Joey had a minute to get there to win. The light showed he'd passed Signpost. Twenty seconds, thirty, forty, there was a machine coming down the road, green and white fairing, yellow helmet, it was Joey. He crossed the line, the crowd went wild, Joey'd done it by twelve point six seconds. He'd won the 1993 Lightweight 125 TT. He'd broken his own race record. He'd beaten Hailwood's record of fourteen TT wins.

At the Prize presentation Joey got a standing ovation. He brought his children up on the stage to share the moment. His fifteenth TT win, more than the legendary Mike Hailwood; the most successful rider in TT history.

Afterwards he said he was glad to get it over, more glad that people didn't hold it against him. We didn't Joey. We never would.

-----oOo-----

William Joseph 'Joey' Dunlop was born in 1952. He describes himself these days as the part-time publican of the Railway Tavern in Ballymoney, Northern Ireland. But to most TT fans he's the 'King of the Roads' or, more commonly, simply 'Yer Maun'.

Joey was encouraged into motorcycle racing by his brother in law Mervyn Robinson and had his first race when he was nineteen. Ironically the seventeen times TT winner almost retired after just one win when Robinson was killed racing in the North West 200. Joey seriously thought of giving up racing. He cancelled all his entries except the TT. But after winning the Classic TT that year he decided to carry on.

His 'King of the Roads' title came after he won five consecutive TT Formula 1 World Championships from 1982 to 1986 inclusive. For his achievements he was awarded the MBE. He's been Irish Sports Personality of the Year. He's taken van loads of food and medical supplies to children in Rumania, Albania and Bosnia. But essentially he's a motorcycle racer - and a TT fan.

He loves the TT and freely admits that, even when he's satisfied with the set-up of a bike, he'll still go out for another practice lap, just for the fun of it. He likes the odd Guiness or Vodka and his first desire when finishing a race is for a cigarette. He likes the atmosphere of a pub and a game of darts with the regulars. He dislikes the occasional razzamatazz and the media coverage that goes with success, though he does what he has to for the sake of the sponsors and fans. He's the fans' favourite; he's one of them.

He's a rider who likes to get his hands dirty and help with the preparation of the bikes himself. Most of his wins have come on Hondas. They've looked after him well and he's responded loyally.

Like many riders, Joey is superstitious and follows the same ritual before a race meeting. This nearly led to disaster in 1985 when, following his routine of travelling to the Isle of Man by fishing boat, the boat sank in Strangford Lough in the early hours of the morning. Luckily all the passengers and crew were rescued. Joey is a bundle of nervous tension before a race. Unlike his brother Robert, who likes to arrive well before the start, Joey likes to turn up at the last possible moment, have a last cigarette, get on the bike and get on with the race.

Joey made his TT debut in 1976 on a 250 Yamaha. He arrived on a fishing boat, signed on and was out in practice that evening. He'd never seen the course before, never even driven round it.

By the following year, however, he'd learnt the circuit pretty well. He finished tenth in the Junior on a Yamsel,

1977: Joey (Yamaha) takes Douglas Corner, Kirk Michael on his way to the first of 22 TT victories in the Jubilee TT.

fourth on the same make of bike in the Senior and seventh in the Classic on a Yamaha. The TT programme that year contained a special four-lap race to commemorate the Queen's Silver Jubilee. Joey, riding the Rea 750 Yamaha, won the race easily setting a race speed of 108.86 mph and a fastest lap of 110.93 mph. Obviously, he was a quick learner.

In the 1978 Junior he finished eleventh on a Yamaha, just ahead of Mike Hailwood, and rode a Benelli in the Formula 2 race to finish fifth. For the Formula One race, he rode a fearsome six-cylinder Benelli, but retired on the second lap. In the Classic he was lying fifth at the end of lap one on the Johnny Rea Yamaha but the exhaust split on the next lap and forced him to retire. He managed sixth in the same event the following year, his only result of note that TT.

It had been a promising start, but, after that first win, an unspectacular one. 1980 was to change all that.

Joey came to the 1980 TT unsure about his racing future. His brother in law and mentor, Mervyn Robinson, had been killed at the North West 200 a couple of weeks before. Joey had just about decided to give up racing. He had cancelled all his other entries but decided to compete in a last TT.

To begin with things went to their accustomed pattern. Joey was sixth fastest in practice on the big Yamaha at 108.54 mph but there was no sign he could give the works stars anything to worry about. In the four lap 250 Junior TT he was off the leader board for the first three laps but crept up to twelfth on the final lap.

His TZ500 Yamaha had given gearbox problems in practice, so Joey elected to ride his 350 Yamaha in the Senior TT After lying in twelfth place for most of the race, he pulled up to ninth by the end, about twenty seconds behind Charles Mortimer [Suzuki]. Things didn't look any more promising for the final race of the week, the six lap Classic.

The Classic, richest race of the week, was expected to be a Honda benefit, with outright lap record holder Mick Grant [114.33 mph in 1978 on a Kawasaki], Ron Haslam and Graeme McGregor all riding factory supported bikes. Charlie Williams on the Mitsui Yamaha, Graeme Crosby on the Yoshimura Suzuki and Jeff Sayle on the George Beale Yamaha were expected to provide the main opposition. Joey had fitted an eight gallon tank on the Yamaha so he only had to stop once during the race but the bike had given trouble in last minute testing and he'd been up until 2.30 in the morning rebuilding the machine.

Joey started at his lucky No. 3. He astonished everyone with a first lap at 112.25 mph to lead Jeff Sayle by six point four seconds. Crosby and Williams were out, McGregor was in third place and Grant was fourth, struggling with a bike that was wrongly geared and would only rev to 8,000 instead of 9,000 rpm. But Joey had his problems too. The tank straps for the big fuel tank had broken and he was having to hold the tank in position with his knees and elbows.

On the second lap Grant got the big Honda moving and lapped at 113.13 mph. With McGregor retiring, this put Grant into third place and only two point eight seconds behind Sayle in second. But at the front, Joey went even faster, lapping at 113.85 mph and extending his lead to twenty-six seconds. Mick closed the gap a little to twenty-two seconds on the next circuit, whilst Sayle's steering damper broke after May Hill and he retired after a spectacular tank-slapper.

Both Grant and Dunlop pitted at the end of their third lap and the resources of Honda, with their dump filler and slick pit work got Grant out in the lead. At the end of the lap he had retained his advantage and led Joey by seven point six seconds with Ron Haslam over a minute back in third. It seemed all over. Dunlop had given Honda a fright but now Grant would consolidate his lead.

That must have been Grant's plan too as he lapped at 113.70 mph. But we were all wrong. Incredibly, on his non-works standard Yamaha racer, Joey beat the absolute lap record at 114.41 mph and reduced Grant's lead to a fifth of a second as they went in to the last lap. Both got their signals urging them on. Grant did his best to respond, but could do no better than 113.24 mph on his final circuit. Joey, on the other hand, went faster again - 115.22 mph, a new lap record - to win by twenty point four seconds. Haslam was third over two minutes behind his team-mate. Grant said afterwards he could go no faster because of the gearing problem. Joey said that, apart from the tank problem, the bike had gone 'as smooth as a Bushmills'.

Honda decided Dunlop would provide no more surprises for them in 1981. They signed him up to ride the works Hondas in the Formula One and Classic events.

It was a year for controversy. Suzuki fielded a strong team of Graeme Crosby and Mick Grant whilst Honda had Dunlop, Haslam and Alex George. The rivalry between the two teams was intense rather than simply competitive. It was made worse by some lingering bitterness over the previous year's Formula One, when Suzuki had protested that Mick Grant had ridden with an oversize fuel tank. The unfortunate atmosphere seemed to spill over into the meeting generally.

It all began with the Formula One Race, the main objective of both teams. Graeme Crosby had chain trouble at the start and was unable to start in his proper position. Eventually he got away at the end of the field. It was not the first time the organisers had allowed a rider who had struck trouble on the start line to start from the back of the field and, depending on the circumstances, they sometimes gave the rider the time allowance appropriate to his revised starting position [the need to pass so many slower riders in front of him being disadvantage enough to any late starter]. But in this case Crosby was given no such allowance.

In the race Joey took an early lead but was forced to change a tyre at his pit-stop at the end of his second lap. Haslam took over the lead and he and Joey eventually finished in first and second positions, to the understandable delight of Honda. After a courageous ride Crosby had got up to third place and would have won if he'd had the time allowance. Haslam was announced as the winner and garlanded as such at the Grandstand. Then Suzuki protested that Crosby should have had a time allowance. The protest was upheld by the FIM

Jury and Crosby was declared the race winner. Honda were furious, Haslam was bitter, Suzuki were embarrassed, and the TT was the loser.

More controversy occurred in the Senior. The race was run in wet conditions and by the end of lap one the rain was pouring down. Chris Guy was leading when the organisers stopped the race after the second lap at the urging, amongst others, of Mick Grant. It was a sensible decision on safety grounds, but when the race was resumed the next day and Guy crashed whilst Grant won there were further mutterings.

By the end of race week relations between Honda and the race organisers hadn't improved and Honda staged their now famous 'black' protest. Their machines for the Classic TT were all painted black and the riders rode in black leathers. Honda were trying to allege that the race organisers were still years behind the times. Unfortunately, in the race, the protest rather backfired. Crosby [Suzuki] took an early lead. Joey, chasing after him, set a new absolute lap record of 115.40 mph but then ran out of petrol. Haslam retired, and Crosby won comfortably from Grant with Alex George third, the only 'black' Honda to finish.

The Honda/Suzuki battle continued in 1982, a little better tempered, thankfully. Grant led the Suzuki challenge whilst Dunlop and Haslam were Honda's best chances. Joey went well in practice until the last practice session when he blew up the race engine of the big Honda. The replacement unit vibrated badly and, after the first lap of the Formula One, the bike's suspension also gave trouble.

Mick Grant took the lead at the beginning of the Formula One with a new lap record of 114.93 mph. Joey was in second place but, as the suspension troubles struck, Haslam took over from his team-mate. Ron was initially twenty-six seconds behind Grant but gradually whittled down the Yorkshireman's lead to six seconds by the middle of the fifth circuit. Then Grant retired at the Gooseneck with an oil leak and ignition problems and Haslam went on to win the race. This time no-one tried to take the result away from him. Joey finished second four and a half minutes behind Rocket Ron after 'touring' at 109.15 mph. It was an important result, however, that helped him win the Formula One World Championship.

In the Classic, it was Charlie Williams on the Yamaha who led both the Hondas and Suzuki. Haslam and Grant were second and third until they both retired on the third lap. Joey could manage no better than fifth with the big Honda still giving problems. Williams led until the gearbox seized at Ballaugh on the fifth circuit leaving Dennis Ireland on a 500 Suzuki to take a surprise win. Joey retired at the Bungalow on the fifth lap with a broken chain.

So far Joey had performed well enough for Honda. But 1983 was to see the start of a remarkable sequence of results. Joey led that year's Honda team for the TT with Roger Marshall and Hartley Kerner [the latter on a standard 750 production Honda]. Suzuki had a strong team with Mick Grant, Rob McElnea and Charlie Williams.

1978: Joey at the Bungalow on the Agrati-entered Benelli 6 in the Formula One race.

1981: Joey on the 'black protest' Honda in the Classic TT.

Riding the new Honda RS 850 V4, Joey set a new lap record of 115.73 mph on the first lap of the Formula 1, and took the lead by seventeen point eight seconds from Mick Grant. Geoff Johnson [Suzuki] was in third, McElnea fourth and Marshall fifth. Joey did another blistering lap at 115.51 mph on the second circuit and refuelled and got away again before anyone else arrived on the roads. By the end of the fourth lap Joey led Mick by nearly thirty-six seconds but felt that the rear tyre needed changing if he was to be sure it would last the full race distance.

Suzuki saw a chance. Honda made ready to change the wheel at the pit stop at the end of the fourth. When Joey came in the Honda mechanics worked as quickly as they could, getting the bike refuelled, the wheel changed and Joey on his

way again in sixty-five seconds. Grant was in shortly afterwards but, although the rear tyre of his bike was already giving problems, Suzuki gambled on not changing it and giving Grant a lead which they hoped he could hold on to. Grant was out of his pit in just thirty seconds and by Ballacraine led Dunlop by twelve seconds.

As soon as Joey got the new tyre warmed up, however, the advantage of fresh rubber began to pay. By Ballaugh Grant's lead was down to two seconds and by the Bungalow Dunlop was ahead again by nineteen seconds. The Suzuki gamble had failed. Indeed, McElnea nearly caught his team-mate until his tyre too began to go off. Joey came home to win by fifty two point eight seconds at a record average of 114.03 mph. But although the winning margin was a comfortable one in the end, it had been a hard race and Dunlop finished it nearly exhausted. As soon as he could he was on the plane back to Northern Ireland to see his wife and one week old baby son, born in practice week.

Joey was back on the Island for the Classic TT at the end of the week but Suzuki, in various forms, dominated the race. New star Norman Brown, on a 500 two-stroke Suzuki, set an absolute lap record of 116.19 mph but ran out of petrol when leading. Rob McElnea on the big four stroke Suzuki was the eventual race winner from Con Law on another 500 Suzuki and Dunlop on the big Honda. Joey didn't mind too much. The Formula 1 was the race he and Honda wanted to win and he went on to retain his Formula 1 World Championship.

1984 was a TT of mixed fortunes for Joey. In the all

important Formula 1 he continued his success. Joey led team -mate Roger Marshall for the first four laps with Tony Rutter on a Ducati in third place. On the fifth lap, though, Marshall took the lead and Joey had to set a new lap record on the last lap - 115.89 mph - to win the class for the second year.

Joey retired in the Junior and Senior races, but only after a terrific Senior battle. The race was a tremendous duel between Dunlop on the 500 Honda-3 and McElnea on the Suzuki. Both led twice and on the fifth lap Joey set a new absolute course record of 118.47 mph. But it was faster than the team had calculated on and on the last lap he ran out of fuel. McElnea won the race from Marshall [Honda] and Trevor Nation [Suzuki].

It was a similar story in the Classic where both McElnea and Dunlop chose to ride their big four cylinder machines rather than the 500 two strokes. Joey led at the end of the first lap but it was Mick Grant [Suzuki] who was in the lead after the second circuit, with Dunlop second and McElnea third. By the end of the third circuit McElnea led but by the finish of the fourth it was Joey back in front, albeit only by one second. McElnea took the lead back on the fifth lap and held on to it to win with a lap record of 117.13 mph and a record race average of 116.12 mph. Joey had the consolation of the Formula 1 win and, later, another Formula 1 World Championship.

On Sunday 26th May 1985, Joey, Brian Reid and other passengers and crew, numbering thirteen in all, were making their way over to the Island on a converted fishing boat. The boat struck rocks at the entrance to Strangford Lough in the early hours of the morning and sank. Joey helped to rescue the other passengers and crew all of whom were saved. Five bikes, Joey's and Reid's, were later recovered from the Lough. Fortunately Joey's works Hondas had arrived at the Island by another route. The incident would have been enough to seriously de-tune many a rider but Joey seemed to shrug it off and went on to have his most successful TT yet.

In the Formula 1 he lead from start to finish with a new class lap record of 116.42 mph.Marshall [Honda] and Grant [Suzuki] both retired when lying second and Joey's winning margin was over five and a half minutes from Tony Rutter [Suzuki] and Steve Parrish [Yamaha].

Joey's Junior win was due to the continuing bad luck of his fellow boat passenger Brian Reid. Dunlop [Honda] led Reid [EMC] by eighteen seconds at the end of lap one. Joey's pit stop gave Reid the lead but when the EMC rider made his stop Dunlop had the advantage again. But on the fifth circuit Reid took the lead back again with a new lap record of 112.08 mph and led by fifteen seconds going in to the last lap. Going through the Bungalow for the last time Reid was still ahead and all set to win when the engine gave out at Hillberry. Joey finished fifteen seconds ahead of Steve Cull [Honda] with Eddie Roberts in third.

For 1985 the Classic TT had been dropped and the Senior restored to its rightful place as the last race of the week. The capacity limit had been increased, however, to include the Formula 1 machines. This time it was Mick Grant's turn for misfortune as he crashed at the Black Dub. Although team -mate Roger Marshall ran Dunlop close, Joey won by sixteen seconds to score a TT hat trick - only managed before by Mike Hailwood. Another Formula 1 Championship added to Joey's rapidly growing reputation as the World's finest road racer.

The 1986 Formula 1 was the race we thought would never get started. Bad weather forced two days of postponements and the reduction of the race distance to four laps. The tension of the various postponements did nothing for the nerves of the riders but Joey put all that behind him and led from start to finish again. He won by almost a minute from Geoff Johnson [Honda] and Andy McGladdery [Suzuki].

The manufacturers were beginning to take increasing interest in the TT's various production races and Honda had Joey ride in Production class C. He finished fourth, his position in the Senior too. The Senior race was full of drama, if not excitement. Roger Marshall on the big Honda led for the first couple of laps but on the third Trevor Nation [Suzuki] took a three point six second advantage at the front. Nation then ran out of fuel at the 32nd Milestone letting Marshall back into the lead. But Roger had to stop with a chain problem, Dunlop had to stop with a steering damper problem and Roger Burnett was left to take the win on the Honda 500-3. Geoff Johnson was second on a Honda and Barry Woodland third on a Suzuki.

Honda had things largely their own way in 1986, but for 1987 Suzuki were back with a vengeance. Roger Marshall had switched to the Suzuki team who also had Phil Mellor riding for them. Mellor soon showed his potential, lapping in practice at 118.03 mph on his Formula 1 bike. Geoff Johnson on a Loctite Yamaha also provided strong opposition.

If Joey was worried by this increased pressure he didn't show it. He never sets fast times in practice in the hope of scaring the opposition. On the contrary he prefers to keep his cards to his chest and let others worry about what speed he may do.

In the race Mellor led at Ballacraine on the first lap. But by the end of the lap Joey was twenty-one seconds in front. Mellor responded with a new lap record of 117.10 mph. But Joey went even faster at 117.55 mph. and increased his lead to twenty-five seconds. Thereafter he stretched his lead further on each circuit to win by fifty-two point two seconds. Johnson was third and Marshall fourth, plagued by fuel starvation problems. Joey admitted afterwards that he'd had to go flat out throughout and this was reflected in his race speed which was a record 115.03 mph.

Dunlop rode a Shell Gemini Honda in the Junior but was never really in contention in a hard fought race. He was fifth at the end of the opening lap but dropped away thereafter and eventually finished eighth.

Everyone was looking forward to the resumption of the Dunlop/Mellor battle in the Senior TT but the weather spoilt the occasion. The race had to be postponed from Friday to Saturday. Even then the forecast was none too good and the race was reduced to four laps. Because of the damp conditions Joey chose to ride the 500-3 rather than the heavier four stroke and, like most riders, used intermediate tyres.

Trevor Nation on the Yamaha was the leader at Ballacraine but Dunlop was ahead by the end of the opening circuit with a lap of 105.08 mph, the fastest of the race. Mellor was second sixteen seconds back with Nation on the Loctite Yamaha third. On the second lap the rain started again and Joey's lap speed dropped to 98.64 mph. His lead dropped too, down to ten seconds, and when Joey pitted and Mellor went straight through, the Suzuki rider took the lead. The two were soon together on the roads but with Mellor ahead of Dunlop on time. Joey gradually started to pull away a little on the road and with Mellor due to pit at the end of the third lap it was all set for a great last lap battle. But as they neared the Grandstand for the third time Mellor dropped his bike at the tricky Nook section. He remounted and reached the pits but he'd damaged his shoulder and the gear lever and was forced to call it a day. Joey went on to win by fifty-eight seconds from Geoff Johnson with Roger Marshall in third. The win, at an average speed of 99.58 mph, gave Joey his tenth TT victory, equalling the number of wins of Stanley Woods and Agostini. But he indicated in no uncertain terms that he never wanted to ride in such conditions again.

TT week 1988 started slowly for Dunlop with no indication of what was to come. Riding a 600 Honda he finished eleventh in the Production Class C race and won, for him, a rare bronze replica. In the Production Class B he did rather better on the 750 Honda, he and Jamie Whitham [750 Suzuki], having a good dice for fourth place. Whitham got the better of him in the end by nine point four seconds. Dunlop had never been really happy on the production machines. He was a racer and needed proper racing bikes to be at his best.

Joey's win in the 1987 Formula 1 had been his fifth in succession, equalling the record of Hailwood and Agostini for winning the same race five years on the trot. Now he was going for an unprecedented sixth successive win. But Honda had not made it easy for him. Instead of the new RVF he wanted, Joey had to make do with an RC30 model. Joey took the lead at the start as usual with a fourteen second advantage over Geoff Johnson on the Bimota Yamaha. When Joey set a new lap record of 118.54 mph on the second circuit, that seemed to be it. But we had reckoned without a rapidly rising new star, Steve Hislop. The Scot had lapped at 118.44 mph and was up to third by the third lap, thirty-six point eight seconds behind Dunlop. By the next lap the lead was down to twenty-nine seconds with two laps to go, and it was looking like it might be another close race. But Hislop's engine seized at Ballaugh on the next circuit and Johnson soon retired too with engine trouble. Joey won at a record speed of 116.25 mph by sixty-eight seconds from Nick Jeffries. Roger Burnett was third, despite having to ride for most of one lap with a flat tyre.

1983: Joey with Marc Beattie, who he adopted as his Manx mascot. Marc was in the Grandstand to watch Joey win his first Formula One race in 1983, and he watched all his subsequent F1 victories.

The Junior TT was now a race for a mixture of 250 and 350 two strokes and 600 four strokes but the 250 two strokes dominated. Joey rode a 250 Honda and started from his favourite No. 3. Brian Reid [EMC], suffering from a broken toe, started No 4, equal on time with Dunlop. Joey led the race from the start and by the pit stops at the end of lap two was twenty seconds ahead of Reid. But Dunlop's stop was a disaster. The filler cap fell into the fairing and the mechanics had to lift the bike up to dislodge it. Joey finally got away, only to find that the cap wasn't on properly and he had to tighten it whilst trying to negotiate Bray Hill. Reid had made up the twenty second advantage and the two were together again on the roads.

Dunlop soon pulled away again and led by four seconds going into the last lap. By the end of the race he had won by nineteen point four seconds and become the first man to lap at under twenty minutes on a 250. His lap record was short lived, however. After a race full of problems, Steve Hislop showed what he might have done by lapping at a new record speed of 113.41 mph on the last lap, finishing fourth. Joey did set a new race record, though, at 111.87 mph. Reid was second and Eddie Laycock [EMC] third.

[Bimota Yamaha] in third. Joey, who had set another race record at 117.38 mph, had achieved another TT hat trick and taken his tally of TT victories to thirteen, just one behind the all time record of the great Mike Hailwood.

A crash at Brands Hatch at Easter 1989 put Joey out of that year's TT, which was dominated by Steve Hislop. The Scot scored three wins in the week and nearly made it four. Everyone looked forward eagerly to a Dunlop/Hislop clash the following year but Joey still looked detuned after his accident and the pressure of the record seemed to be getting to him. The best he could manage was eighth in the Formula 1.

In 1991, though, he showed that he was far from finished with a fine second place in the Senior behind Hislop and ahead of Phillip McCallen. But it was in the Lightweight 125 that he generated the most excitement.

With Joey on such good form it was thought that the Senior would be another Dunlop win. But Steve Cull had other ideas. Joey, riding the 750 Honda, set a new lap record from a standing start at 118.66 mph. But Cull, on a 500 Honda, was only four point four seconds behind in second. On the next lap Joey set another record - 118.77 mph. But Cull went even faster - 119.08 mph. Joey's lead was down to one point four seconds. At Ballacraine on the next circuit Cull was in the lead by one second but by the Bungalow Joey was back in front and he led by four seconds at the end of the lap. Then, just as it looked like developing into a real classic, the expansion chamber on Cull's bike was holed and he started to slow. Worse was to come for Cull. The bike eventually caught fire near Creg-ny-Baa and was burnt out. Joey went on to win by fifty-one seconds from Hislop [Honda] with Geoff Johnson

Joey led the race for the first two laps from his brother Robert. The majority of the crowd felt Robert would let brother Joey have the win he needed to equal Mike Hailwood's record. But Robert was having none of that. He took the lead on the third lap and went on to win from Joey by forty seconds. It was a controversial win with the fans but not, it seemed, with the two brothers. If Joey was going to equal the record he would have to do it fair and square and Joey wouldn't want it any other way.

So to 1992 and another 125 TT. The start was delayed because of bad weather, adding still more to the tension. But eventually the race got underway and the two brothers resumed their dice. For much of the time they couldn't be separated, but towards the end Joey finally drew away and won by just eight seconds. Joey seemed relieved at first that the pressure was off. But then came the pressure of whether to try and break the record, and would the fans turn against him if he did?

Joey did break the record in 1993, but his attitude to it says a lot about the man. During the 70s and 80s we heard and read a lot about the likes of Agostini, Sheene, Roberts and others who had helped to change the image of motorcycle racing. They were smart, photogenic, good with sponsors, articulate ambassadors for their sport. Their achievements deserve to be applauded. But in an increasingly commercial and media led sporting environment, for motorcycle racing as for other sports, there was something comforting and old fashioned about a man achieving greatness whose first thought wasn't 'how much is this worth' but whether the ordinary fans would still love him.

We do, Joey. We do.

We thought it was all over. Now that he'd broken the record, we said, he'd retire. At forty-two he was past his best. It was always good to see him, but he wasn't the force he'd been. He proved us wrong again.

For 1994, Joey was part of a strong Castrol Honda team, with Steve Hislop and Phillip McCallen. The first race of the week was the Formula 1.

It was an eventful one for Joey. On the first lap he came out of Barregarrow only to find a van on the track. An early warning by Marshals gave him time to swerve past the vehicle - later removed. Then the temperature gauge of his Honda failed. Finally, at the Highlander on the second lap, warnings of a stray dog slowed him down.

No wonder that, at the end of the second lap, Joey was only fifth behind team-mates Hislop and McCallen, brother Robert [Honda] and Steve Ward [Honda]. Trouble for Robert and Ward put Joey up to third place by lap five, and brought Joey together on the roads with Phillip McCallen. It seemed to revitalise Joey. He really enjoyed the on-road dice with his compatriot and it gave the spectators a terrific thrill. Both riders recorded their fastest laps on the last lap - McCallen setting the fastest lap of the race at 122.08 mph, and Joey not far behind at 121.49 mph. Steve Hislop was the runaway victor but Joey finished a fine third, a minute and twenty seconds down on McCallen on time but not far behind on the roads. It was a good start to the week, and at the garlanding ceremony Joey got the biggest cheer of the day.

It was a similar story in the Senior at the end of the week. Hislop led from start to finish with McCallen in second and Joey in third. Joey's bike had given endless trouble in practice. But fitting a new set of front forks borrowed from Steve Hislop's spare machine, seemed to do the trick. Joey held on to his third place to give a Castrol Honda 1-2-3, and to complete his best TT week for several years. Once again, he got the biggest cheer of the day from the fans.

For, the middle of the week had seen Joey triumph. He was hot favourite for the 125, but as the race neared it hadn't looked promising. Brother Robert had been badly injured in a crash in the earlier Formula 1 and it seemed at one stage as though Joey wouldn't ride. But encouraging news from the hospital persuaded Joey to compete and to try and add to his fifteen TT victories. He also had the record of the Dunlop family to uphold. He and Robert between them had won the 125 race on its previous five runnings.

Joey, starting No. 56, rode the same Honda RS125 as he had won on in 1993. He led from the start, holding an eight second advantage over Mick Lofthouse [Yamaha] at the end of the first lap and increasing this to seventeen seconds by the completion of the next circuit. Lofthouse kept the lead down to twenty-one seconds on the third lap but then retired when the Yamaha's silencer came loose. Joey went on to win by seventy-one seconds from fellow Ulsterman Denis McCullough [Honda], with a fastest lap of 107.40 mph and a winning average of 105.74 mph. It was a record sixteenth TT victory. 'I won this one for Robert', said Joey afterwards. 'I just wish he'd been out there racing with me'. Thankfully,

1985: Joey exits Ramsey on his way to his sixth successive Formula One win.

Robert was soon showing more improvement.

There was more drama to come. Phillip McCallen was widely tipped to win Wednesday's Junior race, with Brian Reid [Yamaha], and Ian Lougher [Honda], expected to push him close. Joey had other ideas.

At the end of lap one, McCallen led by seven point six seconds from Joey who, in turn, was four seconds ahead of Lougher. Reid, who'd had a first lap fright when his brakes faded, was back in fourth place.

By the end of the second circuit both Castrol Honda men had lapped at well over 115 mph and McCallen was still only eight seconds ahead of Joey. The pit stops would be vital. Joey had a smooth stop in twenty-nine seconds, but McCallen was in and out of the pits in just nineteen seconds, gaining a further ten precious seconds on Dunlop. By the end of the third lap Joey had cut the lead to eleven seconds, but by

Ramsey on the last lap the gap was up to sixteen seconds again - the race looked all over. Then came dramatic news - McCallen was touring down the Mountain. The fast pit-stop had been a terrible miscalculation. He'd failed to take on enough fuel and run out of petrol. Joey stormed on to win by more than twenty-five seconds from Brian Reid despite Reid's terrific last lap effort in setting fastest lap of the race at 115.97 mph. A broken exhaust dropped Lougher from third to fifth with Jason Griffiths [Yamaha] taking the third place position.

Joey had won his seventeenth TT, just as we all thought he'd finished. The crowd went wild - Joey looked happy. His only problem [apart from McCallen], had been that the footrest had been hanging down and he'd had to rest his boot on the bike's exhaust.

It had been Joey's best TT week for years and, to celebrate, he took a hat-trick of wins at the Steam Packet races at Billown on the Saturday after TT Will he add more TT wins to his record? After 1994 I've given up making predictions about Joey Dunlop. One thing I am sure of, however [along with tens of thousands of other race fans]. When it comes to the Isle of Man's TT races, Joey Dunlop is still 'Yer Maun'.

A TT Special

Graham Walker was the voice of motorcycling, the voice of the TT. But in a sense there was another voice. It started, hesitantly, in 1927, doubled in volume in 1928, and trebled again in 1929. In 1930 it extended to practice week and thereafter became as much a part of the TT scene as the Grandstand or the refreshment tent. The voice's name was Geoff Davison, and his chosen instrument was the TT Special.

For some of my early years I was at Boarding school. Unlike the Island's other schools, our holidays didn't always coincide with TT week. A combination of half-terms, exeats, gaps in the timetable and, on some occasions, simple truancy meant I was always able to see some of the racing. But, for the remainder, I and thousands of other motorcycle fans unable to attend relied on the TT Special to convey the atmosphere and excitement of the races we'd missed.

Most of the early race reports were written by Davison himself in his deceptively simple and concise style. They were written in the present tense, as events happened, and with a sense of observation that left you feeling you were really there. You couldn't actually smell the Castrol R or hear the exhaust notes, but you thought you could.

In 1947 Davison wrote 'The Story of the TT'. He mixed the history of the event with his own recollections from his unique perspective of competitor, winner, journalist and observer. It's still the best book ever written about the races.

Davison saw every T.T, from 1921 to 1965 and most of the Amateur races and Manx Grand Prix as well. He recorded them faithfully and added significantly, but never patronisingly, to the understanding of his readers. He inspired with his enthusiasm. The TT Special was informative, enjoyable and latterly, a part of TT history and tradition. But most of all it was a man writing devotedly, and well, about the sport he loved.

-----oOo-----

Born in 1895, Geoff Davison was working for the *Motor Cycling* Magazine when, in 1921, he persuaded the Levis Company to let him have a two stroke 250cc machine for that year's Lightweight 250 TT The Lightweights raced as part of the Junior TT but with their own separate class results. There were twenty one entries for the Lightweight. Six Levis and four Velocette machines led the two stroke entry, three New Imperials and two Diamonds led the four strokes.

Davison started No. 49, the last of the Levis riders. There were no commentaries on the races in those days and no signalling positions. So, during a race, riders had little or no information about their positions. Pit signals were generally limited to 'go faster' or 'ease off'. By the third lap, however, Davison had passed all the other Levis riders, so it seemed to him he might be going reasonably well. At the end of the fourth lap he got a particularly vigorous 'go faster' signal from his pit, so he thought he must be on the leader board. In fact he was battling for the lead. Then, on the last lap, the belt of his Levis broke as he was approaching the Creg. After stopping to fit a new one he rode on to finish second, just two and three quarter minutes behind Doug Prentice [New Imperial] with W. G. Harrison [Velocette] third a further seven minutes behind. Davison's race average speed of 44.33 mph was faster than the previous lap record for the class and 4 mph faster than the 1920 350 Junior race average. It was an impressive debut.

Davison was entered by W. Watson in the 1922 Senior race to ride a 3 ½ hp Sunbeam machine. There were sixty-seven entries in the Senior that year and Davison finished a respectable seventeenth place. But his main target was the Lightweight.

1922 saw the first separate Lightweight TT, although the

1922: Geoff Davison refuels his little, light Levis, the scouts function was to clean the number plates.

race was actually still run concurrently with the Junior. There were thirty-two entries for the new TT with eleven different makes of machine. Once again, the race was expected to be a battle between the four strokes and the two strokes. New Imperial, O.K., Rex Acme, Sheffield-Henderson, Coulson and Massey-Arran led the four strokes with Levis, Velocette and Sun Vitesse leading the two stroke bikes.

Encouraged by his result the year before, Davison decided to do all he could to reduce the weight of his machine. So he and Bob Newey, the Levis designer, chose the lightest components they could find and left off any 'unnecessary' parts like shock absorbers. Davison's race engine only arrived three days before the event, but when it was fitted his machine was around 40 lbs lighter than the other bikes.

Like many riders of the day Davison did not ride in leathers because the material was of poor quality and tended to tear easily. Instead, Davison rode in a cricket sweater and ordinary trousers and in dancing pumps rather than boots. Together the lightly attired Davison and his light weight Levis weighed about four stones less than Doug Prentice and the New Imperial.

The race itself nearly ended quickly for Davison. In a group of four riders at Ballaugh on lap one he found himself on the wrong racing line and nearly came off. At the end of the lap, however, he was only eleven seconds down in second behind Wal Handley on the Rex Acme, despite Handley having broken the lap record on the opening circuit. Handley retired on the next lap and Davison was in the lead, nearly two minutes ahead of Bert Kershaw [New Imperial]. At the end of lap three he made his refuelling stop and was told his position. By then he led Kershaw by almost four minutes and, when the New Imperial rider also retired on the next lap, Davison had a ten minute advantage over Dan Young on a Rex. Davison heeded the 'ease off' sign on the last lap but still won by over thirteen minutes. Young was second and S. J. Jones on a Velocette third. Davison's winning record race speed of 49.89 mph was again faster than the previous lap record and would have given him third place in that year's Junior. Davison had joined the elite band of riders who had won a TT

For 1923 Davison was again entered in the Lightweight and Senior TTs. The Lightweight had been extended to six laps and there were forty starters. In the race, though, the two strokes, including the Levis, were outclassed by the four stroke Blackburne and JAP engined machines. Pike on a Levis was the first two stroke home in seventh place. Davison and his Levis were tenth behind Wal Handley [eighth] and P. Walker [ninth].

In the Senior Davison had no better luck. His Sunbeam broke down early on at Ramsey. Davison and Howard Davies, another early retirement, came back to Douglas on the Manx Electric Railway and then returned to the Grandstand in an open horse-drawn carriage still wearing their crash hats and riding gear.

Davison had by now joined the 'Continental Circus' with other British riders such as Freddie Dixon, Wal Handley and Stanley Woods and as some consolation for his TT results he won that year's 250 French GP.

In 1924 the TT organisers introduced an Ultra Lightweight race for machines of 175cc. Davison rode a Levis in this and the Lightweight TT. Even twenty-three years later it was clear that the Ultra Lightweight was a source of frustration.

Davison had been quickest in practice for the 175s and was a clear favourite with everyone to win the race. The event had the first ever TT mass start and Davison was on the front row of the grid with Jock Porter [New Gerrard] and Alec Bennett [Diamond]. Davison led the field down Bray Hill but, in his understandable enthusiasm, overdid things before the engine was fully warmed up and took the edge off the bike's performance. At the end of the lap he was sixth, the first two stroke but nearly fifty seconds behind Manxman Chris Stead on a Cotton. By the end of the three lap race he was up to fourth but five and a half minutes behind the Manxman. Davison's lap speeds were remarkably consistent - 47.55 mph, 47.55 mph and 47.49 mph - and show he was trying as hard as he could throughout. But these times were four minutes slower than his practice lap and he was bitterly disappointed with the result. He felt it was a race he could and should have won.

For some reason the organisers had decided that the Lightweight race should be run concurrently with the Senior, with the Lightweights starting off first. This meant the Seniors had to pass the Lightweights on the roads, with consequent difficulties for both. In the 250 race the two stroke Levis's were again outclassed and Davison had the added disadvantage of a slow start. He never really got going and finished eleventh out of twelve finishers, forty-seven minutes behind the winner.

Davison soon put his TT disappointments behind him and

1926: Davison waves to the cameraman as he speeds along Braddan straight on the Lightweight New Imperial.

rode his 175cc Levis in the Lightweight and Ultra Lightweight classes of the Belgian GP. He finished third in the 250 and won the 175cc class. At the end of the season, however, he decided to give up racing, returning to journalism and also getting married.

By 1925 the Italians were beginning to take an interest in the TT and there was talk of Guzzi and Bianchi entries soon. So an entry for the 1925 races by a 'Ferodo Vaselini', riding in practice as reserve rider for Scott, Sunbeam and New Imperial caused considerable speculation. It was rumoured the said Vaselini, who appeared each practice session suitably dark hued and moustachioed but disappeared as soon as his

ride was over, was really a spy sent over by Mussolini to try out the course. The speculation continued until one morning the thick black moustache came off at Ramsey and the truth was revealed. 'Vaselini' was really Davison getting the chance to road test various models in practice conditions.

In February 1926, Davison was skating with his wife at the Olton Reservoir near Birmingham when he met up with Norman Downs, Managing Director of New Imperial. Downs explained that New Imperials were now making their own engines [they had previously used JAP engines], and invited Davison to ride for them in the coming season. Since New Imperials had won the last two Lightweight races, Davison quickly agreed to come out of retirement.

The return to racing though was to prove a disappointment. Davison's first major race was the 1926 French GP but a dropped valve at the beginning of lap two meant an early retirement. Then in the Junior TT he retired on the first lap at the Bungalow with engine trouble.

New Imperial had entered a team of five riders for the Lightweight TT including Davison and Doug Prentice. Because of all the mechanical problems with the new engines, Davison decided to go for a steady ride and, hopefully, a finish. The plan nearly came to grief at Quarter Bridge where Davison fell off on the first lap. But neither he or the bike were too badly damaged and he was able to remount and continue the race. Prentice was not quite so lucky and was out on the second lap when lying ninth.

Davison lapped at a steady pace and worked his way up from tenth to sixth as he started his last lap. But as he came through his pit gave him the 'all out' signal and, loyally but foolishly, Davison obeyed. He retired at Barregarrow crossroads when the big end broke. If he had kept at his former steady pace the retirements of others would have given him third.

Post-TT he rode the New Imperial in the Brooklands 200 mile race but retired when the cam gear sheared. The model finally came good, however, at the 250 Belgian GP when

Davison again went for a steady ride and finished second.

For 1927 Davison combined riding in the TT with the production of the first ever *TT Special*. His riding was in a Rex team for the Lightweight of Wal Handley, Davison and McCrae. There were twenty-nine entrants for the race and it was thought that the Rex team had a good chance. But Davison was never on the pace. At the end of the third lap he called in to his pit and, as his own *TT Special* reported, 'caused some amusement by refuelling himself [with beer] as well as his tank with petrol. The pits breaks into the froth blowers' anthem'. He eventually finished ninth, twenty-nine minutes behind winner, team-mate and close friend Wal Handley.

That was Davison's last race as a rider but far from his last TT The TT Special, which had been an initial eight page single issue grew the following year to sixteen pages, then three 16 page issues in 1929, one for each race. In 1930 the first practice issue was produced and so it continued. During the war Davison served in the Signal Corps with the rank of Major. Afterwards, when racing resumed so did the T.T Special. He saw and reported on his last TT in 1965 and so missed the 1967 Senior. How I would have loved to read his report of that. He died in Barnt Green, Worcestershire in February 1966.

Davison called his story of the TT 'A Book for Motor Cyclists and all others who believe that motor cycle road racing is the finest sport on earth'. If you didn't believe that before, you did after reading the book; and there's no doubt who believed it most.

Geoff Davison (left) reminisces with Rem Fowler on their TT victories, with Rem's Peugeot-engined Norton and Geoff's Levis acting as aide memoirs.

TT Heroes - a personal selection